CODENAME TRICYCLE

CODENAME
TRICYCLE

The true story of the Second World War's
most extraordinary double agent

Russell Miller

Secker & Warburg
LONDON

Published by Secker & Warburg 2004

2 4 6 8 10 9 7 5 3 1

Copyright © Russell Miller 2004

Russell Miller has asserted his right under the Copyright, Designs
and Patents Act 1988 to be identified as the author of this work

First published in Great Britain in 2004 by
Secker & Warburg
Random House, 20 Vauxhall Bridge Road,
London SW1V 2SA

Random House Australia (Pty) Limited
20 Alfred Street, Milsons Point, Sydney,
New South Wales 2061, Australia

Random House New Zealand Limited
18 Poland Road, Glenfield,
Auckland 10, New Zealand

Random House (Pty) Limited
Endulini, 5A Jubilee Road, Parktown 2193, South Africa

The Random House Group Limited Reg. No. 954009
www.randomhouse.co.uk

A CIP catalogue record for this book
is available from the British Library

ISBN 0436210231

Papers used by Random House are natural,
recyclable products made from wood grown in sustainable forests;
the manufacturing processes conform to the environmental
regulations of the country of origin

Typeset by Palimpsest Book Production Limited,
Polmont, Stirlingshire

Printed and bound in Great Britain by
Mackays of Chatham plc, Chatham, Kent

To Harvey, Nancy, Archie & Lulu
in the hope they never have to live through a World War

Contents

Dramatis Personae

DUSKO POPOV: double agent. British codename 'Tricycle', though briefly known as 'Skoot'; German codename 'Ivan'.

IVO POPOV: Dusko's older brother, also a double agent, in Belgrade. British codename 'Dreadnought'; German codename 'Paula'.

'JOHNNY' JEBSEN: Popov's best friend. An Abwehr officer recruited by British intelligence. Codename 'Artist'.

DICKIE METCALFE: Popov's sub-agent. British codename 'Balloon'; German codename 'Ivan II'.

FRIEDL GAERTNER: Popov's sub-agent and lover. British codename 'Gelatine'; German codename 'Yvonne'.

LUDOVICO VON KARSTHOFF: Dusko's German controller.

ADMIRAL WILHELM CANARIS: director of the Abwehr, the German intelligence service.

'TAR' ROBERTSON: head of the MI5 section dealing with double agents.

EWEN MONTAGU: naval intelligence officer and friend of Dusko.

WILLIAM LUKE: Dusko's first MI5 case officer.

IAN WILSON: Dusko's final MI5 case officer.

FELIX COWGILL: Dusko's MI6 contact.

FRANK FOLEY: Dusko's subsequent MI6 contact.

WALTER 'FRECKLES' WREN: MI6 head of station, Trinidad.

STEWART MENZIES: head of MI6, known as 'C'.

J. C. MASTERMAN: chairman of the XX ('Double Cross') Committee.

J. EDGAR HOOVER: director of the FBI.

PERCY FOXWORTH: FBI agent in charge in New York.

CHARLES LANMAN: Dusko's FBI handler.

SIMONE SIMON: Hollywood actress with whom Dusko had an affair.

Foreword

UNRAVELLING THE LIFE OF A DOUBLE AGENT IN THE SECOND WORLD WAR, even with full access to the official records in London and Washington, is no easy task since in the murky world of espionage lies become intertwined with the truth. To add to the complications, Dusko Popov, indisputably one of Britain's most successful and courageous double agents, had three wartime lives.

First, there was Popov himself, a wealthy Yugoslav lawyer with a reputation as a ladies' man, he was fluent in several languages, and his charm was captivating. To the outside world he was a businessman, an entrepreneur uninterested in politics. Only his closest friends knew that his louche, devil-may-care lifestyle concealed a deep-rooted hatred of Fascism and Communism.

Then there was 'Ivan', viewed by the German intelligence service as one of its most successful agents, a man with excellent social connections and few moral scruples, apparently willing do anything for money – even risk his life by spying on Britain. Although there were some in Berlin who were suspicious of him, 'Ivan' shuttled back and forth between London and Lisbon for nearly four years, supplying the grateful Germans with a mass of information – much of it bogus – about Britain's military preparations.

Finally there was 'Tricycle', the enigmatic double agent working for British intelligence, fighting a lonely and dangerous war. Troublesome and demanding (who else could ask to be supplied with chocolates and silk stockings for his girlfriends?), 'Tricycle' was a vital player in Britain's top-secret operations to confuse and deceive the enemy. He was required to pass to the Germans as genuine a *mélange* of lies and half-truths concocted by the British. He was never sure, each time he visited Lisbon, if his cover was still intact and if the thread from which his life dangled had been cut. It was because of agents like 'Tricycle' that, when the Allies landed in Normandy in June 1944, the Germans were still waiting for the main assault to be unleashed on the Pas de Calais.

Popov was required, throughout the war, to switch between his various lives and keep track of who he was, in order to stay alive. One slip, one careless remark, one moment of absent-mindedness during interrogation by his German controllers could have cost him his life and put at risk Britain's fragile deception plans.

Yet in some ways he enjoyed a uniquely comfortable war. He never had to wear a uniform, never suffered the tribulations of military life. He was paid handsomely (by the Germans). Since he insisted that his cover as a spy was to act the part of a playboy, Popov took to the role with relish, always stayed in the best hotels, ordered silk shirts by the dozen, squired numerous beautiful women to the best parties and behaved as if he did not have a care in the world. When he was sent on a mission to the United States, he rented a penthouse on Park Avenue in New York, resumed an affair with a Hollywood actress and was a favoured patron of the Stork Club.

Thousands of pages of documents lodged in the National Archives in Washington and London chronicle Popov's astonishing career, although they are a minefield for the unwary researcher. One afternoon at the Public Records Office in Kew I was reading a long and extraordinarily detailed report about how Popov had met an Indian technician in New York, who had agreed to build a radio transmitter for him – only to discover, belatedly, that the whole story had been dreamed up by British intelligence as part of Popov's cover. None of it was true.

After the war Popov liked to say that he was afraid when he started being a spy, and only stopped being afraid when he stopped being a spy. If this is the case, it is certainly not reflected in the record. Nowhere is there even a hint that he was worried for his own safety. Indeed, on one occasion his British case officer warned him not to go to Lisbon as there were indications that his cover had been blown; he faced arrest, torture and execution. Popov would not countenance the idea, but met his suspicious German controller as arranged and literally talked his way out of trouble. However, the tension took its toll and it is perhaps not surprising that he ended the war with nine ulcers.

The recent release of the Popov files by the British government made this book possible, but I would also like to thank many members of the Popov family for their help and hospitality in the south of France and for allowing me access to Popov's voluminous personal records. By an extraordinary coincidence, Popov's older brother, Ivo, also worked as a double agent in Yugoslavia, pretending to collaborate with the German occupiers while secretly assisting the Allies. Ivo's widow, Brigitte, and his sons, Misha and Nicolas, provided valuable assistance. The excellent – and free – research facilities available at the National Archives in Washington and its British counterpart in Kew made the task of unravelling Popov's complicated career much easier, and the US Freedom of Information Act enabled sensitive, and potentially embarrassing, files to be prised from the Federal Bureau of Information. The hard-working staff at the London Library and my local library were, as ever, helpful in tracking down hard-to-find books. Thanks, too, to Geoff Mulligan, who saw the potential of the story and to my editor, Stuart Williams, whose contribution was immense. Finally, I want to pay special tribute to my wife, Renate, without whose loving support during a difficult time this book would never have been written.

Russell Miller
Isle of Wight, England

I

The Arrival of a Spy

ON A COLD GREY DAY IN LATE DECEMBER 1940, A DUTCH CIVILIAN airliner touched down at Whitchurch airfield, on the outskirts of Bristol, in the west of England, after a circuitous flight from Lisbon to avoid the attentions of the Luftwaffe. Among the passengers on board was a young Yugoslav national. He was well dressed, of medium height, with typical Slav high cheekbones, hair brushed straight back from his forehead and startling green eyes. His name was Dusan Popov, 'Dusko' (Dooshko) to his friends. At home in Dubrovnik he had a reputation, unquestionably deserved, as a playboy and a bon vivant. Wealthy, handsome, self-confident and amusing, he liked to say that his primary interests were 'sports cars and sporting women'. But for now his primary interest was staying alive, for he was about to enter a labyrinthine, lonely and dangerous world.

Popov was known to the Abwehr, the German intelligence service, by the codename 'Ivan'. He had been recruited a few months earlier, in Belgrade, to spy for Germany and had made his way across Europe to neutral Portugal to be briefed by his German controller for his mission in Britain. On 20 December, a top-secret signal was dispatched from Lisbon to Berlin to inform Admiral Wilhelm Canaris, wily chief of the Abwehr, that Ivan was on his way. Canaris would have been pleased: another agent in place at a crucial time when the Reich was planning 'Sea Lion', the invasion of Britain, the operation that would undoubtedly win the war for Germany.

Had Popov been an ordinary passenger arriving at Whitchurch, the papers he was carrying might have caused some raised eyebrows. When he was searched, he was found to be in possession of 'some typewritten sheets in Serbo-Croat containing references to Gibraltar and Dakar, and various positions given by latitude and longitude . . .'[1] But immigration officials had high-level orders to wave him through with a minimum of fuss, and so the formalities barely extended beyond recording that he was a Yugoslav citizen, born in Titel, Vojvodina, on 10 July 1912, and that he was travelling on passport number 4822, issued in Belgrade on 16 November 1940.

Popov was hustled through Customs formalities and met by a middle-aged man, a former racing driver, who took his bag and escorted him to an unmarked car, which was driven at speed along the Great West Road towards London, then under nightly attack by wave after wave of Luftwaffe bombers. Popov's first glimpse of the capital was an ominous red glow in the sky. 'If I had any doubts, moral or ethical,' he would say after the war, 'about what I was doing – the lying and treachery and so forth – they vanished when I experienced the Blitz at first hand and saw how the British were standing up to it.'[2]

Seven thousand Londoners had been killed in the first three weeks of the Blitz – an aerial onslaught designed to destroy the morale of the people and bring about a surrender without the need for an invasion. But Hermann Goering, the architect of the policy, misread the British character: the Blitz inculcated a stubborn defiance in the populace, a grim determination to continue business as usual, and the city still functioned, despite the smoking ruins that greeted every dawn.

There seemed to be no let-up in the intensity of the attacks on the capital as Christmas approached. Popov's car crawled through the smoke and flames in the blacked-out western suburbs, round Trafalgar Square and along the Strand to the opulent Savoy Hotel, where a room had been reserved for him. In the hotel lobby he was met by a tall, urbane Scot in civilian clothes who introduced himself as 'Tar' Robertson, welcomed Popov to London and politely suggested 'a drink and a chat' before they got down to business in the morning.

Major Thomas A. Robertson, Seaforth Highlanders, was on the staff of MI5, the British counter-intelligence service, and was in charge of Section B.1A, responsible for handling double agents. All Robertson knew about Popov was that he had been recruited as an agent by the Abwehr and had subsequently offered his services to the British. There was no reason in the world why he should be trusted and every reason to suspect that he might be a German 'plant'. In the espionage business, trust was a rare commodity.

By the end of 1940, Britain had in place the embryo of a top-secret organisation, under the aegis of MI5, that was to run what became known as 'the great game of double cross' for the remainder of the war. Although it had yet to hold its first meeting, it had a wryly appropriate name – the XX Committee. Double X for double-cross operations, using double agents. Its function, primarily, was twofold: to deceive and confuse the enemy at every opportunity by feeding false information into the engine room of the German intelligence-gathering machine; and to divine the enemy's military and strategic intentions by analysis of the instructions given to agents who the Abwehr believed were spying on its behalf, but who were, in fact, working for the Allies.

If Robertson and his team decided that Popov was genuine, he had the potential to become the XX Committee's most valuable asset, since he was able to travel back and forth between London and Lisbon under the cover of being a lawyer negotiating import and export deals. He was thus able to make direct, face-to-face contact with the enemy, deliver or collect documents and infiltrate the Abwehr from within.

It was for this reason that Popov was given the red-carpet treatment when he arrived in London, with a room at the Savoy rather than a cell at MI5's interrogation centre in Latchmere House, a grim Victorian mansion at Ham Common, on the outskirts of the city, which was certainly where he would end up if Robertson concluded that he was a 'plant'. Popov had already been given a codename: 'Skoot', a play on the pronunciation of his name, 'pop-off'. From the date of his initial interrogation onwards, the name 'Dusan Popov' would never feature in MI5 files.

Popov's debriefing at the Savoy by Major Robertson and three other MI5 officers took place in French, a language in which he was more comfortable than English, and continued for four days without interruption. The questioning was merciless as his interrogators probed for any inconsistency that would indicate he was lying. He was made to go over his story time and time again: how, as a lawyer, he had come into contact with the German Legation in Belgrade while negotiating export licences for a client. How, through a friend, he had been introduced to a senior German officer as someone who was well connected, with a wide circle of friends in Britain, and how this officer had suggested that it might be in his best interests to work for Germany. How he had immediately reported this approach, secretly, to the British Legation in Belgrade, and how he had been told to express interest. How he had made it clear to the Germans that, as a loyal Yugoslav, he would never do anything to harm the interests of his own country and that he would only be prepared to work for them if he was well paid.

Popov lied to the Germans that he had a friend in the Yugoslav Legation in London who would be willing to gather intelligence and pass it back to Belgrade in the diplomatic bag. In fact he had no such friend. The Germans gave him three lengthy questionnaires to pass on to his 'friend', which he handed over to his contact in the British Legation. When no answers were forthcoming – Popov explained that his friend had got cold feet – the Germans agreed that he should go to London to collect the information himself.

(What Popov did not know – and certainly was not told – was that much of his story was corroborated by intercepted signals between Belgrade and Berlin. One of the greatest secrets of the war was that British intelligence had cracked Enigma, the enemy's radio code.)

Popov had travelled from Belgrade to Lisbon via Rome and Barcelona. In Lisbon he met his controller, a man called von Karsthoff, who had given him some rudimentary training and a short verbal questionnaire, aimed at identifying prominent people opposed to the policies of prime minister Winston Churchill and who might perhaps be willing to work for peace with Germany. Popov was to establish how best to approach them and what weaknesses – drink, money, women, and the like – could be exploited. He was also to assess which elements of the Blitz were most affecting the morale of the people and what kind of propaganda would be most effective. Finally, he was to try and ingratiate himself with friends of Vice Admiral Sir John Tovey, commander-in-chief of the Home Fleet. He was not told why.

Popov's trump card was that von Karsthoff had unwisely given him the name and address of another German agent in Britain whom he could contact in an emergency. When he produced the name, Robertson accepted the information without blinking an eyelid, and without telling Popov that the man – a Czech by the name of George Graf – had already been turned and was working for MI5 as a double agent under the code-name of 'Giraffe'. But the fact that Popov readily volunteered to disclose the identity of another enemy agent greatly bolstered his *bona fides* in the eyes of his interrogators.

Although some of his Savoy interrogators were leery about Popov's reputation as a ladies' man and a playboy, he generally made a favourable impression, answering questions directly and consistently. He appeared to be completely genuine in his desire to fight the Nazis and perfectly willing to accept the considerable risks of working as a double agent. He knew that if his cover was blown, he could expect no mercy from the Gestapo. Popov said he had been earning the equivalent of £3,000 a year – a very considerable amount of money in those days in Yugoslavia – and was adamant that he wanted no payment from British intelligence, as he anticipated being well paid by his German masters. He explained that he was anxious to return to Lisbon early in January as he was concerned that a business deal he had left in the hands of a Portuguese lawyer, Dr Fernando Pacheco, would go sour without his personal attention.

'Skoot left an exceedingly favourable first impression upon all of us,' noted John Marriott, a young solicitor who was Robertson's deputy. 'His manner was absolutely frank and we all considered without question that he was telling the truth. He particularly impressed upon us that he desired no money from us and only stipulated that he should be allowed to go home as early as conveniently possible in January so that he might attend to his own business.'[3]

At the end of the interrogation, all four inquisitors agreed that it was worth the risk of allowing him to return to Lisbon. At the same time it was decided that Popov should be kept under the closest possible surveillance to guard against the theoretical possibility of a triple cross – that he was working under German orders to present himself as a double agent. Thus his access to the inner workings of British intelligence was strictly limited. He was told nothing of the existence of the XX Committee or of other double agents in Britain who were in contact with Germany by radio. He was not even allowed to know the real name of William Luke, the MI5 man appointed to be his case officer. This led to an embarrassing moment a few months later when they were lunching together at the Royal Automobile Club in Pall Mall and a waiter addressed Luke by name. Since Luke had told Popov his name was Matthews, he blustered something about not really being a member of the club and having to use the name of a genuine member, Luke, to get a table. By then Popov was accustomed to the machinations of MI5 and went along with it.

The initial assessment of Popov's character lodged in MI5 files was a pen portrait of a man perfectly equipped to become a double agent, rather in the mould of James Bond, a character with whom he would come to be closely associated:

> Though not fond of work, particularly routine work, he has undoubted ability and power of concentration when he chooses to call on them. He is courageous, discreet and has great charm. Accustomed to the good life, he spends money freely. In more sense than one he is an adventurer. He is fond of the society of attractive women and seems, from the ease with which he acquires mistresses wherever he goes, to have a greater attraction for women than might be expected from his personal appearance . . .[4]

His po-faced British interrogators were evidently mystified by Popov's success with women, but British men – then as now – did not understand that charm was just as important as looks. Certainly no punches were pulled in putting together a description of Popov for the file:

Hair brown brushed straight back, parted just to the right of centre. Hair receding above temples giving a heart-shaped appearance to the head. Eyes light grey. Complexion rather yellow, tending to be white and blotchy in the morning after a late night. Broad nostrils and flat nose, rather bulbous at the end. Two deep lines at either side of nose extending to the corners of the mouth. Small, well shaped ears. A mole on the left of the lower lip. Good even white teeth. Loose sensual mouth and thick lips. Has the appearance of being a Mongolian-Slav type with rather high cheek bones. Clean shaven. Hands rather podgy, white and well-manicured. Receding forehead and determined chin. Is broad shouldered and thick set. When walking his gait is long-strided and slightly rolling and is the very reverse of military. When talking he gesticulates freely with his hands. He dresses well but carelessly, trousers always seem too long for him, prefers white silk shirts with soft collars and fancy ties. He smiles freely showing all his teeth and in repose his face is not unpleasant, although certainly not handsome.[5]

Once the decision had been made to accept Popov as genuine, nothing was too much trouble to make him welcome. On Christmas Day Robertson took him to a turkey-with-all-the-trimmings lunch at 'Quaggers' (Quaglino's), a fashionable restaurant famous for its rumba band, the only one of its kind in London. They spent an amiable afternoon playing billiards at the Lansdowne Club before heading back to the Savoy for dinner. Robertson dictated a note for Popov's file the following day: 'I think he enjoyed himself thoroughly once he took part in the Christmas bonhomonous rioting, well lubricated by champagne. We were picked up by a couple by the name of Keswick who took us to the Suiva nightclub where we danced. Early in the morning, we returned to the Savoy, both viewing things through rose-tinted spectacles.'[6]

On Sunday, 29 December, the Luftwaffe mounted a huge raid on the City of London – the business district – less than a mile from the Savoy. More than 10,000 firebombs fell on the City's square mile and for a time the fires raged out of control. Like most of the guests, Popov sought refuge in the hotel's own bomb shelter: banqueting rooms in the sub-basement protected by sandbags and reinforced with scaffolding, where food was available from a limited menu for those with an appetite.

Next day Popov lunched with John Marriott, at Marriott's club, to talk about his imminent return to Lisbon – a seat had been booked for him on the first flight the following Friday. There were a number of problems that needed to be resolved. First, the Germans were obsessed with the idea that Popov had a wide circle of friends and business contacts in Britain. In fact, he knew virtually no one. (When Robertson asked him during his interrogation for details of his friends in Britain, he could provide only three names, none of whom he knew how to contact.) His influential 'friends' were supposed to explain, for German consumption, how he was able to obtain a priority seat on an aeroplane to Lisbon (actually arranged by MI5), so Popov was aware that he would be expected to name names. Second, he needed evidence that he had attempted, as ordered, to make contact with someone on Admiral Tovey's staff. Finally, he wanted to be put in touch with the MI5 man in Lisbon in case of emergencies. Marriott took a careful note and promised to be in touch shortly.

On New Year's Eve Popov was invited, somewhat to his surprise but to his considerable delight, to a weekend house party at the family home of Major-General Stewart Menzies, the head of MI6, Britain's secret intelligence service. It was more than just a social occasion: Menzies, known as 'C' (the first head of MI6 was Captain Mansfield Smith-Cumming, known as 'C', which became the acronym for all his successors to the present day), wanted to meet Popov and talk shop. Popov, for his part, had other things on his mind: he had been told that the Menzies' parties were always glamorous affairs and that he 'wouldn't have to worry about popsies' (that is, there would be plenty of attractive women present).

The Menzies were indisputably 'top-drawer'. The family originally owned Dorchester House, a mansion in Mayfair that later became the Dorchester Hotel, and a large estate in Gloucestershire next to that of the Duke of Beaufort. Born in 1890, Stewart Menzies was educated at Eton, won a DSO and MC with the Household Cavalry during the First World War and was, naturally, a member of White's, the most exclusive gentlemen's club in London. Closely connected to court circles, it was bruited in London that he was the illegitimate son of Edward VII.

The party was held at Little Bridley, a Georgian mansion set in rolling parkland in Surrey, which was the country home of Menzies' mother, Lady Pamela Holford (she had remarried following the death of her first husband), a noted society hostess and lady-in-waiting to Queen Mary. Popov was driven to Little Bridley by an MI5 officer and was conducted into the drawing room, where the guests had assembled. Lady Pamela welcomed him effusively and introduced him to her younger son, Major Ian Graham Menzies, Scots Guards, and his stunning Austrian wife, Lisel, but Popov's attention was diverted. Standing in the same group was the most beautiful woman he had seen since arriving in England. She was Lisel's sister, Friedl Gaertner,[7] a singer who regularly appeared in cabaret in London night clubs. Stewart Menzies was delighted to observe that

Popov was smitten, because Friedl had been invited to the party specifically to provide Popov with the entrée into British society that was expected by his German masters. Friedl was a part-time informer for MI5; Menzies thought that she and Popov might work well together. He was right. They would soon become lovers and co-conspirators – Friedl would join Popov's embryonic network of agents under the codename 'Gelatine', because someone in MI5 thought she was a 'jolly little thing'.

Popov flirted outrageously with Friedl throughout the weekend and was far from pleased when Menzies quietly suggested he should tear himself away from her for a few minutes and join him in the book-lined study. There, seated in leather chairs on either side of a roaring fire, Menzies lit his pipe and got down to business. It was immediately clear he had studied Popov's file in minute detail, since he began with an analysis of what he believed were Popov's strengths and weaknesses as a double agent. Much of it was less than flattering. He assessed Popov as being unbothered by conscience, ambitious, ruthless, even cruel. On the positive side he was honest, not prone to panic and, driven by an instinct for self-preservation, coped well in dangerous situations.

Menzies told the younger man: 'You have too many devices on your banner for my taste',[8] but that he had the makings of a very good spy, as long as he learned to obey orders. It was for this reason that Popov was to be entrusted with a special intelligence mission on Menzies' personal behalf. Wearing his 'C' hat, Menzies first gave Popov a detailed briefing about the structure and organisation of the Abwehr and the personalities of the officers in charge of the different *Abteilungen* (departments).

Although the Abwehr had a long and illustrious history (it was founded in 1866), it had become moribund by the time Hitler came to power and in 1935 he appointed a naval officer, Admiral Wilhelm Canaris, to energise and expand the organisation. Canaris was a surprise choice. Forty-eight years old and only five feet four inches tall, he had had a distinguished career in the German navy, but had never joined the Nazi party (and never would) and would eventually harbour profound reservations about National Socialism. As he set about expanding the Abwehr, Canaris filled senior posts with like-minded military men, mainly First World War veterans and officers from the old imperial army and navy, who tended to be aloof from the Nazis. But the Abwehr's reputation for intelligence-gathering grew rapidly and by the beginning of the war it had some 16,000 agents sprinkled around the world, operating in neutral countries under the cover of diplomatic missions.

Menzies explained to Popov that Canaris, while a patriotic German, was not a 'dyed-in-the-wool Nazi' and that at some future date he could become a catalyst for a popular uprising against Hitler. To this end, 'C' wanted to know everything about everyone who was close to Canaris. While Popov's first duty as a double agent was to MI5, the counter-intelligence service, he was to find out what information he could about Canaris' circle, keep his eyes and ears open for any hints about anti-Nazi sentiment within the Abwehr and report directly to 'C', without using an intermediary.[9]

Menzies explained that he was handling the matter personally and that, as Popov was not in a position to assess the importance of whatever he might learn, he was to pass on every detail, no matter how seemingly irrelevant. With an assurance that all MI6 agents abroad would be instructed to give him every assistance, a chastened Popov was returned to the party, where he was soon making arrangements to see the lovely Friedl again.

If Popov was confused about why he should be reporting only to 'C', no one could have blamed him. Relations between MI5 and MI6 were frequently strained. Fundamentally, the difference between the two organisations was that Military Intelligence 5 was responsible for counter-espionage within the British Isles, while Military Intelligence 6 was charged with gathering intelligence overseas. Problems initially stemmed from a marked reluctance by each organisation to share information with the other, but natural rivalry and jealousy also contributed to the tension. Ironically, the British public only learned of the existence of the secret intelligence service when author Compton Mackenzie published *Greek Memories*, an account of his experiences as an MI6 officer during the First World War, in 1932. Mackenzie was fined £100 for breaching the Official Secrets Act and promptly put under surveillance by MI5.

Back in London the day after Menzies' party, Popov had another caller at the Savoy – Lieutenant Commander Ewen Montagu, Royal Naval Volunteer Reserve, the naval intelligence officer on the XX Committee. A barrister and rising King's Counsel in civilian life, Montagu had been recruited by Admiral John Godfrey, director of the Office of Naval Intelligence. Ingenious and visionary, Montagu was a natural for intelligence work and dreamed up the famous 'Man Who Never Was' stunt later in the war, planting fake documents on a corpse floating in the Mediterranean to convince the Germans that Greece, not Italy, was the Allies' next target.

Montagu's job was to assemble a cover story that would convince the Germans that Popov had been using his time diligently on their behalf during his brief trip to London and assure them he really was working as a spy. Montagu also had to record his impressions of the young Yugoslav.

'I found him a most charming person,' he noted in his report of their meeting, 'and I should be most surprised if he is not playing straight with us.'

The meeting was Popov's introduction to the meticulous care that would go into preparing him for every confrontation with his German controller. It had been agreed by MI5 that Popov could name Montagu as one of his 'wide circle' of friends in Britain, and it was therefore necessary to put together an account about how they had met, in case the Germans became inquisitive. Montagu knew that Popov was a keen amateur yachtsman and suggested that they could have been introduced by a friend of his, a member of the Royal Ocean Racing Club who had sailed down the coast of Dalmatia and could easily have run across Popov at that time. Part of the elaborate cover story they concocted was that Montagu was encouraging Popov to bring his yacht, the *Nina*, over to the Solent, on the south coast of England, after the war. Popov could make his base on the River Hamble, where another friend of Montagu's, one Foster-Brown, a Royal Navy lieutenant commander, had a 'convenient house'. Foster-Brown happened to be a liaison officer on the staff of Admiral Tovey – thus allegedly providing Popov with indirect access to the admiral in whom the Germans were so interested.

Popov realised that all of this had been planned in advance when Montagu reached into his briefcase and produced a personal letter that Popov could show to the Germans as proof that they were in touch. Written on Admiralty notepaper and dated the following day, Montagu's letter apologised for not being able to make lunch, but emphasised how much he had enjoyed meeting Popov 'again' the previous evening.

> Please do ring me as soon as you return to this country as I am much looking forward to renewing our conversation. It is so nice in these troubled times to meet another who is as mad as I am about sailing! I hope that you will have a photo of 'Nina' to show me when you get back, as she sounds a grand boat; she must be brought over to the Solent after the war as I told you.
>
> Best of luck until we meet again.
>
> Ewen Montagu, Lt Cdr RNVR.[10]

For the benefit of prying eyes, Montagu made sure the two of them were later seen together in the cocktail bar at the Savoy, animatedly discussing sailing and looking at photographs of Montagu's boat. Popov would tell the Germans that while they were drinking in the bar, Montagu had indiscreetly 'let slip' two interesting snippets of information:

that almost every Atlantic convoy was to be provided with an escort of one or more submarines, and that it was intended to fit aircraft (possibly torpedo-laying) to most of the larger merchantmen.

Montagu had not, of course, let anything slip. All the 'intelligence' that Popov would take with him to Lisbon had been vetted by MI5. A combination of genuine, but essentially harmless, information designed to bolster his status as an agent in the eyes of the Abwehr and deliberate disinformation designed to deceive the German high command, it all had to fit in with the overall picture being painted by other double agents. Most importantly, Popov had to be trusted to pass over to his German controller exactly what had been agreed and nothing more. One slip and the elaborate house of cards being constructed by the XX Committee would collapse.

Robertson and his colleagues were reasonably confident that Popov could handle the pressure. 'We have in him a new agent of high quality,' an MI5 report noted, 'who can plausibly meet persons in any social stratum, who is well established with the Germans at the instance of an Abwehr official, and who has excellent business cover for frequent journeys to Lisbon or to other neutral countries.'[11]

On 2 January 1941, Robertson and Marriott gave Popov his final briefing before he was due to leave for Lisbon the following day. 'We went carefully through the whole of his questionnaire and told him to tell the following story to the Germans,' Robertson recorded:

> He is glad he came over here as he felt that his friend in the Yugoslav Legation had not done all the work that he had expected him to do, chiefly because having his own work in the Legation, he had had little time to give to answering the questions and also he was very frightened being in a foreign country and doing anything which might rouse the suspicions of the authorities. He has, however, been able to obtain certain answers to the questions asked and Skoot is to hand these over. He is also to say that he thinks it would be far better if he could come back to this country at a later date when he himself could set up contacts over here and find some better way to get answers to future questionnaires. He is to give them the names of all the people he has met over here and build up stories around them. He was allowed to keep a copy of the questions and answers which we gave him and has strict instructions from us that before going to the interview, he is to destroy these papers and I think we can rely on him to do this . . . The only thing he is anxious about in connection with the questionnaire was how he would get this out

of the country without being detected. I said that I would arrange this for him with the SCO [Security Control Officer] Bristol. He is also very anxious that he should be put in touch with one of our people in Lisbon to whom he can give future questionnaires for transmission to the UK and to whom he can go for advice.[12]

Popov was told he had *carte blanche* to answer the five questions he had been given in Lisbon however he liked, and he was offered the names of Lords Brocket, Lymington and Londonderry as among those opposed to Churchill and likely to accept peace terms with Germany. None of these names would have raised an eyebrow in Berlin. Lord Brocket was vice-president of the Anglo-German Fellowship and Hitler's personal guest at the Führer's fiftieth birthday celebrations in April 1939. Lord Lymington owned the right-wing journal, the *New Review*, was Oswald Mosley's second-in-command in the British Union of Fascists and was widely rumoured to be Hitler's choice for Gauleiter after Germany's successful invasion of Britain. Lord Londonderry resigned from Stanley Baldwin's government in 1935 to promote Anglo-German reconciliation, was a friend of Goering and Ribbentrop and was regularly castigated in the media for being 'pro-German'.

On 3 January, the Security Control Officer at Avonmouth noted the departure of one Popov, Dusan, exit permit 363438, destination, Palace Hotel, Estoril. He added in the log:

In accordance with instructions from Maj Bardwell [MI5], Popov was treated as an ordinary passenger and during the routine examination of his documents, an unsealed envelope stamped Savoy Hotel was noted. This envelope contained about eight typewritten quarto sheets in the form of a questionnaire and answers with pencilled notes . . . There was also a sheet of Savoy Hotel notepaper with various notes in Yugoslav, and the names of Lord Brocket, Lord Londonderry and Lord Lymington scrawled on the reverse.[13]

Popov was on his way to his lonely, dangerous and peculiar war.

2

An Unlikely Agent

DESPITE GROWING UP IN A FLEDGLING COUNTRY HOVERING ON THE brink of anarchy, Dusko Popov had an idyllic childhood. Modern Yugoslavia rose from the ruins of the Austro-Hungarian empire in 1918 as the Kingdom of Serbs, Croats and Slovenes, created artificially after the First World War by the Treaty of St-Germain, signed in September 1919, under which Austria ceded Slovenian and Dalmatian territory to the new kingdom, and by the Treaty of Trianon, signed in June 1920, under which Hungary similarly ceded Croatia, Slavonia and part of Banat.

Also transferred to the new kingdom were many of the nationalist problems that had plagued the old Habsburg and Ottoman empires before 1914. German, Magyar, Albanian and Romanian minorities competed with Muslims and Slovenes, while the two largest nationalities, the Croats and the Serbs, manoeuvred for dominance. Fervent nationalism, religious differences, ethnic tensions, widespread poverty and political intrigue led to constant internal strife, culminating in the assassination of a former Croat Cabinet minister by a Serb during a session of parliament in 1928. King Alexander scrapped the constitution, which had done little to heal the fissures within his divided kingdom, proclaimed a dictatorship, dissolved all political parties and renamed the state Yugoslavia (land of the south Slavs). Six years later King Alexander himself was assassinated in Marseilles by a gunman from the Internal Macedonian Revolutionary Organisation. His place was taken by his brother, Prince Paul, who attempted to make a rapprochement with the Croats in the teeth of fierce opposition by the Serbs, but bitter ethnic divisions endured and still exist today.

To some extent, the Popovs were shielded from the turmoil by their position in society. The Popov family was wealthy and well connected and enjoyed a lifestyle – large houses, servants, yachts, foreign travel – indistinguishable from similarly influential families elsewhere in Europe.

Dusko's grandfather, a banker and industrialist, founded the family fortune with a business empire that eventually included textile factories, coal mines and even a hat shop in Paris. His father, Milorad Popov, savoured the cosseted and leisurely life of a man with inherited wealth, never felt the need to work for a living, took mistresses and travelled frequently to Monte Carlo, Switzerland and Paris.

Born in the autonomous province of Vojvodina, Serbia, where his grandfather endowed a library that is still named after him, Dusko was just a baby when the family moved permanently to their large summer house in Dubrovnik. The most picturesque of all resorts on the Adriatic coast and a favourite watering hole for European royalty, the liberal and democratic city of Dubrovnik played a major role in forging Dusko's character, developing his self-assurance, independence and determination to live life to the full. Throughout his life he would always claim to be a Ragusan first (Ragusa was the original name for the city).

It was in Dubrovnik that the Popov boys (he had an older brother, Ivo, whom he worshipped, and a younger brother Vladan) learned to swim, fish and sail and cause mischief. All three were keen sportsmen, played ferocious water polo and were expert riders, tennis players and skiers. Dusko's mother was determined he would learn to play the violin; Dusko was equally determined he would not. He never left the house without his swimming costume packed in his violin case and always headed straight for the beach in preference to a music lesson. By contrast, tolerance and indulgence symbolised Milorad Popov's relationship with his sons; when the boys were in their teens he built a separate house for them in the garden where they could entertain their friends – girls included.

No expense was spared on Dusko's education. Although his first language was Serbo-Croat, he was soon fluent in Italian, German and French. After four years at a *lycée* in Paris, he was sent, at the age of sixteen, to school in Britain – Ewell Castle, a minor public school in Surrey. Unfortunately he did not take kindly to the rigours of English boarding-school discipline, which included beating with a cane for a whole range of misdemeanours. In the spring of 1929, during his second term, he was expelled for grabbing the cane with which a master was about to beat him and breaking it in two over his knee. He had taken one beating for smoking behind the bicycle sheds, but objected to another for refusing to identify the boy he was with. Dusko's father took the news of his son's expulsion with his usual equanimity and suggested he should return to Paris to the tough Lycée Hoche, which was much more to Dusko's liking, despite the fact that the students were woken at six every morning by a roll of drums. After two years in Paris he moved back to Yugoslavia to take a law degree at the University of Belgrade.

The Popovs owned a large house in the centre of Belgrade and Dusko became a familiar figure in the city's raucous night clubs, often with a pretty girl on each arm. Dusko made no secret of the fact that, like his father, he loved the company of women – and women usually returned his affection. He was charming, funny, excellent company and, on occasion, completely mad. He once stopped at a horse-drawn cart loaded with flowers in the centre of Belgrade, intending to buy a bouquet for a girl-friend. He could not make up his mind what to choose, so he asked the flower seller how much he would charge to deliver the entire cart-load to his lady friend. They struck a deal. The horse and cart headed off in the direction of the girl's house, leaving Dusko standing in the street, grinning furiously.

After graduating from the University of Belgrade, Dusko, not in the least anxious to begin a career, enrolled for a doctorate in law at Freiburg University, in the heart of the Black Forest in southern Germany. In 1935 Adolf Hitler had been in power for nearly three years and was well embarked on constructing a regime of unparalleled barbarity: the Nazi grip on the country had tightened to a stranglehold; opposition was tantamount to suicide; civil rights and liberties had disappeared. Books by non-Nazi authors were ceremonially burned, the first concentration camps had opened and the systematic persecution of the Jews was well advanced, with barely a voice raised in protest.

It was a deeply depressing picture, but in truth Dusko was not much concerned with politics or, indeed, what was happening in Germany. A carefree twenty-three-year-old with a lust for the good life, he wanted to improve his German and chose Freiburg for no better reason than that it was not too far from home, was a nice place to live, with a medieval old town and cobbled streets, had a vibrant student life, a reputation for pretty girls and fine restaurants, and was close to first-class ski slopes.

Freiburg University, founded in 1457, was one of the oldest in Europe and was a renowned centre for philosophical debate and scientific research. As a foreign student, Popov was afforded privileges and a measure of freedom denied to Germans. He was under no pressure, for example, to join the youth section of Himmler's SS (the blackshirts) or the *Sturmabteilung* (the brownshirts), as German national students were. He felt able, within reason, to speak his mind; he could ignore the Nazi propaganda that was everywhere, and he did not have to curry favour with party apparatchiks to safeguard his future career.

Foreign students had their own club, the *Deutsche Ausländische*

Gesellschaft, in a handsome house on Badenstrasse and it was there that Popov met Johann ('Johnny') Jebsen, a young man from Hamburg who would become his best friend and, coincidentally, provide the connections that would lead Popov into the shadowy world of espionage. Jebsen, the heir to a shipping empire based in Hamburg, was aristocratic, aloof, always impeccably dressed, with a monocle clenched in his right eye. At first sight he would appear to have little in common with the easy-going Popov, but the two of them shared twin passions – for sports cars and what Popov would describe as 'sporting girls'. Jebsen drove a super-charged Mercedes 540K convertible, Popov a BMW; the prettiest girls in Freiburg rotated through the front passenger seats of both cars.

Popov soon discovered that Jebsen's apparently haughty demeanour concealed a keen intelligence and warm personality infused with irreverence towards authority and an irrepressible sense of fun. Jebsen also despised the Nazi regime. When restaurant owners in Freiburg were ordered to post signs stating 'Jews and Dogs Not Allowed', Jebsen, Popov and their friends ostentatiously patronised the one establishment – the Billiger Café on Bertholdstrasse – where the owner refused to comply. When SS troopers were posted at the door to intimidate potential customers by demanding their names, Jebsen and Popov loudly gave theirs and, without pausing, swept inside and sat at a prominent table in the window.

On one well-remembered occasion, Popov got involved in a trivial argument with another student (about a girl, naturally), which escalated absurdly and ended with Popov being challenged to a duel. Popov asked Jebsen to be his second and together they decided, as Popov had the choice of weapons, that he should insist on pistols rather than the traditional sabres, particularly as it was common knowledge on the campus that Popov was a crack shot and had won a snap-shooting contest two years running back in Dubrovnik. Choosing pistols for a duel was considered outrageously bad form in German student society, and a court of honour was convened to adjudicate. Jebsen gravely explained that, as a reserve officer in a cavalry regiment back home in Bosnia, his friend was honour-bound to duel only with pistols. The court decided that Popov could not be obliged to dishonour his regimental code, but neither could his opponent be forced to duel with pistols against his will, so the incident was quietly forgotten. Thereafter Jebsen, who delighted in stirring up mischief, warned anyone who crossed their path that Popov would not hesitate to challenge them to a duel – with pistols.

Every other Friday evening, a debate was held at the Ausländer Club after a formal, black-tie dinner known as the *Herrenessen* (gentlemen's dinner). Girls were allowed to join the party, for dancing, only after eleven o'clock. Popov regularly attended, as much for the girls as for the debate, but was depressed by the extent to which the other foreign students seemed to be swayed by arguments supporting Nazi ideology. When he mentioned this to his friend, Jebsen explained that German students attending the *Herrenessen* were all hand-picked party members, who not only always chose the subject for debate, but carefully rehearsed their speeches beforehand in order to impress the foreign students.

Popov persuaded Jebsen, who was president of the club, to find out in advance the topics for debate and then recruited English and American students to prepare forceful counter-arguments to the Nazi position. Freedom of speech was allowed during the debates, except for criticism of the Führer, which was strictly forbidden, and thereafter the tenor of the debates swung dramatically against the Germans. Popov himself made two impassioned speeches in defence of democracy and began contributing articles to a Yugoslav political weekly, *Politika*. Although he did not know it at the time, he was gaining a reputation as a political meddler and making powerful enemies.

When he had completed his doctoral thesis in the summer of 1937, Popov decided to celebrate by taking a trip to Paris, a city he knew well and where he had many friends – a number of them, inevitably, female. At six o'clock on the morning he was due to leave, he was woken by hammering on the door of his apartment. He struggled out of bed, blearily opened the door and found himself face-to-face with four members of the Gestapo, who pushed past him into the apartment and ordered him to dress.

While one man kept a close watch on him, the other three conducted a thorough search of the apartment, emptying drawers and cupboards, poring over his papers and books, checking the pockets of his clothes and poking through the garbage. Popov knew it was pointless to protest, but he made an indignant attempt and kept asking them what they were looking for. They ignored him. When they had finished they were obviously furious that they had found nothing incriminating. They pulled him roughly to his feet, dragged him out the door, down the stairs to a waiting car and drove him to the local Gestapo headquarters in Freiburg.

Popov was kept in Gestapo custody for eight days and questioned relentlessly, day and night. His interrogators seemed to want him to account for every minute of every day he had spent in Freiburg, whom he had seen and what he had talked about. They told him one of his girl-friends was a Communist, asked why he was dating her and were not amused when he answered: 'Because she's pretty.' They seemed to want him to confess that he was a Communist and a Jewish sympathiser and used his contribution to the *Herrenessen* debates as evidence against him. Popov would learn later that, while he was being questioned, other Gestapo officials were talking to almost everyone with whom he had ever come into contact: his professors, friends, fellow students, even the waiters at restaurants he frequented. Such was the fear generated by the Gestapo that many of those questioned were ready to agree that Popov was a troublemaker and quite possibly a Communist. One professor who, a few weeks earlier, had lavishly praised Popov's work, told the Gestapo that he was both a mediocre student and an anarchist.

Popov was eventually transferred to Freiburg prison, a grim red-brick building in the north-east quarter of the town. Kept in solitary confinement for most of the time, he learned from a whispered conversation with a fellow prisoner, during a brief exercise period, that he (Popov) was destined for a concentration camp in the not-too-distant future. It was a prospect that sent a chill through his bones.

Fortunately his best friend did not forsake him. When Jebsen realised that Popov had disappeared, he began making frantic enquiries to try and find out what had happened and where his friend had been taken. He got nowhere, beyond establishing that Popov was somewhere in the Gestapo headquarters. No one would tell him why Popov had been arrested or what was going to happen to him. Unwilling to risk being overheard on a German telephone line, Jebsen drove across the nearby border into Switzerland and telephoned Popov's father in Dubrovnik. Milorad was shocked to hear what had happened to his son; fortunately his wealth and prominent position in society meant that he had no shortage of influential contacts. He went straight to the Yugoslav prime minister, Dr Milan Stojadinovic, who promised to raise the matter with Hermann Goering, then a rising star in the Nazi party and soon to be appointed Hitler's deputy, whom he was due to meet in the next few days.

Popov, of course, had no idea that strings were being pulled on his behalf at the highest levels of the Nazi government. All he knew was that he was suddenly summoned to the prison governor's office one morning in September 1937 and coldly informed that he was being released immediately, providing he agreed to leave Germany within twenty-four hours. No one could have been keener to leave. Warned that he was to communicate with no one, Popov returned to his apartment, packed a bag, settled a few bills, scribbled a note to Jebsen explaining what had happened and asking him to make arrangements to sell his BMW, then caught a taxi to the station to wait for a train to Belgrade. He was secretly hoping that word of his expulsion might have spread and that a few friends might turn up to see him off, but no one appeared. Only later did he learn that they had been intercepted by the police and prevented from entering the station.

The loyal Jebsen was not so easily thwarted. Changing trains in Basle, Popov stepped down onto the platform to find his friend waiting for him, smiling broadly. When he had been denied access to the station in Freiburg, Jebsen had jumped into his Mercedes and raced the train the forty-five miles to Basle. Popov was overwhelmed with gratitude for what his friend had done to secure his release and swore that if he could ever help Jebsen in return, in any way, he had only to ask. It would be nearly three years before Jebsen called in the favour.

Back home in Dubrovnik, Popov set up a small private practice in commercial law and picked up the threads of his former life as an eligible young man about town. He had plenty of time for socialising, a full calendar, a house overlooking the sea on a peninsula just outside the city and a large staff of servants to care for his every need. He could usually be found in his office only between nine and eleven on weekday mornings, but he was always ready to do 'favours' for clients, using his high-level political and official contacts to obtain import/export licences or revisions of Customs duties. His annual income was equivalent to around £3,000 (more than £80,000 today), which enabled him to travel widely throughout Europe and spend at least a month every year in Paris, where he counted among his numerous lovers a divorced French marquise, Pinta de la Rocque. Life, unquestionably, was good.

He remained in regular contact with Jebsen and was concerned about his well-being in Germany as the international situation deteriorated. Jebsen had made no secret of the fact that he disliked the Nazis, and Popov knew, perhaps better than most, that even covert opposition to the harsh regime in Germany was foolhardy, if not downright dangerous: thousands of innocent people perceived to be enemies of the state had already been corralled into concentration camps. It seemed inexplicable to someone as free-spirited as Popov that an entire nation could be brought to heel and primed to follow the Führer with unquestioning obedience into war.

At 4.45 a.m. on 1 September 1939, German tanks rolled across the border into Poland. Two days later Britain and France, fulfilling their pledges to Poland, declared war on Germany. The Second World War had begun. Yugoslavia, fearful of an attack from Italy, mobilised 500,000 men, and Prince Paul, the pro-Nazi regent, hurried to Berlin to seek German protection from Italian aggression and, not coincidentally, protect Yugoslavia's valuable trade links with the Third Reich.

For the first few months of the war Yugoslavia managed to sustain a fragile neutrality and in February 1940 the annual festivities in Dubrovnik in honour of St Blaise, the city's patron saint, went ahead as usual with street fairs, extravagant costume parties and masked balls. As an enthusiastic party-goer, it was Popov's favourite time of the year and he was not best pleased when, on the morning of 4 February, he was woken early by his manservant and handed a telegram.

It was from Jebsen, in Berlin. 'Need to meet you urgently,' it said. 'Propose 8 February, Hotel Serbian King, Belgrade.'

Popov was shocked by the change in his friend when they met in the wood-panelled bar of the Hotel Serbian King, overlooking the silvery Danube, a few days later. Jebsen's supreme self-confidence seemed to be shattered; he was clearly nervous, chain-smoking and throwing back one whisky after another. His teeth and moustache were stained with nicotine and his hair badly needed the attention of a barber. He quickly explained why he needed Dusko's help. Jebsen had joined his family's shipping business after graduating from Freiburg University and wanted to pull off a risky deal that could eventually land him in trouble with the ruling Nazi party. Five German merchant ships, one of them belonging to Jebsen, were trapped by an Allied blockade in the harbour in Trieste, Italy. Jebsen had managed to obtain authorisation to sell them to a neutral country, provided they would not be used to trade with England or France; he wanted Dusko to use his contacts in Yugoslavia to set up the deal before the German government woke up to the fact that once the ships were in the ownership of a neutral country any guarantee not to trade with the Allies would be worthless. Jebsen was motivated by more than just a desire to make money – he wanted to deny the ships to Germany. 'Hitler is making fools out of the Germans,' he confided to his friend, 'and with their help he may take over the world.'[1]

Popov thought the quickest way to close the deal was to secretly offer the ships to the British, using a Yugoslav company as cover. Through his friendship with Bozo ('Bosho') Banac, the most influential businessman in the country and a man with many interests in Britain, Popov knew the British commercial attaché for the Balkans, a Mr Sturrack. He set up a meeting with Sturrack for the following day and put the proposition to him. Sturrack was enthusiastic and promised to get approval from London in a couple of days.

Meanwhile, Jebsen flew back to Berlin to organise the documentation and Popov approached Mrs Djurdjina Racic, the widow of a shipping magnate and a close family friend. Mrs Racic was the daughter of Nikola

Pasic, the first prime minister of Yugoslavia and the man revered as the father of the country; she was also staunchly pro-British. She unhesitatingly agreed that her shipping company could be used as the notional purchaser of the five ships in Trieste. Within two weeks the deal was done.

When Jebsen returned to Belgrade, he had surprising news for his friend – despite his virulent anti-Nazi views, he had volunteered to join the Abwehr as a *Forscher* (researcher), which would allow him to travel on private business and financial affairs so long as he was willing to submit reports on information he had obtained from his business contacts. His primary motivation, he admitted, was to avoid being called up for military service, but he also felt that as an Abwehr agent he stood a better chance of staying in touch with what was happening in the world outside Germany than if he were forced into uniform. Popov was mystified and felt there was much his friend left unsaid, but did not press for further explanation.

Jebsen had another favour to ask. His first task as an Abwehr *Forscher* was to solicit independent views for a report identifying which French politicians would be most likely to cooperate with Germany after the fall of France – which, he explained, Germany considered was both inevitable and imminent. Would Popov, who had good contacts in France, be willing to contribute? After some thought, Popov agreed that he would do so, but only as a friend. He made it clear he had no interest in helping the Abwehr, let alone the Nazi regime. But in truth he was intrigued by this invitation to skirt the fringes of an intelligence operation and was flattered that his opinions were sought. He also, privately, wondered if his report might be of interest to someone at the British Legation in Belgrade.

Over the next few weeks Popov sounded out family friends, French diplomats, government officials, experts on French affairs, businessmen trading with France – anyone, in fact, with inside knowledge of the country. He usually raised the subject casually at social functions to avoid drawing attention to himself. It was interesting that almost everyone agreed there was only one obvious candidate to govern France on behalf of the Germans: the former prime minister Pierre Laval, whose collaborationist views were well known and who had spoken frequently about creating a military alliance with the Third Reich.

Popov typed out his report, in duplicate, and took a copy with him when, a few nights later, he was invited to a reception at the British Embassy. He was not quite sure what he was going to do with it – he did not want to be considered either a meddler or, worse, an informer for the Abwehr – but thought that if an opportunity presented itself to pass the report on, he would take advantage of it. At one point, midway through the evening, he noticed that the First Secretary, a man he knew only as Mr Dew, had stepped out onto the terrace for a breath of fresh air. Popov followed him. Grateful there was no one around to overhear their conversation, Popov quickly told Dew about his friendship with Jebsen, the background to the report and Jebsen's assertion that the Germans were confident that France would fall. Dew was attentive, asked a lot of questions and made it clear that he would be interested in seeing a copy of the report, which Popov instantly handed over. Before they returned to the party, Dew tucked the report into an inside pocket and quietly suggested that Popov should stay in touch with his Abwehr friend.

Jebsen's prediction that France was doomed soon proved correct. On 14 June 1940, four months after Jebsen's approach to Popov, German troops marched triumphantly into Paris after less than forty days' fighting. Two weeks later Pierre Laval was named as the head of the Vichy government.

Not long after Popov had given the top copy of his report to Jebsen he noticed a subtle change in the attitude of staff at the German Legation in Belgrade. He was negotiating a concession to manufacture an explosive, known as penta-aeritrite, for a client who needed to import machinery from Germany. In previous dealings with staff at the German Legation, Popov had always found them cold and unfriendly, and assumed it was because they were aware of his run-in with the Gestapo in Freiburg a few years earlier. Now they seemed to be all smiles, falling over themselves to offer him assistance. Popov knew he had been named as the author of the Laval report and deduced, rather uncomfortably, that the Germans now considered him an ally. One of the legation secretaries, a certain Herr von Stein, even insinuated that since Popov knew the Banac family well, and therefore had easy entrée into British social circles, he might do well to work for the Germans.

Jebsen spent a lot of time in Belgrade that summer, as much on business as on his duties for the Abwehr, and one day he asked Popov, without any explanation, if he could bring a colleague from the German Legation to dinner at Popov's house. Jebsen simply said it was someone he wanted his friend to meet. The uninvited guest turned out to be a pompous individual by the name of Müntzinger, who did not explain who he was, but wasted little time making it clear why he wanted to meet Popov.

While Jebsen sat at the dinner table smoking silently and avoiding his friend's eye, Müntzinger talked first about the certainty of German victory. In a couple of months, he maintained, Britain would be invaded and would collapse in the face of the mighty German army, just as France had. Germany would become the supreme power in Europe – invincible.

Müntzinger wanted to thank Popov for his recent help (Popov assumed he was talking about the Laval report) and congratulated him on its content. He was aware of the 'unpleasantness' in Freiburg and could only attribute it to an excess of zeal on the part of the local Gestapo; but that was in the past, and someone with Popov's talents and connections could be very useful in the future. Müntzinger seemed impressed that Popov was a friend of the Duke of Kent, although in truth he was not. (He had met the Duke when he visited Yugoslavia a few years earlier and had arranged for him to have honorary membership of the Argosy yacht club in Dubrovnik.) With connections like that, Popov could render invaluable service to the Reich, and the Reich was of course generous in showing its appreciation . . .

Incredulous, Popov realised that Müntzinger was trying to recruit him as a spy. 'I can't really say that I was shocked,' he recorded in his memoirs, 'or that I was surprised – subconsciously I must have been prepared for the offer – but I did feel a burst of adrenalin running through me.'[2] Popov said nothing for a while and let the German continue. Germany had plenty of agents in Britain, Müntzinger said, but none with Popov's access to society and his ability to open doors; what they wanted, he explained, was someone who could mix in the highest social circles and report back.

When Popov finally asked what kind of 'reports' would be required, the German blustered, saying he was only seeking an agreement 'in principle' and that Johnny would fill in the details later and introduce him to the proper people, if he were to accept. Popov asked for time to think it over; Müntzinger immediately agreed and stood up to leave.

Jebsen, clearly agitated, was pouring himself a drink in the sitting room when Popov returned from showing Müntzinger to the door. Popov angrily demanded that his friend come clean and Jebsen poured out the whole story. Müntzinger was his boss, the chief recruiter for the Abwehr in central Europe, and Jebsen had 'taken the liberty' of putting his (Popov's) name forward as a possible agent. Germany was going to win the war and had enormous economic influence over the Balkans; it would do Popov no harm to have friends in Berlin. Before leaving for the night, Jebsen made a curious comment about the advantages of opposing an organisation from the inside, which left his friend wondering exactly where Jebsen's loyalties lay.

For Popov there was no such dilemma. He had already decided that he would only accept Müntzinger's proposition if he was able to use it in some way that would be beneficial to the Allies. The next morning he was sitting in Dew's office in the British Embassy explaining word for word what had happened the previous evening. Dew warned him that he was entering dangerous territory and that he could pay with his life for a single mistake; Popov simply shrugged. Dew was pleased and said he would arrange for Popov to meet one of his 'friends' later that day at the offices of British Passport Control, just down the street from the embassy.

Dew's 'friend' turned out to be the head of the Belgrade Station of MI6, the British secret intelligence service, who operated under the cover of Passport Control Officer. He told Popov his name was Fickis, although Popov never knew if this was just a pseudonym. Fickis made Popov repeat the story of his meeting with Müntzinger and questioned him at length, extracting every last scrap of information. When he was satisfied that Popov could tell him no more, he said that he was very interested in what Popov had to say and would be contacting London for further instructions.

Two days later, Popov was summoned back to Fickis' office and told that London wanted him to accept the German offer. He was to be friendly, but not too enthusiastic, and was to contrive some business excuse for a visit to London where, he was to tell the Germans, he had a diplomat friend who needed money and might be prepared to help. In fact, MI5 wanted to get a look at Popov, check him out thoroughly and make certain that he really was working for the Allies and not playing a triple game.

Müntzinger could barely conceal his satisfaction when Popov told him he was ready to cooperate with the Abwehr. The German boasted that he was an excellent psychologist and had sensed all along that Popov would recognise where his best interests lay; he was delighted to be proved correct. Jebsen would in future be the go-between, providing contact between Popov and Müntzinger. Popov had already told Jebsen about his 'diplomat friend' and Müntzinger pressed for a name, but Popov insisted that his friend had agreed to cooperate only on the basis of his name not being revealed. Müntzinger was unhappy about it, but Popov stood firm. He also made it clear that he would never be prepared to undertake any mission that would damage Yugoslavia and that his primary motivation was financial – he wanted to be paid well and he wanted his family to be looked after. Müntzinger hastened to reassure him that would be no problem and even offered to pay for Popov's younger brother to complete his schooling in Italy. Before their meeting ended, Müntzinger fished in his briefcase and pulled out a small metal phial. It contained, he said, secret ink. Popov was to give it to his friend, along with a questionnaire with which he would shortly be supplied. His friend was to write the answers in secret ink.

The questionnaire, when it arrived, was exhaustive. It contained twenty-one separate questions and called for information about the coastal defences in south-east England from the Wash to Southampton ('Why during night air-raids are there few anti-aircraft guns active and more searchlights and fighter aeroplanes? Is reason tactical or lack of anti-aircraft guns?'); the location of military units and the names of commanding officers; the state of arms production, particularly anti-tank weapons; a list of Churchill's enemies; the names of politicians or civic leaders in favour of opening peace negotiations with Germany; and details of organisations campaigning for a quick end to the war.

Popov passed the questionnaire to Fickis, who studied it carefully and said that it was valuable inasmuch as it indicated what the Germans did not know at that time. London would contrive some 'answers' in due course. Popov would be given two more lengthy questionnaires over the next few weeks, both of which he pretended to the Germans had been sent to his friend in London in the Yugoslav diplomatic bag, but both of which he passed to Fickis.

Meanwhile, Popov was trying to set up the import/export business in Belgrade that was supposed to provide him with cover – and an excuse to travel – in his new role as a fledgling double agent. During this critically busy time his car broke down and the mechanics at his garage warned him they would have to strip the engine completely to get it back on the road. His father's chauffeur, Bozidar, who was not needed in Dubrovnik, offered to drive him round in the family Buick. Popov was grateful, but amazed – Bozidar's laziness was a legend in the family, although everyone was fond of him. He had worked for the family for a long time, had taught Popov to drive when he was fifteen and, being cross-eyed, was teased endlessly about being able to see in two directions at once.

The arrangement with Bozidar seemed to work well until Jebsen burst into Popov's bedroom very early one morning in a state of high excitement. He shook his friend awake and waved a sheaf of papers in his face. 'You're being sold out by Bozidar,' he shouted. Popov sleepily sat up in bed and tried to focus on his friend. Jebsen explained that he'd been telephoned the previous night by Müntzinger and told to pick up some papers from Bozidar. He had just done so. The papers (nine pages of them) contained a list of every address at which Popov had called in the previous two weeks. Bozidar, it was clear, was spying on Popov for Müntzinger. It was stupid of Müntzinger to involve Jebsen, who he knew was a close friend of Popov, but presumably, as a faithful party man, he could not envisage anyone putting friendship before loyalty to the party.

Popov felt no need to ask his friend why he was risking his career, and perhaps even his life, by warning him what was happening. He did not know what game Jebsen was playing, and did not want to know, but he recognised that the bonds of their friendship were stronger than Jebsen's dubious loyalty to the Abwehr and knew he could trust him – that was all that mattered.

At first, Popov thought he had nothing to worry about. He looked through the list of addresses and made a wry crack about it only including a few of his girlfriends, but Jebsen pointed, with a nicotine-stained finger, to a visit to an address on Milosa Velikog, and another the following day, and another a few days later . . . six in all. When Popov protested that it was only the office of British Passport Control, Jebsen shook his head sadly. Everyone in the Abwehr knew, he said, that it was the headquarters of British intelligence.

It was at that moment Popov realised he was in serious trouble and that his career as a double agent could well be at an end before it had begun – not to mention the danger to his life. If the list was sent to Müntzinger, he would immediately realise that his new recruit was in cahoots with the British. There would be no way Popov could talk himself out of trouble; he would be arrested and would be lucky if he ended up in a concentration camp. There was also a strong possibility that his family would be targeted, if for no other reason than as a warning to others.

Jebsen offered to delay submitting the list to Müntzinger long enough to rewrite it, omitting the damning visits to 'Passport Control'. That was simple enough: the problem was Bozidar. All the time he was around, Popov risked exposure. Popov considered threats, bribes, dismissal, sending Bozidar far away or even getting him arrested by the Belgrade police on some trumped-up charge. But none of the options guaranteed Bozidar's silence – and his silence was necessary for Popov's future.

Two days later Bozidar was found shot dead in a Belgrade railway yard. The police said he had apparently been in the process of carrying out a burglary and was killed by security guards. Popov, who had some unsavoury friends in the Yugoslav capital, paid for the funeral and sent flowers. He lost no sleep over the casual dispatch of a long-time family retainer; as far as he was concerned, the chauffeur was Yugoslavia's first collaborator and got what collaborators deserved. Popov's cold ruthlessness would stand him in good stead for his career as a double agent. His expansive personality and great personal charm concealed a core of steel and he never allowed emotions or personal feelings to interfere with his work. Much later in the war he almost killed his German controller when he thought he was going to be arrested.

Meanwhile, the Germans were getting restless that no answers were forthcoming to the questionnaires Popov had sent to his 'friend' in London. Popov played for time by explaining that his friend had become nervous and was frightened to use the diplomatic bag. Finally Müntzinger agreed that the best solution would be for Popov to go to London to collect the answers himself; he cabled Berlin for authorisation to apply for the necessary exit permits and transit visas.

For the next few weeks Popov waited with increasing impatience for permission from Berlin to leave for London. Jebsen explained that the delay was probably caused by continuing security checks. To prompt the Germans into action, MI5 devised an ingenious 'carrot'. At Popov's next meeting with Fickis – now conducted extremely discreetly after the scare with the unfortunate Bozidar – he was given a handwritten letter, ostensibly from his 'diplomat friend', on the headed notepaper of the Yugoslav Embassy in London. 'Dear Dusko,' it read:

I understand your impatience. I have collected quite a number of the Ming porcelain you want as a present for your mother, but unfortunately I cannot send it through the diplomatic pouch. For one thing, it is too fragile and too bulky. More important, the British Foreign Office is becoming sticky and we have been asked to limit our mail to the strictly essential. I suggest you collect the porcelain yourself when you come to London, or arrange for it to be collected. Otherwise, you'll have to wait until my next trip to Belgrade. Incidentally, the money you advanced for the purchases has been spent. If you want to complete the collection, I suggest you bring more funds. Yours, Bata.

Popov immediately passed the letter to Jebsen, who gave it to Müntzinger. There was no need to explain that the 'Ming porcelain' was code for answers to the questionnaire. A few days later Popov was told he should make arrangements to travel to London as soon as possible.

Before leaving, Popov was briefed by both Fickis and Müntzinger. He arranged to meet Fickis in a park outside Belgrade, where, on the steps of a massive monument to the fallen of the First World War, the MI6 man ran through basic principles: Popov was to act at all times until he reached Britain as if he really were working for the Germans; he should expect to be under constant observation; he was to keep his eyes and ears open, but write nothing down; he should memorise names and addresses as far as possible. In particular, Fickis added, British intelligence wanted to be given any scrap of information, no matter how trivial, about German plans for the invasion of Britain. The codename for the operation, he explained, was 'Sea Lion'.

Coincidentally, Müntzinger, too, mentioned Operation Sea Lion at his final meeting with Popov. The German was in excellent spirits, mischievously greeting Popov as 'Ivan', before announcing this was to be his codename, and then expounding at length on his belief that victory was in sight: Britain was on its knees, the Luftwaffe ruled the skies and a huge invasion force was being readied to cross the Channel and deliver the *coup de grâce*. Popov thought he might as well get straight down to work and pumped Müntzinger for more information, but concluded either that the German knew nothing more or that he was cannier than he appeared. Popov was given the notepaper of a shipping firm to use for correspondence, and crystals with which to make secret ink.

On 17 November 1940, Popov left Belgrade by train for Rome, from where he was due to fly first to Lisbon and then to England. His career as an Abwehr spy began somewhat inauspiciously with a ludicrous misunderstanding straight out of the pages of a comic novel. In Rome he was to sit on the terrace of a café on the Via Veneto, reading a copy of a Yugoslav newspaper, the *Politika*, with a packet of Morava cigarettes on the table. He would be approached by a man who would strike up a conversation with him and offer to show him the sights. Popov was to say that he would like to see the Vatican, and the man would then offer to hail a fiacre, which would in fact take him to his *Treff*, or rendezvous.

Popov arrived at the café an hour early, intending to pass the time watching the girls go by, and was surprised when, after only a few minutes, an elderly man settled into a chair at the next table and asked him, conversationally, if it was his first trip to Rome. The man had the demeanour of a retired professor, slightly untidy and down-at-heel, not exactly an obvious candidate for the Abwehr, but, Popov assumed, excellent cover. They chatted for a few minutes and Popov got round to saying how much he would like to see the Vatican, whereupon the man offered to be his guide and suggested hailing a fiacre.

Off they went – on a tour of Rome. Popov had no idea what was going on, but waited for his contact to make the first move. Only after they had traipsed round the Vatican and St Peter's and were admiring the Michelangelo ceiling in the Sistine Chapel did Popov finally whisper to his 'guide' that perhaps it was time they got down to 'serious business'. The old man leered knowingly, beckoned him into an alcove, then reached into an inside pocket for a much-thumbed bundle of photographs. They were all of women and girls in various stages of undress. While Popov tried to stop himself from laughing out loud, the man began to describe in colourful and lascivious detail the services each of the women offered. Popov professed to be offended and beat a hasty retreat, leaving the furious Italian muttering dark threats. When a surly Abwehr agent finally caught up with Popov at his hotel later that afternoon, Popov was reprimanded for failing to be at the café at the appointed time. He felt no need to explain his encounter with the elderly Italian pimp.

Popov was instructed to call at an office on the fourth floor of 7 Via Torino the following day. The name on the door was that of a lawyer, a Signor Ardanghi, but the man waiting for him inside was Major Conti, a senior officer in Italian counter-espionage operations. Conti explained that he was arranging a reservation for Popov on a flight to Lisbon, via Barcelona. As soon as he arrived, Popov was to send a brief message to a cover address in Bilbao, from where it would be relayed to Müntzinger. The message was to state: 'Still [number] wagons deliverable' – the number indicating the number of days Popov expected to stay in Lisbon.

Things went better in Lisbon, where Popov was instructed to wait outside a shop on the Rua Augustus and follow a girl who would wink at him. This was much more his style, although the preamble was, as always, cautious and elaborate. Popov had first to telephone a particular number from a particular public telephone box in the city centre, ask for a Karl Schmidt and say that Schmidt's cousin in Stuttgart had told him to call. Schmidt requested him to ring back in ten minutes, when Popov was told to go to the shop on Rua Augustus. He had already been warned, in Rome, that he was to show up an hour earlier than whatever time Schmidt gave him.

Popov was pleased to note that the girl who, on cue, winked at him was extremely pretty. He followed her for several blocks to a black Opel car waiting at the kerbside with its engine running and a driver behind the wheel. The girl opened the rear door and slid onto the back seat, indicating that Popov should join her. As soon as he had slammed the door, the car moved off, stopping a few minutes later to let the girl out. The only words she spoke were to tell Popov to stay in the car, which headed out of the city centre towards Estoril. Shortly after passing the casino, the driver politely asked Popov to lie down on the back seat so that he could not be seen, and to stay down until the car had stopped and the engine had been switched off. Popov did as he was told. When the car finally came to a stop and the ignition was killed, he sat up and realised that they had driven into a garage; the doors were already closing behind them. Another door led directly to the interior of a large Moorish-style villa where a tall, aristocratic-looking man was waiting to greet him, his hand held out in welcome. 'I am von Karsthoff,' he said. 'We are happy to have you here.'

Major Ludovico von Karsthoff's real name was Kremer von Auenrode and he would be Popov's Abwehr controller for the duration of the war. A cultured and urbane man who originated from Trieste, he was head of the Abwehr station in Lisbon, working under diplomatic cover at the embassy, a post in which he could enjoy the lively pleasures of the Portuguese capital, then a veritable hotbed of spies, while at the same time keeping the Nazi regime at arm's length. Like many Abwehr officers, von Karsthoff was ambivalent about National Socialism and its benefits to Germany. His young blonde secretary, Elizabeth Sahrbach, was also his mistress and lived with him in the villa in Estoril, where he kept a pet monkey and two boisterous dachshund dogs, named Ivan I and Ivan II. There was no connection, he hastily assured Popov with a broad smile, between his dogs and Popov's codename.

Popov instinctively liked von Karsthoff, an affection that the Austrian returned. During this first visit, von Karsthoff took Popov under his wing, personally tutoring him in the arcane fieldcraft of spying – how to use dead-letter boxes and secret ink, how to avoid being followed, how to code and decode messages. Von Karsthoff gave Popov a Leica camera and taught him how to use it, although Popov never got the hang of developing his own pictures. The shutter action on a Leica is almost silent, enabling it to be used secretly without attracting attention, but von Karsthoff claimed it was extraordinary what you could get away with, if you posed as a tourist and put a pretty girl in front of whatever it was you were actually trying to photograph. This was the kind of tip Popov really appreciated.

Von Karsthoff gave Popov $400 in cash and a new set of questions clearly aimed at assessing the mood of the British population prior to the planned invasion:

1. Who are the people opposed to Churchill and working for peace with Germany? How can they best be approached? Who are their contacts? What are their hobbies and weaknesses – money, drink, et cetera?
2. What type of bombing attack has the greatest effect on the morale of the population?
3. What kind of propaganda would be most effective?
4. Which class of people is most susceptible to propaganda and how can they be best approached?

Finally Popov was ordered to try and make contact with 'the circle surrounding Vice Admiral Sir John Tovey, commander-in-chief of the

Home Fleet'.[3] He was not to attempt to send the information by mail to a cover address, but was to bring the answers back to Lisbon personally. Von Karsthoff casually added that if Popov happened to be in England when the invasion took place, he was to remain where he was and make contact with the nearest commander of German troops as soon as possible. 'When our troops are there,' he said, 'just ask to be taken to the Commander, tell him who you are, mention my name and everything will be all right. The Commander might give you new orders, just do what he tells you to do.'[4]

But despite their mutual regard, von Karsthoff was powerless to intervene when Abwehr III, the German counter-intelligence organisation, set up a sting to test their new agent's loyalty. Popov already suspected that his room at the Hotel Aviz had been searched at least twice, but he had been careful not to carry anything that could link him to British intelligence and remained unconcerned. What was of more interest to him was the beautiful young woman he occasionally encountered in the hotel dining room, who, he felt certain, was making eyes at him. Her name, he ascertained from the desk clerk, was Ilena Fodor.

Popov's subsequent account,[5] after the war, of his tryst with Ms Fodor could easily have come from the pen of Ian Fleming. He said he emerged from the shower to find the sultry Ms Fodor in his room clad only in a silk negligee. She had already helped herself to a drink from the bottle of whisky he had ordered from room service, and during the next couple of hours they practically finished off the bottle between them while Ms Fodor displayed an extraordinarily keen interest in where Popov had come from, what he was doing in Lisbon and where he was going. Popov lied throughout, claiming that he was trying to recover three post-Impressionist pictures that had been stolen from a Belgian client. He swore that he manfully resisted her amorous advances and eventually packed her off with the remains of the whisky and the admonition that she had had her 'bedtime story'.

Despite his reputation as a playboy, Popov was no fool. He was certain that the luscious Ms Fodor was hoping to get information from him in bed that he might be more reluctant to divulge in less passionate circumstances, and it was a game he did not want to play. He was gratified to have his suspicions confirmed at his next meeting with von Karsthoff, who drily suggested that he should not waste any further time looking for 'post-Impressionist pictures'. Von Karsthoff also quietly warned him that Abwehr III was both merciless and ruthless in its pursuit of suspected traitors.

All this while Popov was trying, unsuccessfully, to get to England in the guise of a businessman representing import/export interests in Yugoslavia. Almost as soon as he had arrived in Lisbon he had called at the British Passport Control Office with a letter of introduction from the corresponding Belgrade office, but was told he would simply have to wait. His visa was approved on 5 December, but he was still unable to get a seat on a plane. Lisbon in the latter part of 1940 was crammed with the human detritus of war – refugees, speculators, smugglers, arms dealers and spies from all sides. Wealthy refugees took suites at the Palacio Hotel in Estoril and whiled away their time in the casino; poor refugees sold whatever they could – sometimes their bodies – to stay alive. Almost everyone was waiting to go somewhere else, and as a result every berth in every departing ship was booked months in advance and seats on departing aeroplanes were impossible to obtain without influence in high places.

As in Belgrade, MI6 operated in Lisbon under the dubious cover of the British Passport Control Office, on the Rua Emenda. It kept tabs on Popov's futile and frustrating attempts to find a passage to England, but only when an angry message was dispatched from London insisting that 'Skoot' arrive before Christmas did the station chief in Lisbon bestir himself and start to pull strings.

Midway through December, a message arrived, out of the blue, at Popov's hotel to inform him that a seat had been reserved for him on a KLM flight to England, departing on 20 December 1940.

3

The Great Game Begins

BRITAIN IN DECEMBER 1940 WAS AT A LOW EBB. STRICT FOOD RATIONING had been introduced earlier in the year (the cheese ration was one ounce per person per week); paper shortages curtailed the printing of books and newspapers; house owners were urged to dig up their beloved lawns to grow vegetables in the 'Dig for Victory' campaign; the BBC broadcast a relentless diet of light music and comedy to cheer up the weary populace; more than 120,000 children had been evacuated from London to rural areas to escape the Blitz; and many Londoners remaining in the capital spent their nights sleeping fitfully under blankets on the dusty platforms of underground stations, never knowing if their homes would still be standing when they emerged in the morning.

While more than 300,000 members of the British Expeditionary Force, encircled on the French coast in June, had been rescued from annihilation by sea, no one could pretend that the 'miracle of Dunkirk' was anything other than a humiliating defeat at the hands of the apparently invincible German army. The Low Countries had been overwhelmed, France had swiftly surrendered, victorious Nazi storm troopers had been photographed parading along the Champs-Elysées in Paris, and it was grimly accepted in Whitehall that the next phase of the war could be a bloody battle on British soil.

Prime minister Winston Churchill prepared the nation for the worst with his defiant warning to the enemy: 'We shall defend our island, whatever the cost may be. We shall fight on the beaches, we shall fight on the landing grounds, we shall fight in the fields and in the streets, we shall fight in the hills. We shall never surrender.'

As fears of an invasion grew, Britain was swept by spy scares, stimulated by lurid stories in the newspapers about the 'enemy within' and 'Fifth Columns' – a term that originated in the Spanish Civil War when a Nationalist general broadcast that he had four columns of troops advancing on Madrid and a 'fifth column' in the city itself. The 'Careless Talk Costs Lives' advertising campaign, with its implication that informers were everywhere, paradoxically stoked public fears, as did the government's decision to remove signposts and place names, as if an assault were imminent. In September all German males resident in Britain between the ages of sixteen and sixty, already subject to severe travel restrictions and curfew, were interned. Police stations across the country were inundated with panicky reports of suspicious activities: there were rumours of coded messages being left on lamp posts for parachutists, of strange comings and goings in the dead of night on remote stretches of coastline and of German agents disguised as nurses, monks, nuns and postmen.

In fact, plans for Operation Sea Lion – the German codename for the invasion of Britain – were well advanced. Over the course of many months the Abwehr had drawn up a lengthy intelligence summary, *Informationsheft Gross Britannien*, which included a list of those people who were to be arrested immediately by the Gestapo as German forces took control of the country. But it had no way of knowing, of course, that its intelligence operations in Britain were fatally compromised and that its principal agent, number A.3504, was controlled by British intelligence.

A.3504, a weaselly Welshman by the name of Alfred George Owens, was MI5's first double agent. Although doubts about his allegiance were never completely resolved, the Owens case demonstrated to sceptics what could be achieved by running a double agent and spurred British intelligence into wholehearted participation in the great game of double cross. An electrical engineer who had emigrated to Canada in his twenties, Owens returned to Britain in 1933 and established a company manufacturing battery accumulators, which were sold to the Royal Navy, amongst others. His work required him to travel frequently to Germany on business, as a result of which he brought back snippets of technical information, which he loyally passed on to his contact at the Admiralty. In 1936 Owens suggested he could provide even more information, if the British government was interested. He was put in touch with MI6 and, with some reservations, taken on their books as an informer and given the codename 'Snow', a partial anagram of his name.

MI6 was right to be chary of Owens. Only a matter of weeks after he had been recruited, a letter he mailed to a post-office box in Hamburg was intercepted. It indicated that he had been in regular contact with the Germans for months and wanted to arrange a meeting in Cologne in a few days' time. Owens was followed to Cologne and observed arriving at and leaving the meeting; more of his mail was intercepted, confirming that he was playing a double game. In December 1936, he was confronted with the evidence and immediately confessed that the Germans had made overtures to him to switch sides, but pleaded desperately that his objective all along was to penetrate the German secret service on behalf of British interests.

For the time being he was given the benefit of the doubt, although he was kept under close observation, followed everywhere he went and his mail continued to be intercepted. He struggled to establish his *bona fides* with British intelligence, offering bits and pieces of information both to MI6 and to Scotland Yard's Special Branch about connections he had made in Germany. But even when he reported that the Germans had appointed him their chief agent in Britain and wanted him to set up a network of secret transmitters to broadcast propaganda in the event of war, Owens was still regarded by his handlers with the deepest suspicion.

Everything changed in January 1939, when Owens informed Special Branch that the Germans were about to send him a wireless transmitter, which he had been asked to store 'until an appropriate time'. Here, at last, was apparent proof that Owens was on the side of the British. Why, otherwise, would he admit that he was being given a radio? A few days later he received a letter from Hamburg with instructions on how to work the radio and a ticket for the left-luggage office at Victoria station, where, he was told, the set had been left for him in a suitcase. Special Branch officers accompanied Owens to the station and took possession of the suitcase as soon as he had retrieved it. It did, indeed, contain a wireless transmitter, which was immediately passed on to MI6 to be examined by technical experts. A few days later the set was returned to Owens and he was ordered to open communications with Germany and await instructions. In fact, he was unable to make the set work when he got it home – the plaintive letter he sent to Hamburg complaining that it was faulty was routinely intercepted and read by British intelligence.

In August, serious doubts about Owens once again surfaced. Without warning, he suddenly took off to Hamburg with his lover – an English woman of German extraction – and an unidentified man. A week later, his wife and son, left behind in Britain, denounced him to the police as a German agent. Owens returned to Britain on 23 August, but slipped through the port of entry without being noticed and disappeared.

All this while the international situation was deteriorating rapidly. Having swept into Czechoslovakia, Germany now threatened to engulf Europe in a major war by invading Poland. As early as April the British government had announced plans to conscript young men into military service and to evacuate two and a half million children in the event of war. In May, Germany and Italy signed a 'Pact of Steel' committing both countries to support each other with 'all military forces' in time of war. And by August, with Germany becoming more belligerent by the day, all hope of preventing conflict had more or less been abandoned.

On 1 September, German armoured troops and infantry, supported by the Luftwaffe, launched a lightning attack on Poland, introducing a terrifying new word into the language of conflict – *Blitzkrieg*. Two days later, British prime minister Neville Chamberlain announced to a hushed and sombre House of Commons that Britain's ultimatum to Germany to suspend its attack on Poland had expired and therefore 'This country is now at war with Germany.'

The following day, out of the blue, Owens telephoned his contact at Special Branch – a police inspector – to ask for a meeting. The inspector was delighted to oblige since it had been decided that 'Snow' should be arrested as soon as he could be found. A rendezvous was arranged at Waterloo station. The inspector turned up with a detention order, immediately arrested Owens, escorted him to a waiting car and conveyed him, protesting vigorously, to Wandsworth prison.

In the grim confines of a Victorian prison cell, Owens' options were laid out for him. He could be charged with spying for Germany and, in the very likely event of being found guilty, would almost certainly be sentenced to death – hanging was the British government's preferred method of execution at that time. He could, however, escape the gallows if he were to operate as a double agent and open radio communication with Germany under the direction of MI5. Faced with such a choice, it was hardly surprising that Owens readily agreed; 'Tar' Robertson was appointed as his case officer.

Owens' first mission was to go to Holland to meet his German controller, a Major Nikolaus Ritter, who masqueraded under the pseudonym 'Doktor Rantzau', and convince him that he was back in business. The radio set was located and brought to Owens' cell, where an MI5 technician got it working. After some difficulty, contact was made with Hamburg and a cryptic message was dispatched: 'Must meet you in Holland at once. Bring weather code. Radio town and hotel. Wales ready.'

One of Owens' duties was to transmit daily weather reports to Germany and he needed a shortened code to reduce the length of transmissions, now that war had been declared. 'Radio town and hotel' was simply a request to identify a rendezvous, and 'Wales ready' referred to his instructions to find renegade members of the Welsh Nationalist Party who might be willing to undertake sabotage operations against England.

In late September, Owens travelled to Rotterdam – commercial flights and cross-Channel ferries were still operating between Britain and the Continent – met Ritter at a safe house in Antwerp and received more instructions, which he duly passed to Robertson of MI5 when he got back to Britain. Two weeks later he returned to Holland in the company of Gwilym Williams, a retired police inspector who played the role of a rabid Welsh Nationalist anxious to strike a blow against the hated English. Williams was presented to the Germans as Owens' 'chief agent' and was enrolled as A.3551. At a third meeting, on 21 October in a suite at the Hotel London in Antwerp, Ritter introduced Owens and Williams to 'the commander', an Abwehr officer who talked at length about shipping arms and explosives to Wales by submarine to encourage an insurrection by the Welsh Nationalist Party. Williams assured the Germans he was an explosives expert, ready to start sabotage operations as soon as he was provided with the necessary explosives, and was given detonators hidden in a block of wood.

The two men returned to Britain with a wealth of information, including a new cipher to use for radio transmissions, a series of five-figure groups which turned out to be the basis for a number of Abwehr codes and would prove invaluable, enabling cryptologists in Britain to decipher Abwehr radio traffic transmitted from a ship off the Norwegian coast, and helping MI5 to create a card index for every case officer and agent mentioned during these broadcasts. It was a major step forward for British intelligence.

Owens was also given by Ritter a letter of introduction to a man in Liverpool who turned out to be a British subject, born of a German father, who had been recruited by the Abwehr under duress in 1938 after they made threats against his brother, then resident in Germany. This man was an expert photographer and was working on the development of micro-photographs, about the size of a postage stamp, which the Germans planned to use to communicate with their agents in the United Kingdom. When approached by MI5, he readily agreed to switch sides.

While Owens was away, MI5 had intercepted two letters addressed to him at his home in London, each containing a £20 note stamped 'S & Co.'. Robertson's assistant, Richard Stopford, discovered that 'S & Co.' referred to Selfridges, the large department store in the West End of London. With remarkable perseverance, he tracked down an assistant who remembered serving a middle-aged, foreign-sounding woman who had asked for two £20 notes in exchange for notes of smaller denomination. She had also, extremely unwisely, given her name as Mathilde Krafft and asked for her purchases to be delivered to her home address in

Bournemouth. No action was taken against her, for fear of compromising Owens, but she was kept under surveillance in the hope that she would provide leads to other enemy agents.

Owens had unquestionably produced results for MI5, even if his true allegiance remained obscure. The Germans, too, were impressed. By the end of 1939 Owens was regarded by the Abwehr as the 'lynchpin' of their intelligence operations in Britain. As far as Berlin was concerned, the 'Welsh ring' was functioning superbly well, with 'Snow' making almost daily reports to Hamburg, and Williams allegedly engaged on a dastardly plot to poison the reservoirs in Wales that provided water for Britain's industrial heartland.

In April 1940, Ritter suggested to Owens, at their last meeting in Antwerp before Germany invaded the Low Countries, that he should recruit an agent for training by the Abwehr in the Fatherland. Owens pretended to go along with the idea and a plan was hatched for the new recruit to be handed over to a German U-boat at an agreed rendezvous in the North Sea. MI5 was enthusiastic when Owens returned with this news: planting a double agent inside Germany, albeit only temporarily, was an opportunity too good to be missed. Owens' 'recruit', posing as an RAF deserter, was a reformed petty criminal and confidence trickster who went by the name of Sam McCarthy and was apparently willing to volunteer for this extraordinarily dangerous mission. There was, however, a fatal flaw in the planning: McCarthy did not trust Owens any more than Owens trusted McCarthy.

With the discreet help of MI6, Owens was provided with a Grimsby trawler, the *Barbados*, and set out on the evening of 19 May with McCarthy to rendezvous with a German submarine just south of Dogger Bank in the North Sea. The operation rapidly descended into farce. Both men were nervous and both were sea-sick, and somewhere out at sea each became convinced that the other was a genuine German agent who would reveal his true identity to Ritter, effectively signing a death warrant. When, two days before the rendezvous, an enemy seaplane circled the trawler and gave the agreed recognition signal, McCarthy acted. He locked Owens in his cabin and ordered the skipper of the trawler to extinguish its lights, turn around and set a course back to Grimsby.

Interviewed by Robertson on their return, each man blamed the other. McCarthy claimed that Owens had been drinking heavily and had hinted, while drunk, that he had duped MI5 and was, in reality, working for the Germans. Owens claimed that he acted as if he were a German agent because he suspected that McCarthy really *was* an Abwehr agent and was leading him into a trap.

With an uncharacteristic lack of forethought, MI5 then decided to keep the North Sea rendezvous, this time in a trawler with a Royal Navy crew and with a shadowing submarine, in an attempt to capture Ritter. Fortunately, the plan was thwarted by thick fog. Had Ritter been captured, Owens' cover would certainly have been blown and the foundation for future double-agent operations would have been destroyed.

Owens' protestations of innocence during his interrogation were not helped when he was searched and a report about the organisation and operations of MI5 was found. Its provenance was traced back to William Rolph, the manager of a restaurant in Piccadilly who had occasionally worked for MI5 as an informer. Robertson and Stopford confronted Rolph in his office in Dover Street. He admitted he had been secretly recruited by Owens as a German agent because he needed the money, and swore that he would cooperate fully with MI5 if he could avoid prosecution. He must have realised his predicament was hopeless: as soon as the two MI5 men left, he killed himself by putting his head in a gas oven.

In August, intercepted signal traffic indicated that Germany was planning to dispatch a number of agents to Britain on short-term missions in preparation for Operation Sea Lion. That same month the Abwehr asked Owens to supply specimen names and numbers for a dozen forged identity cards. MI5, acting on Owens' behalf, was more than willing to oblige.

From June 1940 onwards, legal entry into Britain from Europe was possible only through Sweden or Portugal and all entrants were rigorously screened. Germany responded by attempting to insert agents clandestinely – landing by rubber boats from submarines at night or parachuting into remote rural areas. Unfortunately for the Abwehr, the British security services usually knew when and where they were arriving and were waiting for them.

In April, British scientists at Station X (the government's code and cipher school, based in a rambling red-brick house at Bletchley Park, fifty miles north of London) had finally cracked the Enigma code, used for all Germany's signal traffic worldwide. The Germans were confident that Enigma was unbreakable, but a development team under Professor Alan Turing had been working at Bletchley Park for nearly two years to eliminate the bugs from a data-processing machine, codenamed Ultra, that was able to unravel the code. It was one of the most important breakthroughs of the war and was of unparalleled strategic value, since it enabled British intelligence to intercept secret signals from the enemy's high command. Perhaps the most valuable, and most closely guarded, secret of the war, Ultra was never referred to by name in official reports, but was described, obliquely, as 'special intelligence'.

Although more than 10,000 people were made aware of the existence of Ultra during the war, incredibly not a word leaked out about it for more than thirty years. Security was so tight that none of the double agents run by MI5 was ever allowed to know that the British were reading German traffic. This sometimes meant that agonising decisions had to be made. At one point later in the war signals were being intercepted clearly indicating that the Germans suspected Popov had been turned and was playing a double game – yet he could not be warned. As far as MI5 was concerned, preserving the secrecy of Ultra was more important than the life of an agent, even one as valuable as Popov.

'Special intelligence' meant that the careers of most German agents ended before they had even begun. Even those who escaped immediate arrest were so poorly trained and equipped that their freedom was soon curtailed. Some carried forged identity documents put together with information supplied by Owens, instantly identifying them as spies; some were given contact addresses that had been bombed months earlier; some could barely speak English and others were so ill-informed about everyday life in wartime Britain that they quickly gave themselves away. One was arrested after he had offered food coupons for a meal in a London restaurant at a time when coupons were not needed. Another came a cropper after he tried to buy a ticket at a railway station; told the price was 'ten and six', he handed over ten pounds and six shillings, instead of ten shillings and sixpence. Agents' orders were generally to pose as refugees and report troop movements, anti-aircraft defences and civilian morale, but their equipment was pathetic – a wireless transmitter, a revolver, material for secret writing, local maps and a small amount of money in £5 notes, presumably on the assumption that they would only need to survive until Germany invaded Britain.

'All this inefficiency made us wonder whether it really was due to incompetence,' a British intelligence officer noted, 'or whether such agents were being planted on us so that the Germans would know that their traffic was being controlled by us. Could any intelligence service, let alone one run by the super-efficient Germans, be so incompetent?'[1]

To 'Tar' Robertson, the routine imprisonment of suspected German agents was a shameful waste of a potentially valuable asset. He had seen what could be achieved by a single double agent, even someone as untrustworthy as 'Snow', and was convinced that running a number of double agents could pay handsome dividends for the Allies. Robertson had been persuaded in 1933 to give up his career in the regular army in favour of counter-intelligence work by his friend Guy Liddell, then deputy director of MI5's B Division, responsible for counter-intelligence.

At that time recruitment to MI5 was by personal introduction only, which was thought to be the best guarantee of loyalty and integrity. Robertson possessed both qualities in abundance, but more importantly he was not hidebound by rigid military thinking.

After a fifth convicted spy had been executed, Robertson went to his immediate superior in MI5, Colonel Dick White, with a radical proposal to set up a network of bogus spies, which would feed disinformation to Germany and coax intelligence out of the enemy. He believed that many of the captured agents awaiting trial or execution could be 'turned' and used in a systematic deception campaign. While they could not be offered their freedom in return for cooperation, they could be offered their lives, providing they were willing to reopen radio contact with Germany and transmit under the strict supervision of British intelligence.

Dick White was an energetic, erudite and imaginative individual who would later head both MI5 and MI6. He immediately recognised the potential of Robertson's proposal and took it up with Guy Liddell, by then director of B Division, who put it forward to the intelligence direc-tors of the three services. Cabinet approval swiftly followed and Robertson was put in charge of B.1A, the MI5 section that was to be responsible for the turning and running of double agents. A separate organisation, the XX Committee, was set up to vet the information and disinformation that was to be passed to the enemy.

The XX Committee held its first meeting on 2 January 1941, in the inauspicious surroundings of Wormwood Scrubs prison, in west London, which was acting as the temporary headquarters of MI5. It would later move to the top of St James's Street, agreeably close to all the London clubs and some of the best restaurants. In the chair was a tall, thin Oxford don by the name of John Cecil Masterman, who had been recruited by MI5 at the outbreak of war for his brilliant, shrewd and unconventional mind. Always referred to by his initials, 'J. C.', Masterman got a First in modern history at Christ Church, wrote mystery thrillers as a hobby and was a passionately enthusiastic cricketer, a sport that he would insist stood him in good stead as a spymaster.

'Running a team of double agents is very much like running a club cricket side,' he wrote after the war:

Older players lose their form and are gradually replaced by new-comers. Well established veterans unaccountably fail to make runs, whereas youngsters whose style at first appears crude and untutored for some unexplained reasons make large scores. It is not always easy to pick the best side to put into the field for any particular match. In addition, some of the players required a good deal of net practice before they were really fit to play in a match. The prime difficulty was that we never knew the date where this decisive match would take place, and our best batsmen and the ones we had most carefully trained might be past their best or even deceased before the date of the final game.[2]

Masterman laid out the objectives of the XX Committee simply and clearly:

1. To control the enemy's intelligence system
2. To catch fresh spies as and when they arrived
3. To gain knowledge of personalities and methods of the German Secret Service
4. To obtain information about codes and ciphers
5. To get evidence of enemy plans and intentions from the questions they asked
6. To influence enemy plans by information supplied
7. To deceive the enemy about Allied plans.[3]

Masterman liked to claim that the most important decision he ever made as chairman of the XX Committee was to arrange for tea and buns to be provided at every meeting – no easy matter in the days of rationing – thus ensuring a nearly perfect attendance record. It was a false modesty: the XX Committee under Masterman was instrumental in bringing about an extraordinary coup – control of the entire Abwehr espionage operation in Britain.

'Dimly, very dimly,' Masterman wrote, 'we began to guess at the beginning of 1941 that we did, in fact, control the enemy system, though we were still obsessed by the idea that there might be a large body of spies over and above those whom we controlled.'[4] After the war it was confirmed there was no such body, large or small. The astonishing truth was that every German spy in Britain was controlled by MI5 for the duration of the war: what the Abwehr believed be an efficient espionage network was nothing more than a mirage. Some 120 German spies worked at various times during the war for the Allies; thirty-nine of them were effective, full-time double agents. 'In retrospect,' Masterman noted, 'it is clear that we were slower in using the weapon in our hands than we need have been, but extreme caution was justified since an early failure might have wrecked the whole system.'[5]

The XX Committee held weekly meetings throughout the war to

decide what genuine information could safely be passed to the Germans in order to 'build up' double agents and establish the trust of their handlers. Obviously agents could not ignore demands for information and it was a tricky balancing act, fraught with danger, trying to decide what the Germans could be told, without causing too much damage: the aim was to provide just enough information to convince them that the lies they were being fed were true. 'In communicating with the enemy almost from day to day,' Masterman noted, 'we were playing with dynamite.'

To ensure a continuous flow of harmless, or undetectably false, information, all chiefs of staff were informed that while the security services had 'means of getting misinformation to the enemy', it would be necessary at the same time to provide genuine intelligence. The directors of intelligence for each of the services were instructed to collate the information (true and false) and pass it on to the XX Committee, which was responsible for convincing the Germans that it had in place a genuine spy operation, rather than a chimera. As 'evidence' of an agent's dedication, extraneous information, known to the committee as 'chicken-feed', was often included in reports. Answers to direct German questions, on the other hand, had to be carefully calculated. What was the potential damage of the truth? What was the potential advantage of a lie? Should an answer be avoided altogether by excuses – no reliable information available, or information very difficult to obtain?

'The answers and the chicken-feed', Ewen Montagu recalled:

> were a mixture of truth, wherever possible, and falsehood where the truth could not be told and where the falsity could not be detected or the detection, when it came, would not matter. From our bogus, or weighted, answers we could try to put them off our own plans and deceive them as to our naval, military and air strength and our weapons development. It had to be delicately done. Explanations which the Germans could check, even some time later, could only be slightly exaggerated or altered. It had also to be credible but from our point of view, not too exact. All this was part of the building up of the agent's credibility with the Germans, so that the Germans would believe the untrue information that we were passing through simultaneously and so that eventually their reputation would be so high that when the moment came for a major deception, the Germans would be more likely to swallow the bait.[6]

Montagu ran an early deception operation when the director of naval intelligence indicated to the XX Committee that it might be helpful in close-quarter naval actions if the Germans believed that King George V-class battleships had been fitted with torpedo tubes. It would have been simplicity itself for an agent to merely report this as a 'fact' to the Germans, but Masterman shrewdly preferred to 'paint a picture', gently prompting the enemy to make deductions that would lead them to conclude, inexorably, what the XX Committee wanted them to conclude.

In this case, Agent A first reported that he had been in a dockyard pub and had overheard two sailors, both the worse for drink, arguing about how much leave they would get while their ship was in dry dock. One had said that it must be at least a week, as 'fitting torpedo tubes was not as simple as all that'. Agent B then reported, to the same spymaster, that he had been on a train going through the same dockyard town and had seen a King George V-class battleship in dry dock. Finally Agent C reported overhearing two factory workers on a bus moaning about loss of overtime while their production line was being converted to manufacture more torpedo tubes.

Another successful long-term deception, confirmed by Ultra intercepts, was to persuade the Germans that the range of British radar was considerably shorter than it was in reality. Information was fed to the Abwehr in apparently random pieces, which could be fitted together like a jigsaw puzzle. After the war, Admiral Wilhelm Meisel, chief of German naval operations, admitted that the German navy had been informed that the range of British radar was exactly that which the XX Committee had intended it should deduce, a mistake that led in part to the loss of the *Scharnhorst*, the pride of the German fleet, sunk by the British battleship the *Duke of York*, off Norway on 26 December 1943.

The XX Committee rarely dealt directly with the agents themselves. Handling the agents was the responsibility of Section B.1A, under 'Tar' Robertson. Arrested agents were taken to a top-secret detention centre set up at Latchmere House, the rambling Victorian manor house in wooded grounds near Ham Common, to the south-west of London, which was originally used as a convalescent home for officers during the First World War. Intense psychological pressure was applied on new arrivals to capitalise on the unnerving experience of their capture and to exacerbate their sense of isolation and desperation: they were quickly made aware, for example, just how much British intelligence knew (from intercepted signals and other double agents) about their missions. Unlike Allied agents, Abwehr spies were given no training in how to withstand interrogation, and when their interrogators got round to suggesting that there was a way they could escape execution and be treated as prisoners of war rather than spies, a surprising number (even hard-line Nazis) were amenable. Coercion or brute force seldom worked – the aim was for agents to experience a real 'Damascene' conversion.

J. C. Masterman observed:

Many spies are willing to commit treachery under pressure or for self-preservation. Some are genuinely anxious to serve the side against which circumstances have obliged them to operate, some have a natural predilection to live in that curious world of espionage and deceit and attach themselves with equal facility to one side or another, so long as their craving for adventure of a rather macabre type is satisfied, some are ready to play for both sides at the same time and appear to maintain a kind of professional pride in doing a good job.[7]

Every double agent was lodged separately in a safe house and assigned an MI5 case officer, usually an older man, who was obliged to play many roles – part guardian, part companion, part social worker and, ultimately, jailer. Case officers were encouraged to develop close relationships with their charges, both to obviate any lingering feelings of guilt and to make the agent dependent on the case officer's goodwill. Providing the agent continued to cooperate, the case officer did everything in his power to ensure that his charge was comfortable and content, providing money, cigarettes, booze and, occasionally, discreet female company.

It was necessary to organise not only their day-to-day activities, but the 'notional' lives that the Germans supposed them to be living. Agents had to be vested with plausible, yet completely bogus, existences – a home, a job, friends, interests, et cetera – to convince the Germans they were functioning successfully. Some agents recruited an entirely fictitious network of sub-agents, all of whom similarly had to be provided with lifestyles and characteristics to make them real to the Germans. None was allowed to step out of character for fear of provoking enemy suspicion. An agent allegedly working as a waiter in a London restaurant, for example, could reasonably be expected to report gossip that he had overheard at a table, but not the technical details of a new weapon. An agent asked for information about a heavily guarded airfield would only report what he could be expected to see either by walking or driving past.

'To build up the agent's value in the Germans' eyes,' said Ewen Montagu:

we sometimes let them have a scoop. For instance, one of them might report accurately that eight major ships were sailing to Malta where their arrival would eventually be reported by the German agents watching that port. In such a case, we had to plan very carefully so that the information could only reach the German operational authorities after the ships had arrived so that there was no chance of their being intercepted.[8]

After every meeting of the XX Committee, individual case officers were briefed on the intelligence that was to be transmitted to Germany by their charges. While it was important that case officers closely supervised all contact with Germany, either by secret writing or by radio, to ensure that the message was exactly that required to be sent by the XX Committee, it was also vital that the message sounded as if it had been put together by the agent himself. Agents operated their own radios, since wireless operators had a recognisable 'fingerprint' in the way they worked the transmitting key, but only with their case officers sitting alongside them and watching every move. There was always a danger, in this intricate web of treachery, that a new double agent was simply waiting for an opportunity to warn his Abwehr masters that he had been turned, or even that he was operating as a triple agent, still working for the Germans. Every case officer was acutely aware that a man who had switched his allegiance once was perfectly capable of switching it again. In fact, very few tried it. One man, suddenly smitten by conscience, made an attempt at escaping on a stolen motor-cycle, but he was arrested long before he reached the coast and spent the remainder of the war in prison.

Fundamental to the success of the operation was the need to convince the Germans that their agents were moving freely about Britain, insinuating themselves into everyday life while acting on orders from Germany. When those orders involved committing acts of sabotage, considerable cunning was required to convince the Germans that the sabotage was actually happening. Helga Moe and Tor Glad were two young Norwegians specifically trained as saboteurs by the Abwehr for operations in Britain. They were flown in a seaplane to the Moray Firth in Scotland in April 1941, paddled ashore in a rubber dinghy and promptly surrendered when they were met by MI5. Offered the usual stark alternatives, they agreed to be turned and were given the codenames 'Mutt' and 'Jeff', after the comic-strip characters.

Since the primary objective of their mission was sabotage, the Germans needed to be convinced they were actually carrying out raids. At first they managed to avoid arousing Abwehr suspicions simply by claiming credit for whatever acts of sabotage were reported in the newspapers, but it soon became clear that an actual 'raid' would have to be organised on their behalf by MI5 to satisfy their German controllers. The first attempt was to blow up a food dump near Wealdstone, in Essex, in November 1941, but local people quickly gathered to put out the fire and the incident never made the newspapers. The next job was almost too successful. The plan was to blow up an old powder factory in the New Forest, but the resulting explosion was so enormous that almost all evidence of sabotage was destroyed, including 'Mutt's' pocket compass, which had been left on the scene to 'incriminate' him. However, on this occasion the explosion was reported in the newspapers, satisfying the Abwehr that their saboteurs were active.

To minimise the risks, agents were kept in isolation and encouraged to believe that they were working alone; certainly none of them knew there was an entire orchestra of double agents all playing together under the direction of British intelligence. Every scrap of information supplied to the Abwehr had to be monitored and cross-referenced to make certain that no report significantly contradicted another, since a single careless slip could have alerted the Germans to what was going on. The information had to be believable, enticing and sometimes slightly contradictory, as no two agents could be expected to obtain exactly the same intelligence.

It would be illogical for agents to be immune to the trials of everyday life in wartime Britain, so they occasionally fell sick, were sacked from their jobs or were obliged to move house. And because it would be too much to expect that every agent could avoid capture, every now and again one would be made to 'disappear', sometimes after warning Hamburg that the British security services were hot on his heels. It was a complicated and elaborate façade that required great ingenuity, finesse, skill and patience to maintain.

Curiously, the work of Section B.1A and the XX Committee was made immeasurably easier by the fact that the Abwehr, under the erratic direction of Admiral Wilhelm Canaris, was badly organised and riddled with petty jealousies. At the Hamburg *Stelle* (station), which was responsible for infiltrating Britain, Abwehr case officers competed shamelessly with each other to bolster the reputation of their agents and thus increase their own status. It engendered a potentially dangerous environment in which case officers had a vested interest in their charges; they *wanted* to believe what they were being told. It got to the point that when, occasionally, intelligence arrived from an independent source apparently contradicting information supplied by an agent in Britain, the agent was almost always believed.

Certainly at the end of 1940 the Abwehr was not, given the difficult circumstances, dissatisfied with its efforts to penetrate Britain. It was aware that a number of its agents had been arrested, but that was only to be expected; a number had also simply disappeared without trace, but that, too, was not unexpected. On the plus side, A.3504 was still operational and at least five other agents were reporting regularly and providing valuable intelligence. The Abwehr was unaware, of course, that all were under the control of British intelligence. Most importantly of all, 'Ivan', the young Yugoslav recruited in Belgrade and of whom great things were expected, was safely in place in London and was about to report, in person, to his controller in Lisbon.

How were the Germans to know that they would become the victims of perhaps the greatest deception in the history of warfare since the Trojans dragged into their city the wooden horse left by the departed Greeks?

4

The Lisbon Connection

NO ONE WATCHING POPOV DESCEND THE STEPS FROM A KLM AIRCRAFT IN the pale winter sun at Lisbon airport in the late afternoon of 2 January 1941 would have imagined he was anything other than a businessman on a routine trip. Certainly no one would have guessed, from his demeanour, that he was a spy and a gambler, staking his life on his good fortune. Popov would return to Lisbon many times during the war and he would never know, on each occasion he was due to meet his Abwehr controller, if this was to be the meeting at which he would be exposed: a simple slip of the tongue, a false move or an injudicious untruth could seal his fate and deliver him, at any time, into the arms of the Gestapo.

Even when a surly immigration official told him that his visa was not in order he remained serenely unruffled. For a while it looked as if he might be refused entry, but entirely by chance a Yugoslav friend, a diplomat based in Madrid, was passing through the airport and stopped to see if he could help. He got the problem sorted out with a quiet word in the official's ear and a handshake that probably involved transferring escudos from palm to palm. Popov was suitably grateful and unusually vague when his friend asked him what he was doing in Lisbon.

Safely through immigration and Customs, Popov took a taxi to the Palacio Hotel, Estoril, where he was greeted by the manager like an old friend – he had stayed at the Palacio in December – and told that his 'usual' suite, on the third floor overlooking the gardens, had been reserved for him. That evening Popov could be found, in a dinner jacket, at the baccarat table in Estoril casino.

Lisbon was the espionage capital of Europe in the Second World War, teeming with spies, adventurers, political refugees, deserters and riff-raff of all kinds who had gravitated to the historic city to escape the war or to make some money out of it. Information was a form of currency quite as valuable as the escudo, and the city's cafés and bars were infested with *bufos*, paid informers who came from all ranks of society, from domestic servants to politicians, from labourers to bankers.

The German Legation faced a handsome square on the Rua do Pau de Bandeira in Lapa, a smart quarter to the west of the city centre, bordering the River Tagus. It was within shouting distance of the British Embassy, a pink-painted edifice on the Rua de Sao Domingos. *Bufos* would loiter outside both places, hoping to pick up scraps of information or report on the arrival of new faces. Britain's secret intelligence service, MI6, formerly occupied a room in the embassy, but the increasing importance of the station after the outbreak of war justified its own offices, at 37 Rua Emenda. Allied agents were said to prefer the Palacio Hotel, in the fashionable resort of Estoril, while their Axis counterparts favoured the Hotel de Parque, just across the gardens.

Both establishments had their share of exotic guests. At one point the Germans asked Popov to keep an eye on the Marquis Pescara de Castelluccio, an Argentine staying at the Palacio. He was said to telephone Vichy frequently and was intriguingly described as an agreeable adventurer and inventor, aged about forty, balding and with a slight stoop, who appeared to have no money, but played bridge a lot and was seen out and about in the company of a blonde who looked twenty, but was in fact sixteen.

Ian Fleming, Malcolm Muggeridge and Graham Greene all savoured the cosmopolitan delights of Lisbon during the war while serving with British intelligence. The first James Bond book, *Casino Royale*, drew on Fleming's frequent visits to the casino in Estoril, while in Lisbon on a mission for the director of naval intelligence. Muggeridge was a major in the Intelligence Corps, and Greene, responsible for keeping track of German agents in Portugal, reported to Kim Philby, who ran MI6 operations on the Iberian peninsula. They became friends and remained so even after Philby's defection to the then USSR. Greene wrote the introduction to Philby's memoirs, *My Silent War*. Greene and Popov also became good friends after the war.

Although Portugal was officially neutral, the government of António de Oliveira Salazar was, in reality, unashamedly pro-German. The Portuguese dictator even asked the Gestapo to help train his secret police, the PVDE, which was deployed to enforce Salazar's own dubious standards of moral rectitude, along with wide-ranging censorship, by rooting out blasphemers, heretics and other undesirables. Despite Salazar's authoritarian regime and the irritating fact that cigarettes were rationed, Popov liked Lisbon, with its broad, tree-lined avenues, cobbled streets, black-and-white geometric-patterned pavements, its cathedral, squares and palaces and its pink stone, neo-classical arcades. Lisbon had good restaurants, attractive women and, most importantly for a man who loved to gamble, a large casino in Estoril, right opposite the Palacio Hotel.

On the morning after his arrival Popov called his controller, von Karsthoff, from a public telephone box, identifying himself as 'a friend of the Major's cousin from Italy', and was told that an appointment had been made for him at the legation at four o'clock that afternoon, which actually meant he should go to von Karsthoff's home, the Villa Toki-Ana in Estoril. Popov said he would take the train, which indicated that he wanted to be picked up at a prearranged spot on the Avenida da Liberdade in Lisbon; if he said he was taking a taxi, it meant he wanted to be picked up on the Lisbon road outside Estoril.

Von Karsthoff clearly enjoyed the cloak-and-dagger element of his job. At one point Popov received instructions in code by watching the numbers von Karsthoff's dour secretary and mistress, Elizabeth, played on the roulette table in the casino at Estoril. The MI6 representative in Lisbon, Captain Ralph Jarvis, was similarly taken with intrigue, occasionally arranging to meet Popov in the lavatory of a restaurant or bar.

Popov assumed that if his cover were blown, he would be arrested at the moment he first made face-to-face contact, so it was always something of a relief when the initial rendezvous passed without incident. He was picked up, as arranged, on the Avenida da Liberdade by an anonymous car, told to lie down on the back seat and driven directly into the garage of von Karsthoff's villa, as before. That evening he enjoyed a convivial dinner with von Karsthoff and Elizabeth, and held forth at length about everything he had done, and everyone he had met, in England. In London, meanwhile, Robertson was told that a signal had been intercepted from von Karsthoff informing Berlin that 'Ivan' had arrived.

Dinner was an amiable prelude to real work the following day, when von Karsthoff subjected Popov to an intensive grilling, which continued throughout the day and into the night. Popov had to account for his movements day-by-day from the moment he had arrived in Britain: where he had gone, what he had seen, to whom he had talked, what they had said. No detail was too minor to be of interest, no anecdote too boring to be repeated, no conversation too facile to be reported, no incident unimportant – von Karsthoff wanted to know everything: time, date and place; names, titles, descriptions, circumstances. Popov did not feel that the German was trying to entrap him, but was acutely aware, with Elizabeth taking shorthand notes, of the vital need to keep his stories straight and not get bogged down in too many lies. He was grateful to be able to cite Ewen Montagu as one of his sources and glad to be able to show von Karsthoff the letter 'proving' they were old friends.

Von Karsthoff did not seem particularly interested in the naval intelligence Popov had brought with him, but questioned him closely on aviation matters, particularly the new Beaufighter, a versatile bomber-fighter-ground-attack aircraft that had recently gone into service with the Royal Air Force. At one point von Karsthoff was checking Popov's answers with some papers he had in front of him, and baulked at Popov's spelling of the word 'Whitchurch'. Popov assured him that his spelling was correct. 'Well, I have it here from a Dutchman,' von Karsthoff replied, 'perhaps he spelled it wrong.' Popov was immediately alert. 'Oh, a Dutchman from the airline?' he asked. Von Karsthoff laughed and agreed. Popov got the impression that von Karsthoff was talking about a pilot and made a mental note to pass on the information, when he got back to London, that a KLM pilot was feeding intelligence to the Germans. It was one of his strengths as a double agent that he never missed an opportunity to garner information, even under interrogation, when he was supposed to be divulging it.

The following day von Karsthoff left for Paris with Popov's report. When he returned, he again invited Popov to dinner at his villa. This time Albrecht Kramer, Lisbon head of Abwehr III, the counter-intelligence branch, was present. Compared to the urbane von Karsthoff, Kramer was almost a caricature Nazi – a red-faced, heavily built, humourless ideologue utterly committed to the party and the Führer. Popov disliked him on sight, a sentiment that Kramer clearly reciprocated. He looked on with obvious disapproval as von Karsthoff explained that his masters were a little disappointed with the information Popov had brought over, since it was far too general in nature. In future, von Karsthoff advised, it would be better to answer a few questions in the utmost detail rather than attempt to answer all the questions vaguely.

A few days later Popov realised he was being followed. His shadow was a tall, thin man with unfortunately large, and therefore distinctive, ears. Von Karsthoff denied absolutely that the man was acting on his orders, as did Colonel Jarvis of MI6, when Popov called him from a public telephone box. Popov concluded that Kramer was probably responsible.

Popov continued to have regular meetings with von Karsthoff, always at the Villa Toki-Ana after dark. The German seemed very keen to pump Popov about life in England. He wanted to know about the conditions in the underground stations in London, where thousands of people took shelter every night from the Blitz. He asked if any epidemic had broken out because of the overcrowding and was so intent on the subject that Popov wondered if the Germans had plans to introduce some kind of bacteria into the underground system. Popov got the strong impression that von Karsthoff, backed by Berlin, trusted him completely. The German said that if Popov did well, he could be offered an agency for the Wolff industrial conglomerate in Yugoslavia after the war as a reward for his services.

Shortly before Popov was due to leave Lisbon, von Karsthoff handed him a lengthy questionnaire, comprising nine typed foolscap pages with more than fifty questions, many with subordinate queries, demanding a daunting amount of information, largely on the strength and disposition of British forces:

> *Vickers Armstrong.* Do Vickers Armstrong possess factories at Brighton and Hawarden to the west of the aerodrome? Have the buildings which were near the aerodrome and which were used for army purposes now been taken over by Vickers for manufacturing? How many Wellingtons do Armstrong make each month? Where else are Wellingtons or parts of Wellingtons made? We want sketches showing sites for Vickers at Weybridge and Vickers near Crayford.
> *Battle Flying Groups (Fighters).* Numbers? Under what Command? Are they placed under the Army Co-operation Command for purposes of organisation and for tactics, or do they remain part of the organisation of the Bomber Command? [. . .]
> *Night Fighter (Independent) Group*
> (a) What is the number of this Group?
> (b) Which squadrons (with what types) [of aircraft] belong to it?
> (c) Squadrons 600–632: Has squadron 612 been given fresh armament? Specially interesting would be details about Squadrons 622–632.
> *First Destroyer Group.* Is it true that the First Destroyer Group has been given the number 15? Was it until now a Group of the Coastal Command? Confirm, please. Where is No. 14 Group? More details wanted about Squadrons Nos 21, 67, 146, 189, 303, 309, 317 . . .[1]

Popov read it through and asked sarcastically if von Karsthoff would also like to know what Churchill had for dinner. Von Karsthoff smiled indulgently, then warned Popov to memorise the questions as far as possible and only make minimal notes if absolutely necessary. Popov was also given a phial of invisible ink crystals, with instructions on how to mix a very small quantity in a wineglass three-quarters full of water; and three cover addresses in Lisbon to which he could safely send answers written in invisible ink on the back of ordinary letters.

That evening, reluctant to leave the questionnaire in his hotel room,

Popov slipped it into the inside pocket of his dinner jacket when he left the Palacio Hotel for the casino night club with an exotic French marquise, Pinta de la Rocque. Popov and the marquise had become lovers when they first met in Paris; he was delighted to find her staying at the Palacio while waiting for a visa to Argentina.

The evening was not a success. A correspondent for the *Daily Mail* at an adjoining table was hosting a large and noisy party, which included a young woman with foolish pretensions as a singer, who took it upon herself to entertain the clientele by warbling into a microphone in front of the long-suffering band. Finally Popov could stand it no longer. He called over a waiter, put a champagne cork on his silver tray and asked him to present it to the singer with his compliments. There was plenty of laughter as the waiter solemnly presented the singer with the cork and indicated that it had come from Popov. She signally failed to see the joke, rushed across the dance floor, picked up Pinta's glass and made to dash the contents in her face.

Popov just managed to catch her arm, but by then the incident had attracted the attention of the adjoining table. The *Daily Mail* correspondent, gloriously drunk, got up from his chair, staggered over to Popov and accused him of insulting his guest. Popov tried to explain that it was just a joke and offered to apologise, but the newspaperman, who had one arm in plaster, was having none of it and swung at Popov with his good arm. Popov ducked and hit back with a jab that left the other man sitting, unceremoniously, on the dance floor. Several other people at his table were already on their feet and heading for Popov, when he suddenly remembered the questionnaire in his jacket pocket. He would be in trouble if the police were called and found him in possession of what was clearly espionage material. He slipped the questionnaire into Pinta's handbag and told her to leave and wait for him in the hotel lobby. Pinta, who was terrified, needed no second bidding, but as Popov turned to face the newspaperman's angry friends he noticed, out of the corner of his eye, that the man with the big ears was following Pinta out of the door.

Popov promptly ran for it, with the jeers and taunts of the drunken party, exultant in their sudden victory, ringing in his ears. Outside, in the gloom, he could just make out two figures struggling in the small park separating the casino from the Palacio Hotel. The man with the big ears was trying to wrench Pinta's handbag from her grasp. The bag flew open and the contents spilled onto the grass but, as the man was stooping to pick them up, Popov arrived and kicked him in the head with all the force he could muster. He went down like a felled bull and at that moment the manager of the Palacio bustled into view carrying a large revolver. He took in the scene, recognised Popov and the marquise as hotel guests and advised them to return to the Palacio immediately. He said he would deal with the police, who were on their way, and tell them that the man had been attacked by ruffians. It was good advice and Popov took it, hopeful that the shaken Pinta would need extensive comforting.

Next day von Karsthoff, who had already heard what had happened, admitted to Popov that the man with the big ears was an Abwehr III agent. Completely guileless, he explained that Kramer had told him that morning that a tail had been assigned to Popov simply to ensure that he was not being followed by British intelligence. The German quickly changed the subject, suggesting that on his next visit to Lisbon Popov should leave enough time to make a trip to Paris, on a German diplomatic passport, to visit the Abwehr headquarters at the Hotel Lutetia for training. Popov was far from keen, and told von Karsthoff that he was worried he might meet someone he knew.

Popov returned to England on 4 February 1941. It appears from MI5 records that from the moment of his arrival he was kept under close surveillance; every movement and every contact he made was meticulously logged. This report was filed on his journey from Whitchurch airfield:

On the train between Bristol and London after tea, Skoot fell into conversation with a stranger who gave him his card. It was Mr Knut H. Onssager, General Motors Overseas Operation, New York. Age 29, looks 35, tall, strong, always smiling, blond slightly thinning hair, no glasses. Factory address: Westbay Road, Western Docks, Southampton. His telephone numbers are Whitehall 3737 and Southampton 72401.

On arrival at Paddington, Skoot and Onssager shared a taxi and had a drink together at the Cumberland Hotel before Onssager went home. Having drinks together, they met a friend of Onssager's, a small, smiling man, an American of Norwegian origin, living in the Cumberland. Skoot later saw this small man dressed in English Naval uniform.

Yesterday evening Onssager came to the Cumberland for a drink and asked for Skoot. He introduced Skoot to a colleague or business associate of his by the name of 'de la Vitre' (?), an American who came over here a month ago and is also working for General Motors. He lives in the Cumberland. De la Vitre is small, dark, aged about 30, has dimples when he smiles. After 11, they all went to the

Lansdowne for some more drinks and did not get back to the hotel until 1 o'clock. The conversation was entirely of a social description . . .[2]

There was a good reason why Popov was being watched: during his absence in Lisbon two of his greatest supporters – Ewen Montagu and his case officer, Bill Luke – had both had second thoughts about his trustworthiness. Montagu had been turning over in his mind his chat with Popov at the Savoy. They had talked a lot about sailing, but for someone who claimed to be an experienced yachtsman Popov seemed, to Montagu, to have little nautical knowledge. He thought a possible explanation was that Popov's sailing experience was perhaps confined to owning a yacht and that all the work had been done by a paid crew, but he was sufficiently worried to voice his concerns to his colleagues on the XX Committee. A much more likely explanation was that Popov was not familiar with British nautical terminology – he had, in fact, been sailing since he was a small boy and was a long-standing member of the prestigious Orsan Yacht Club in Dubrovnik.

Luke's disquiet was more serious inasmuch as it was based on a gut feeling that Popov was fooling them all. 'I cannot help regarding him with a good deal of suspicion,' he noted in a top-secret report to the XX Committee:

He is supposed to be a wealthy man and yet has no particular preferences in the way of food or drink, being satisfied always to leave it to his host to choose the meal – probably this is due to his sparse knowledge of the English language. I have just the general feeling that he may be a most accomplished liar. In fact, if he was able to persuade the Germans that he had influential English connections, whereas the truth is that he only knows three rather insignificant people in the whole country, he must be a good liar.[3]

The great problem for the XX Committee was that although they could keep the closest possible tabs on Popov while he was in Britain, it became much more difficult to do so when he was in Portugal. And, of course, there was no possibility of ever knowing precisely what passed between Popov and von Karsthoff at their meetings in von Karsthoff's villa. The best they could hope for was that Popov reported their encounters accurately, but they could never be sure that he had not informed the Germans from the beginning that he had been recruited by British intelligence and that the Germans were running him as a triple agent. A third scenario was that von Karsthoff had guessed Popov was working for the Allies and was using him as a stooge to pump disinformation back to Britain.

A week after Popov's return, Robertson and Luke invited him to lunch at the venerable Naval and Military Club – always known as the 'In and Out', from the prominent signs on the gateposts of the clubhouse in Piccadilly. Their intention was to try and make some further assessment of where Popov's loyalties lay, but he disarmed them completely by announcing, as soon as he arrived, that he was being followed and expressing the hope that it was MI5 on his tail. The more his *bona fides* were tested, he jauntily informed his lunch companions, the more pleased he would be. The lunch was inconclusive.

Meanwhile, Robertson was trying to set Popov up with a 'suitable girlfriend', who would be instructed to 'entertain' him and make a note of his contacts and acquaintances. This MI5 pimping operation apparently came to nothing, perhaps because, to judge from his diary, Popov was not exactly short of female companionship or social contacts:

9.2.41 – Lunched at Berkeley Buttery with girl friend.
17.2.41 – Saw business friend at his office in morning; lunched Conservative Club and met a number of people; evening cocktails American Bar, met a number of interesting people at dinner; later visited Piccadilly Club.
25.2.41 – Cocktails at 25 Grosvenor Square; Dinner at the Mirabelle; later at 400 Club with friends.
03.3.41 – Met in Mayfair Lounge at 7.30; Dined at Claridges and visited Coconut Grove and 400 Club.
13.3.41 – 12.30 Yugoslav Legation; In and Out 5.30; dined Gwennie and later took her to 400 Club.[4]

Since Bill Luke was Popov's principal sceptic, it was decided that he should be sent, with Popov, on an extended trip to Scotland on what was supposed to be an intelligence-gathering jaunt for the Germans. Its real purpose was to enable Luke to spend time with Popov, talk to him at length and keep a close eye on his behaviour and reactions as they travelled around the country. The two men met for lunch at the Royal Automobile Club in Pall Mall to discuss the trip. 'Over coffee,' Luke noted in his report, 'he hinted that a little high-class feminine society would be most acceptable but I understand this point is already being attended to.'

Popov arrived in Glasgow late on Saturday, 15 February, where he was met by Luke, who had gone ahead to organise the trip, and by Luke's brother, a polyglot who could speak six languages. He had been briefed by Luke to test Popov's claim to be multilingual. The following day the three men took off in a hired car for a tour of Scotland's scenic attractions, including Loch Lomond and Gareloch, where there was a huge naval base. Luke was encouraged by the fact that Popov evinced no interest in the large number of ships moored in Gareloch and asked no questions about them. His brother chatted amiably with Popov in French, German and Italian and was impressed by his command of all three languages. That evening, after Popov had gone to bed, Luke's brother expressed the somewhat unhelpful view that he did not think Popov's personality would appeal to the Germans – he was a type whom the Italians would be much more likely to employ.

For the remainder of the week Popov and Luke travelled extensively, using Glasgow as a base. Luke, who was a Scot, introduced Popov to many of his friends and pre-war business acquaintances, all of whom were briefed that he was using the pseudonym 'Bill Matthews'. The evenings, Luke later reported, were 'filled with jovial entertainment in congenial company'.

Much as Popov admired the scenery, it was obvious to Luke that he wanted to talk when they were on the road together. He spoke bitterly about his hatred of the Nazis, particularly Joseph Goebbels, the regime's master propagandist. He thought that Goering, whose gallantry in the First World War he much admired, was the brains behind the German military machine. If Germany violated Yugoslavia's neutrality, he was sure, he said, that his country would be ready to defend itself. Although much of the north was very vulnerable to attack, the south-west could be defended by blowing up mountain roads and could even survive aerial attack if the Allies came to the rescue quickly enough. Personally, Popov was convinced that Britain would win the war within two years, probably following Germany's economic and moral collapse.

Popov took the opportunity of their time together to try and enrol Luke's support for his commercial activities. If he could obtain the necessary Navy Certificates (navicerts), he explained, he could ship desperately needed goods into Yugoslavia – including coffee, tea, wool, rubber, sisal, jute, cotton and linseed oil – in exchange for valuable raw materials such as antimony (a metallic element used for alloy castings) and bauxite, 90 per cent of which was at that time going to Germany. Such an arrangement would not only provide excellent cover for his presence in Britain, but would also enable him to make some money over and above what he was being paid by the Germans. Popov slyly reminded Luke that he had asked for no payment from British intelligence for his services. Luke could not help but be impressed by the Yugoslav's acumen.

Their last day in Scotland was due to be spent in Edinburgh, from where Luke had arranged for them to return to London on the overnight sleeper train. In Edinburgh they spent a leisurely day visiting the castle, St Giles' cathedral and the Palace of Holyroodhouse, only to discover, on arriving at the railway station, that there was a problem with their sleeper reservations and the train was full. Luke managed to obtain the last two rooms at the Caledonia Hotel.

Popov was obliged to register as an alien and within half an hour two officious and overbearing police officers in plain clothes arrived at the hotel to question him. Luke attempted to intercede, showed them his War Office pass and intimated that he would prefer them not to interview Popov, but they would not be deterred. Luke then asked them to telephone the chief constable of Glasgow (with whom he and Popov had lunched a few days earlier), but they refused. When, as a last resort, Luke whispered that he was working for MI5, they became even more truculent, claiming that MI5 was constantly making work for them, sending them off on futile enquiries. They insisted that Popov could not remain in Edinburgh overnight – he would either have to leave for London or go back to Glasgow.

Luke, by now exasperated, warned the two officers that he was a personal friend of the chief constable in Glasgow, who had expressly asked to be contacted in the event that Luke had any difficulties with the police in Scotland. At this, one of the officers, by now extremely surly, left to make a telephone call. He returned half an hour later, red-faced with fury, and without a word wrote out a permit authorising Popov to stay in the city for one night.

Popov and Luke set off for London by train early next morning, but a heavy overnight snowfall, combined with a goods train accident outside Newcastle, caused considerable delays and it took them a total of thirty-six miserable and exhausting hours to get back to the capital. It was, said Luke, a 'horrible adventure'.

The good news, for Popov, was that the trip entirely resolved Luke's concerns about his loyalty, and he gave the Yugoslav an enthusiastic endorsement in a long report to Tar Robertson. 'After spending a week almost exclusively in Skoot's company,' he wrote:

I have come to the conclusion that he is definitely working for us and not for the Germans . . . Apart from the unfortunate episode in Edinburgh, which incidentally left Skoot unperturbed, and the formidable return journey, the trip was quite an enjoyable one. Skoot is an ingenuous, cheerful and amusing companion of whose sincerity and loyalty I, personally, am satisfied . . .

As to his personal character, he is clever, versatile and firm of purpose. He knows what he wants and it will not be his fault if he does not get it. He has obviously been brought up in an atmosphere of comfort and ease and has had plenty of money with which to indulge his fantasies. He is fond of the society of attractive women, who are apparently plentiful in Dubrovnik. He spends a month or more of every year in Paris where his amorous exploits would provide good material for Maurice de Kobra [a French author noted for his erotic thrillers]. He does not drink much and is naturally extremely discreet about his work . . . He has personality and charm and would feel at home, I should think, in society circles in any European or American capital, being much the usual type of international playboy.[5]

Whether Popov knew that he was on trial in Scotland and that Luke was his judge is not on record, but he clearly enjoyed himself and liked to tell a story, after the war, about the drive from Glasgow to Edinburgh. 'There was a law that existed at that time that you couldn't have a drink unless you had travelled five miles and so my case officer, being a true Scotsman, interpreted the law that you *had* to stop and have a drink every five miles. The last few miles of that journey to Edinburgh was probably the most dangerous time I had in the whole war.'[6]

With Luke's glowing testimonial finally lifting the shadow over Popov, the XX Committee agreed he should be used in a plan to palm off on the Germans a bogus chart of minefields in the English Channel and the North Sea. A series of minefields had been laid along the east coast of Britain, but there were sizeable gaps to give fishing trawlers and other shipping access to ports. The Germans knew, from aerial surveillance, roughly where the gaps were, but it was thought that if they could be given an apparently authentic chart with the minefields marked in slightly the wrong position, there was a good chance, particularly in the event of an invasion, of German ships blundering into the real minefields. A chart was prepared and suitably 'aged' to make it seem as if it had had extensive use on a Royal Navy chart table. The initial problem was devising a credible explanation for how Popov could get his hands on such a document. It was Ewen Montagu, who was also responsible for the original idea, who came up with the solution, encompassed in a letter that Popov wrote in secret ink to a cover address in Lisbon:

An English naval officer friend, who is a Jew, is afraid of what may happen if there is an invasion – he has read the atrocity stories of concentration camps! When he was staff officer at Hull, he made ready for the Admiral there a chart showing the secret clear passages in the English East Coast minefield for the trawlers and small boats to pass through and back . . . He realised that there would be no mines there. Knowing this information would be valuable to the enemy, he did not burn it after the orders had been made out. He kept it to give in return for his safety if he was made prisoner. When he learned that I might be going back to Lisbon, he described it to me and asked me if I could make contact with the German embassy in Lisbon and find out if there is a means of exchanging it for a letter of safe conduct. It is most important . . . Please send me instructions if you want me to handle it before I leave.[7]

At his regular meetings with Luke and Robertson, Popov frequently urged them to consider recruiting his friend, Johnny Jebsen, who, he said, was only acting as a loyal German because of the circumstances in which he found himself. He felt sure that he could persuade Jebsen he was fighting on the wrong side, and that Jebsen would be willing to work for British intelligence against the Nazis. But Popov may not have helped his case with MI5 by cheerfully suggesting that Jebsen would be even more amenable if Popov could arrange to meet him in Madrid and 'provide him with vivacious and beautiful female society and lose money to him at poker'.

All this while members of the XX Committee were working to provide answers to the long questionnaire that Popov had brought back with him from Lisbon. On the one hand, the questionnaire was encouraging as it indicated to MI5 that the Germans were not at all well informed about what was happening in Britain; on the other, it created enormous problems because of the extraordinarily detailed nature of the questions. These were the German demands about the Beaufighter, for example:

We want an exact account of the Beaufighters still in course of development and testing at Speke, if possible with sketches. What is the equipment, engines and armament, if possible pictures? What is its performance and fighter capacity? We know that the Beaufighter, since it is more like the Blenheim than the Beaufort, is a technical improvement on the Blenheim. Is this new type the same as the Blenheim V? Is the construction of the Beaufort type discontinued?

Every question had to be considered at the highest level and a decision made as to whether to answer with the truth, a half-truth or a lie, or to avoid answering at all.

Popov, never the most patient individual at the best of times, worried that the answers were not forthcoming quickly enough and that those answers that had materialised lacked the detail on which von Karsthoff had insisted. On the evening of 5 March he had dinner with Luke to discuss his concern (MI5 seemed to conduct an extraordinary amount of business during the war over lunch or dinner, either in clubs or fashionable restaurants). 'Yesterday evening Skoot dined with me at the Berkeley,' Luke reported the following day, 'and either as a result of so many late nights or as a result of his feverish activities in the past few days, he was in particularly bad form.'

Popov had a whole litany of complaints. First he considered that the answers so far provided to the questionnaire were so flimsy that his status with the Germans would be dangerously jeopardised. Unless he could give the Germans more solid information, he said, it was hardly worth continuing the operation, particularly as von Karsthoff had warned him, on his last trip, that he would be expected to improve.

Becoming increasingly gloomy as the meal progressed, Popov told Luke that he was beginning to think he had made a mistake in agreeing to work for the British. He had given up a comfortable and almost perfect life in Dubrovnik and now faced the prospect of being stranded either in Britain or Portugal, with no money and little hope of being able to return to his own country. He had nothing to show for being away from Yugoslavia for many months and had been unable to obtain the navicerts that would at least have given him the opportunity to start a business.

Popov had several reasons for wanting to maintain his business connections: first, as cover for travelling backwards and forwards between Britain and Portugal; second, to help his country obtain vital supplies; and third, and not least, because he wanted to try and make some money. Prior to his arrival in Britain, the Yugoslav government in exile, which had been set up in London, had had little luck in persuading the British government to grant navicerts for the export of goods to Yugoslavia, since Britain was concerned – correctly as it turned out – that Yugoslavia would eventually be overrun and the goods would fall into German hands.

Luke was sympathetic and did his best to cheer up his companion, pointing out that the work he was doing was extremely valuable, both to Britain and Yugoslavia, and promising that the final answers to the questionnaire would be sufficiently detailed to impress the Germans. It would be unreasonable of them to expect more during the short time

Popov had been in Britain, he said. Popov remained unhappy. 'I am afraid', Luke reported later, 'that his anxiety to appear to the Germans as a clever spy is warping his judgment. When I pointed out that the Germans might be suspicious if he took back more information, he airily stated that no matter how much information he took back, the Germans would never be suspicious as they were so certain that he knew so many influential people in this country.'[8]

A few days later Luke discussed Popov's complaints with Tar Robertson and both men agreed that it would be in MI5's best interests, and Popov's, if he were operating as a genuine businessman. A deal was quickly put together under which Popov, representing a consortium of Yugoslav banks, would be granted navicerts to buy goods that were not critical to the war effort. To ensure they did not end up with the Germans, the goods were to be held in Egypt and shipped to Yugoslavia on a monthly requirement basis. Popov was delighted, rented an office on the sixth floor of Imperial House, at 193 Regent Street in London's West End, and set up a company called Tarlair Limited – Import-Export. (The 'Tar' part of the name was in honour of Tar Robertson.) Imperial House accommodated at least sixty other small firms and also provided a safe place for Popov to meet MI5 colleagues.

Not long after the deal had been agreed, Popov was invited to lunch in London with the Yugoslav ambassador, who sourly demanded to know how he had managed to pull it off. When Popov made it clear he was not willing to explain, the increasingly irritated diplomat accused him of bribing the Admiralty. Popov, unabashed, told him not to be an 'ass'.

With Popov in a much happier frame of mind, MI5 turned its attention to finding suitable candidates whom he could offer to the Germans, on his next visit to Lisbon, as recruits. He was to tell von Karsthoff that he wanted to create his own network in Britain to spy on Germany's behalf. What better evidence could there be of his dedication to the Reich?

The first choice was Dickie Metcalfe, a former army officer who had already done work for the intelligence services under the codename of 'Balloon' – an unkind reference to his rotund figure. The plan was to present Metcalfe as a man with expensive tastes who had supposedly been cashiered from his regiment for passing dud cheques, felt he had been badly treated and was now desperate for money. At a meeting with Metcalfe attended by Robertson, Masterman, Luke and others, the terms were spelled out to him:

> We explained to him that much would depend on the success
> which attended Skoot's interview with the German Secret Service

in Lisbon, but we had every reason to hope that they will be glad to avail themselves of Balloon's services and pay handsomely for them. It was made clear to him of course that we would regard any money which he might receive as being our property, although he would receive a proportion of it.[9]

That evening Popov was taken to meet Metcalfe at Metcalfe's flat. The two men had similar tastes – Metcalfe, too, fancied himself as something of a playboy – and seemed as if they would get along well together. It was agreed that Popov should tell the Germans he had met Metcalfe through his friend at the Yugoslav Legation, who was originally supposed to supply answers to the first questionnaire but who had got cold feet. Popov was to explain that his Yugoslav friend had in any case intended to obtain most of his information from Metcalfe and, as he no longer wanted to get involved himself, he had put Popov in direct contact with Metcalfe.

They had several more meetings to perfect their respective stories and, as Metcalfe was Popov's purported source of information, he spent two entire days – 9 and 10 March – at Imperial House painstakingly writing out in secret ink the messages Popov was to take to Lisbon in a few days' time.

Communicating with Lisbon in secret ink was a laborious process, particularly if the message, written in block letters, was technical:

One of the reasons for the diminution in the quantity of shells used in AA barrage is that instruments which measure the height have been installed some distance in front of the gun line and there is also some means of finding the position of the sound. This information is sent back to the gun positions in some way and enables them to fire more accurately . . .

The water used to mix the crystals had to be free of chlorine, otherwise it discoloured the paper, and the steel nib of the pen had to be spotlessly clean. The writing could be 'developed' with a hot iron – when the paper turned brown, the 'secret writing' materialised.

Popov amused himself by writing notes to the Germans on the back of letters from girlfriends, some full of innuendo: 'Darling Dusko, I'm sorry I can't see you tomorrow as Charles is coming back to town unexpectedly . . .' Occasionally he used letters from friends to reinforce his playboy image:

Dear Dushka, I have been trying to talk to you on the telephone several times but you always seem to be out. Leading the gay life I suppose! The name of that taylor [*sic*] which you asked me about is Hawkes & Son, 1 Savile Row, W1. They are rather expensive but good. Actually if you want a tweed coat I suggest that you try my man Hunstman at No. 11 in the same street. I will ring you up tomorrow about meeting in the evening as I must look in at Vanity Fair after 7 p.m. tomorrow evening. Gwennie has asked us both to come and have drinks on Saturday. Yours, Dick.

Since MI5 had failed in its attempt to find a girlfriend for Popov who would be willing to spy on him, Robertson felt a woman recruited to his network might perform the same role, 'simply to entertain him and keep him out of mischief, at the same time to keep us informed of the various curious associations which he is making in this country'. The lovely Friedl Gaertner was the obvious choice. Although she was now only one of Popov's many lady friends in London, she was intelligent, well connected and her mother and sister both lived in Germany, making it logical (to the Germans at least) that she would want to work on behalf of the Reich. In fact Friedl had already done some work for MI5 in the months leading up to the war, posing as a Nazi sympathiser and infiltrating pro-Nazi organisations; after the Anschluss, she had called at the German Embassy in London to offer her congratulations in order to establish her supposed sympathies. Discreetly sounded out by MI5, she readily agreed to become involved, reporting to the Germans as a sub-agent in Popov's network with the codename of 'Gelatine'.

It was left to Popov to decide how he should introduce her to the Germans, although it was suggested that he should initially mention that she was a young woman he had met in London and with whom he had formed an attachment. If von Karsthoff expressed interest, Popov could let drop that when they first met they both evinced strong pro-British sympathies, but as they got to know each other, it became more and more evident that both were pro-German. Popov was advised that if it seemed von Karsthoff was going to swallow the bait, he could mention that Friedl had provided some of the information he had brought with him.

With an embryonic 'network' in place, MI5 decided to change Popov's codename to 'Tricycle', reflecting the fact that he was about to run an operation with two sub-agents. Years after the war scurrilous rumours circulated, without the slightest evidence, that his new codename more accurately reflected his proclivity for what British tabloid newspapers were usually pleased to describe as 'three-in-a-bed sex romps'.

On the afternoon of Thursday, 13 March, Robertson, Masterman, Marriott and Popov met at the 'In and Out' club to run through the final details of his forthcoming trip. That evening, an intelligence report noted, Popov dined with an unnamed lady friend he had met at the Cutty Sark Club with Metcalfe and continued on to the 400 Club. A note was made in the file to obtain the lady's name from Metcalfe and run a check on her.

On Friday, 14 March Luke met 'a somewhat tired' Popov for lunch at the Savoy, during which he confessed that he had not enough money to pay his hotel bill. 'From this,' Luke reported, 'it would seem that his previous evening must have been an expensive one.' At this early stage of their relationship, MI5 was perfectly prepared to indulge Popov's high living, and Luke telephoned Robertson, who sent over £35 in notes. Popov paid his bill and caught the 4.15 train from Paddington to Bristol, with seconds to spare, after a hair-raising journey from the Savoy. In the panic he left behind in the car a small attaché case containing his sleeping clothes and sponge bag, which Luke sent down on the 6.30 train. Luke later reported to MI5 that Popov had expressed 'great concern' about his luggage and had asked Luke to ensure it was all taken on board his flight.

Popov had every reason to be anxious about his bags, since they contained a number of innocuous letters he had asked Metcalfe and Friedl to write to him. On the back, in secret ink, were the answers to the questionnaire.

5

Plan Midas

'EACH TIME DUSKO WENT BACK TO LISBON TO REPORT TO THE GERMANS,' Ewen Montagu pointed out after the war, 'he was warned his life was in their hands and we could do nothing to help him if things went wrong.' When Popov arrived at the Palacio Hotel in Estoril on the evening of 15 March 1941, he found a message at the reception desk instructing him to go directly to the Villa Toki-Ana to meet von Karsthoff. This was unusual and Popov immediately wondered, with a sudden stab of fear, if something had happened to jeopardise his position, and if the Gestapo would be waiting for him at the villa. In fact it turned out that nothing sinister was going on: von Karsthoff was simply anxious to get his report as soon as possible. The German greeted him warmly, seemed genuinely pleased to see him back in Portugal and showed every sign of being impressed by the intelligence Popov was able to produce, along with the answers to the questionnaire. Disappointingly, he seemed less interested in the prospect of obtaining the minefield chart, expressing the view that it was probably out of date.

As usual, von Karsthoff wanted to know everything about Popov's six weeks in Britain. This was always a tricky time for Popov. Bill Luke had advised him to stick to the truth as far as possible, but there were pitfalls everywhere. 'In Britain I had to go through the process of getting the information, even if it had been handed to me by my case officer,' he explained after the war, 'just so that I could answer all their questions. They would ask me what station I used, what hotel I stayed in, where was the lobby, where was the bar, what was the pattern of the wallpaper in my room? You could never be sure that your interrogator did not know the hotel, so you had to make certain that you answered every question correctly.'[1]

Von Karsthoff was particularly pleased to hear that Popov had enrolled two potential recruits to his 'network'. As he had been briefed, Popov described Dickie Metcalfe as a disgruntled ex-army officer, who had been obliged to resign his commission after a little difficulty in balancing regimental accounts and who considered he had been very badly treated. Largely as a result of gambling, racing sports cars and expensive girlfriends, Metcalfe was in desperate financial straits and ready to do anything for money. Although high-spirited, he had excellent contacts since he was now employed by a company manufacturing small arms. Friedl, Popov explained, was probably already known to Berlin through her frequent visits to the German Embassy in London before the war, when Joachim von Ribbentrop was ambassador. Popov emphasised that she moved in the highest social circles, through whom she had access to political gossip and the top tiers of the British intelligence structure. Von Karsthoff rubbed his hands together with pleasure.

The German's news was not so good, as far as Popov was concerned. Abwehr headquarters in Berlin wanted Popov to go either to Berlin or to Madrid to meet Abwehr 'specialists'. Popov again argued that it would be risky for him to travel to Berlin because he had too many friends in the city and might be recognised. Von Karsthoff agreed and said he would contact Berlin suggesting Madrid as a preferable venue.

Popov was happy to linger in Lisbon since he had companionship there in the shapely form of a glamorous Brazilian blonde by the name of Maria Elera. MI5 paid close, not to say prurient, attention to Popov's exotic amorous exploits and a black-and-white picture of Maria, posing on the steps of an aeroplane in a saucy white hat with a feather, a cigarette in one gloved hand, is lodged in Popov's file, along with a sour note that another of his lady friends, a Señora Martha Castello, was nothing more than a 'high-class procuress'.[2] Popov was not, of course, neglecting affairs in London. MI5 intercepted a cable he sent from the Palacio Hotel: 'Missing you terribly darling. I adore you. Hope to be back soon. D.' This missive, his file records, was addressed to one Gwennie, 'a girl friend of his to whom he had paid a good deal of attention'.

While Popov was in Lisbon canoodling with Maria and waiting for instructions from Berlin, Yugoslavia was dragged into the war. On 27 March 1941, the pro-Nazi Regent of Yugoslavia, Prince Paul, was overthrown in a *coup d'état* organised by a cadre of patriotic Serbian officers. Hitler reacted with fury and ordered a full-scale attack. For three days and nights the Luftwaffe bombed Belgrade. The German army, assisted by troops from Romania, Hungary and Bulgaria, swept across the border into Yugoslavia and within twelve days the country, ill-prepared to face such an onslaught, had surrendered. Popov, frantic with worry about his family, finally received a message, via his friend Johnny Jebsen, that they were all safe, at least for the time being. With Yugoslavia occupied, Popov had to face the grim fact that his work as a double agent now placed his entire family – his parents, two brothers, sister-in-law and innumerable cousins – at risk. He was in no doubt that, in the event of being exposed, the Gestapo would not hesitate to exact retribution on them.

Popov also realised, in the light of the coup, that his own loyalties might be questioned and thus he was not surprised to receive a message at the Palacio that von Karsthoff wanted to see him urgently. Barely bothering with the usual civilities, the German demanded to know if Popov was a Serb or a Croat. Serbs, by and large, were pro-Allies, whereas Croats supported the Ustashe Fascist movement agitating for an independent Croatia under the protection of the Third Reich. Popov, who was a Serb, got the strong impression that von Karsthoff wanted him to say he was a Croat and thus convince Berlin there was no problem, but he knew that such a claim would not have withstood even superficial investigation. He prevaricated, claimed that his allegiance was to Ragusa (the historical name for his home town of Dubrovnik) and that he thought of himself primarily as a Ragusan rather than a Serbian or a Croat. This, surprisingly, seemed to satisfy von Karsthoff.

Four days later, Berlin telegraphed von Karsthoff with instructions for Popov to leave for Madrid, where he was to contact a 'Mr Lenz' at the German Embassy. A room had been booked for him – naturally, at the Ritz, the best hotel in town. 'Mr Lenz' had good news for Popov: Jebsen was coming to meet him in a few days' time, on 6 April.

It was a matter of some irritation to Popov that he had been expressly forbidden by MI5 even to hint to his friend that he was working for the Allies. Popov's assurances to his controllers in London that Jebsen was utterly trustworthy, vehemently anti-Nazi and would probably make a good double agent himself, had fallen on deaf ears. So it was that when the two friends met in Madrid they conducted their usual circumlocutory conversations, with Jebsen pretending he was a loyal Abwehr officer and Popov pretending he was a genuine Abwehr agent.

Jebsen had much to report. First, all the indications from Berlin were that Popov had been accepted as a fully fledged agent. Three 'specialists', led by a Dr Warnecke, were on their way to Madrid to talk to Popov and settle the financial terms of his employment; Jebsen's orders were to keep him happy until they arrived. The two friends talked for hours whenever they could be certain they could not be overheard. Popov was never sure whether Jebsen guessed that everything he said was being passed to Allied intelligence, but if he did guess, it did not seem to inhibit him. He talked freely about the ambivalent attitude of some members of the Abwehr hierarchy towards the Nazis and how intelligence from Britain played an important role in helping Canaris, the head of the Abwehr, maintain his status. Von Ribbentrop, now the minister for foreign affairs, hated Canaris, and Canaris hated von Ribbentrop; Canaris took every opportunity to score points over his rival by furnishing the Führer with information about what was happening in Britain. Jebsen went on to mention the technical problems being experienced by the Dresden Institute of Technology in developing something called a microdot, which – if it could be perfected, as Popov would subsequently discover – would enable German intelligence to reduce documents to the size of a full stop on a typewriter. He said life was getting tough for ordinary people in Germany and that clothing was in very short supply, while factories across the Reich were turning out 3,000 aeroplanes every month. All of this, and more, Popov later repeated to Ralph Jarvis, the MI6 station head operating under the cover of the Passport Control Office in the British Embassy in Lisbon.

Travel in Europe during the war involved daunting paperwork and endless complications with visas and permissions, so it was entirely natural that Popov should have to pay frequent visits to the Passport Control Office. His instructions on his first visit were to ask about his 'Nigerian visa', which enquiry immediately alerted Jarvis to his presence in town. Popov was able to pass a wealth of intelligence to Jarvis, including a list of the principal Abwehr officers in Lisbon, their codenames, specialities and private addresses.

On 9 April, Dr Warnecke and his two colleagues arrived in Madrid and held a number of long meetings with Popov at the Ritz Hotel. Their mission, it became apparent, was to decide if Popov was the right man to be sent to the United States to set up a new spy network. German espionage operations in the United States were in chaos, they explained; J. Edgar Hoover, the director of the FBI, had files on all members of the German-American Bund, a group of Americans with German ethnic background, and was picking them up 'like whores on the Reeperbahn'.[3] Warnecke said they were looking for someone to start from scratch creating an entirely new network untainted by individuals already known to the FBI. Popov was flattered by the Abwehr's apparent confidence in him, despite recent events in his home country. He pretended to be enthusiastic, but privately wondered how MI5 would react.

'The game was tempting,' he would write after the war:

The mission the Germans wanted me to undertake was extraordinary. It would put us in control of the enemy's American espionage organisation so that when the United States entered the war – as we all felt was inevitable – it would have one leg up. For the moment perhaps the FBI had matters under control and was netting all existing German spies, but that was creating a vacuum which the Abwehr was bound to fill. What better than to have our own men sent in?[4]

Warnecke also wanted to settle Popov's terms of employment. It was agreed that the Germans would continue to pay all his expenses and regular fees, conditional on his performance. In addition, the Abwehr would guarantee to protect his family in Yugoslavia and make its best efforts to release any of his friends who had been arrested. After the war, Popov would be rewarded for his services with an exclusive agency to represent the Wolff industrial conglomerate in Yugoslavia.

Popov returned to Lisbon on 23 April and busied himself with commercial matters – a fifteen-ton consignment of turpentine stalled at the Yugoslav border, a barter deal involving coconut oil, and an attempt, on behalf of Jebsen, to purchase shipping in Peru through the agency of a mysterious middle man called Tchichatcheff. Neither the Germans nor the British interfered with Popov's complicated personal business affairs, both accepting that his activities as a wheeler-dealing lawyer/entrepreneur provided excellent cover for his travel between Britain and Portugal. Astonishingly, von Karsthoff never even asked Popov how he always managed to find a scarce seat on an aircraft to Lisbon and then back to London. Popov let him believe it was due to the influence of the powerful Banac family.

On 27 April Popov was summoned to another meeting with von Karsthoff, who wanted to tell him that both Metcalfe and Gaertner had been accepted as his sub-agents. Berlin had at first rejected Gaertner, and it was only when von Karsthoff had pointed out that her name was already on their files that Berlin finally agreed she might be useful. Metcalfe was given the codename 'Ivan II', while Gaertner was to be 'Yvonne'.

Popov had explained that Friedl was prepared to work for patriotic motives only, whereas Metcalfe would certainly demand money up front, but when von Karsthoff produced £300 to give to 'Ivan II', Popov initially put on a show of reluctance about taking the money into England, pointing out the risks. The serial numbers of all currency entering Britain were noted. If Metcalfe was arrested, the money in his possession would lead immediately to Popov, and to his inevitable arrest.

None of this was going to happen, of course, since both men were working for the British, but it was important that Popov, when dealing with von Karsthoff, rigorously maintained the façade of being a German spy, facing all the travails that involved. When in Lisbon, he not only had to act like a German agent, he had to *think* like one to maintain the confidence of his German masters and thus ensure his survival. 'It was like an actor learning a part,' Popov said after the war. 'When I was with the Germans I tried to play the part that I am a real German spy. I had to keep in my mind not to make a slip because in that kind of work you are allowed only one mistake and that is the last one you ever make.'[5]

Popov did his best to present himself to the Germans as someone who, while making no secret of the fact that he was in the business for money, was also utterly reliable. When von Karsthoff wanted to send a wireless set to 'Ivan II', Popov said he could make the arrangements through a Yugoslav diplomat who was on his way to Britain and who would not be told what he was carrying. But he subsequently returned the set to von Karsthoff, explaining that he had discovered at the last minute that the 'diplomat' did not in fact have diplomatic immunity and he therefore thought it was too risky to try and smuggle the set into Britain. Von Karsthoff complimented him on his judgement and made sure Berlin knew about it.

On 30 April Popov flew back to Britain with $2,000 in his pocket as payment for his services to the Abwehr. He was met at Whitchurch airfield by MI5 officers who searched him and took possession of all his papers, which were placed in a sealed dispatch case and deposited with the Night Duty Officer. Popov was then driven to the Royal Hotel, Bristol, where Bill Luke was waiting to greet him. 'On the way up [to London] in the car,' Luke reported to the XX Committee, 'Tricycle discussed with me some of his experiences and I am still satisfied that he is playing straight with us . . . He said the Germans were extremely pleased with the information which he had provided them with and that he is now being built up very satisfactorily . . .'

The news that the Germans wanted Popov to go to the United States was greeted with a distinct lack of enthusiasm in London. By the early summer of 1941 he was the XX Committee's most productive and important asset − not just an agent in whom the Germans apparently placed complete trust, but the only agent able to make frequent face-to-face contact with his German controller and with a close friend well placed in the upper echelons of the Abwehr. As far as MI5 was concerned, there was little to be gained from Popov operating out of the United States, but little they could do to prevent his departure without the risk of blowing his cover. The best they could hope for was increased cooperation with the FBI.

Although the general view was that the Tricycle case was developing well, there remained a nervousness within MI5 that running Tricycle was proving all too easy – that the Germans were too ready to swallow everything he gave them. In his debriefing report, Luke raised the alarming possibility that the Germans knew Popov was a double agent and were using him for their own purposes: 'It has occurred to me previously that the Germans may know he is doubling but may consider that they get more information by letting him continue doing so than they would if he disappeared. I am not suggesting that Tricycle is aware that they know he is doubling and I am still convinced that as far as he is concerned we can rely upon him . . .'[6]

MI6 had also raised questions about Popov's allegiance after hearing that he was negotiating a $14 million deal to sell German merchant ships currently lying in South American ports. MI6 had notified Tar Robertson about the transaction in April and had queried, under the circumstances, if 'Tricycle is still on our side'.[7] At a meeting with Popov on 5 May Luke asked him what was going on. Popov had a complete explanation. The ships were of no use to the Germans, he said, and were accruing large harbour dues. His plan was to arrange their purchase through a nominee in South America, who would offer a guarantee to the Germans that the ships would not be used to transport goods to Britain, or be resold to the British. But once the deal was done, there was no reason why the nominee could not break his word, 'all being fair in love and war'.

Luke was intrigued, noting:

From our point of view, such a proposition cannot fail to be attractive, but the person who would have to be persuaded that it is an equally attractive proposition from the Germans' point of view is Admiral Raeder [commander-in-chief of the German navy], who has already objected to the transfer of the ships. One way of possibly forcing the Germans' hands would be for us to spread a rumour through our entirely efficient propaganda machinery in the South American countries that the ships may be seized by the South American governments concerned. Admiral Raeder's reaction to this might be that it would be worthwhile selling them while he could still obtain dollars for them. The approximate purchase price of the ships would be in the neighbourhood of $160 per registered ton.[8]

In fact the plan came to nothing since the British government refused to recognise the transfer of enemy ships to a neutral flag. Popov also had a similarly impractical scheme for exporting perfume from France, paying with francs bought cheaply with dollars from French refugees in Portugal. It would have been against regulations concerning the export of goods from France, but Popov was airily confident that the Germans would be prepared to grant him a waiver. This, too, never came to fruition.

When he was not pursuing ambitious business opportunities, or women, Popov was kept busy sending a stream of messages to Lisbon written in secret ink, usually between the lines of letters, but sometimes on the back of bills. So it was that in early May von Karsthoff received a note about the disposition of Allied forces on the back of a bill for £47 16s. 10d. for three lounge suits from W. Millen, tailors of Savile Row. A few days later another message arrived on the back of an invoice for a dozen and a half monogrammed silk shirts from A. J. Izod, 'Court hosiers and shirtmakers by appointment to His Majesty King George VI'. Cost, £67 13s. 0d.[9] Popov was never restrained by the deadly seriousness of his job. On one occasion he scribbled troop dispositions in secret ink between the lines of a letter to his contact in Lisbon, Arthur Soares, which began: 'Dear Arthur, I have been experiencing great difficulty in obtaining sufficient supplies of port wine in this country. My wine merchant is only allowing me four bottles per month, which is scarcely sufficient under the present trying war-time conditions . . .'

On 15 May he reported:

There has been a new issue of battle dress which is treated against gas. This has the appearance of the old battle dress but has faint white stripes. Owing to its smell it is unpopular and the story is told of one NCO who refused to wear it as it was and sent it straight to the cleaners unworn. The smell came back unaffected, the only change being that the white stripes became more distinct. The inference is that this must be an extremely satisfactory protection owing to the way it stands up to cleaning.

Regular convoys sailed during the week 30.3.41 to 5.4.41 to the Middle East with 7,000 trained recruits from the Army and RAF to reinforce troops. In the above convoys were 360 aeroplanes, including medium bombers, fighters and scouting planes; at least 150 of these were destined for the Balkans.

Machine-gun ammunition is now being manufactured which is 'streamlined'. This makes for higher velocity, greater accuracy and greater armour penetration.[10]

Finally he noted that a new rifle was shortly going to be introduced into service, with a seven-inch round bayonet that would make for 'much easier withdrawal from Huns' – a little joke he added for his own amusement, although it was unlikely to generate much mirth in Lisbon. He also answered German questions about the construction of five King George V-class battleships, electronically controlled land mines and other new arms, and made sketch plans of the new Vickers Armstrong plants in Surrey and Kent and a detailed map of an imaginary underground factory producing parts for Wellington bombers.

All this intelligence had, of course, been cleared through the XX Committee, which went to inordinate lengths to avoid arousing German suspicions about its provenance, even instructing the Post Office on the date Popov's letters should be posted, to allow for suitable censorship delays, and on what postmarks should appear on the envelopes. One internal memorandum advised that the Post Office should not use a W14 postmark as 'I can't imagine Tricycle going out to Putney to post a letter'.[11]

MI5 had been disappointed that the Germans had shown little interest in acquiring a copy of the bogus minefield chart, but refused to give up on the idea. Popov was instructed to write to Lisbon to say that he had seen the chart and was convinced of its authenticity and value. His contact, Ewen Montagu, had recently been transferred to the Admiralty's legal department: all instructions for cancelling previous orders passed through his hands, so he knew the minefield had not been altered. When there was still no response, Popov wrote again to say that Montagu would be prepared to hand over the chart personally to a senior German officer, in return for a guarantee of safe conduct. A meeting was suggested at the Shelbourne Hotel in Dublin in July. But Berlin refused to take the bait – a rare example of accurate intuition on the part of Abwehr chiefs, since they swallowed, hook, line and sinker, almost everything else Popov offered them.

In order to perpetuate the myth that Popov had an extensive range of influential contacts in Britain, the XX Committee arranged for him to meet, usually over a convivial lunch, a number of 'highly placed individuals', including peers and Members of Parliament, whom he could then describe to his German employers. These individuals, in turn, reported on Popov to his MI5 controllers. Among them was Victor Cavendish-Bentinck, heir to the Duke of Portland and chairman of the Joint Intelligence Committee at the Foreign Office. Cavendish-Bentinck reported to Luke on 8 June:

You asked me to give you a short record of my conversation with and impressions of the friend whom you invited me to meet on June 5th . . . My impressions of your friend are that he is quite a well educated and high class Croat or Dalmatian; that he is by temperament an adventurer who is very partial to the flesh-pots of this world and that he realises that a person of his type can enjoy the flesh-pots better under democratic than under totalitarian conditions . . . During part of the conversation when you had left us I was much struck by his statement that his employers genuinely do believe that possibilities of Fifth Column activities exist among British subjects and that there are important elements in this country who long for the conclusion of peace and would gladly work against Churchill with this object in view. According to your friend, his employers would even gladly assist in Churchill being supplanted by someone else equally hostile to them in the conviction that such a person would not have the same hold over the country and that they could thereafter worm their influence in. When he was recounting this I am quite certain that your friend was really telling the truth and that this was the point on which his employers are most anxious to obtain information.[12]

During his discussions with Luke, Popov repeatedly reopened the question of attempting to recruit Jebsen to work for British intelligence. He told Luke that his friend had previously made it clear that if Popov were caught and imprisoned by the British, he would be prepared to make his way to Britain and tell all he knew on condition that Popov's life was spared. 'Tricycle seems keen for us to find a way of getting Jebsen over here,' Luke reported, 'but of course it would be impossible to do this, and in any case I am not at all sure that we should gain very much by having him here; he seems to be very much the playboy type who may not know a tremendous amount about the different intelligence branches in Germany.'[13]

While MI5 was not in the least interested in providing asylum for Jebsen in Britain, it was more than willing to take advantage of Jebsen's friendship with Popov. Luke suggested to Popov that when he was next in Lisbon he should ask Jebsen if he would be willing to obtain a plan of the German secret-service organisation. Popov should tell his friend he would memorise the plan and use it to barter for his life only if he were arrested by the British. 'Needless to say,' Luke pointed out in his report, 'immediately he received such a plan or information Tricycle would hand it over to Captain Jarvis.'[14]

In truth, Luke had little time to worry about Jebsen since he was deeply involved in making arrangements for Popov to leave for New York. Secret negotiations were opened up with the US Embassy in London to set up Popov with the Federal Bureau of Investigation. The military attaché at the embassy was assured that 'there was no question concerning his honesty, reliability and loyalty' and was informed that Popov 'might be of use' in developing information about the German espionage organisation in the US. Word eventually came back that the FBI was prepared to take him on, although in reality the Bureau was deeply unenthusiastic at the prospect. FBI director, J. Edgar Hoover, had agreed only after being promised that Popov 'could be kicked out at any time' if the arrangement did not work to the Bureau's satisfaction. Hoover's distinctly luke-warm response was an ominous portent of trouble ahead.

To provide Popov with cover, Sir Walter Monckton, the minister of information, was asked to approach the Yugoslav Legation in London with a formal request for Popov to be released from his obligations as a reserve officer in the Yugoslav army (Popov had volunteered his services as soon as he returned to England after his country had been invaded) to undertake special duties for the ministry. 'A good deal of care will have to be taken in the manner in which this approach is made,' Luke warned in an internal memorandum. It was envisaged that the Yugoslavs would agree, that Sir Walter would ask the legation to make the approach to Popov, and that Popov himself, with a great show of reluctance, would finally consent to undertake the 'special duties'. All this was designed to prevent the Yugoslavs from knowing what was really going on. Luke also pointed out that such a course of action might obviate difficulties in obtaining a US visa: 'Realising that he is doing good work for the Allied cause, the Yugoslav Legation would probably be only too pleased to send him to the United States with a diplomatic visa or as a courier.'[15]

MI5's confidence that the Yugoslav Legation would cooperate proved entirely unfounded. When Sir Walter approached the Yugoslav prime minister, he proved to be unhelpful, asserting that Popov was 'not very brainy and unsuitable for the job' and that there were a number of other, older Yugoslavs better qualified whom Sir Walter could more profitably employ.[16] (It may be that Popov's altercation with the Yugoslav ambassador a few months earlier, when he had accused the diplomat of being an 'ass', had not helped his cause.) Sir Walter did not press the matter, but retired gracefully and reported his failure to a furious Robertson, who decided that MI5 would go ahead without the help of the Yugoslavs and pull whatever strings were required to get a US visa for Popov.

In the meantime Popov, anticipating that he would shortly be off across the Atlantic, had come up with an excellent idea that would lead to an audacious operation known as Plan Midas. Simple in both conception and execution, like all the best ideas, Plan Midas provided a method for the Abwehr to finance what it believed to be its growing network of spies in Britain, while ensuring that the funds were passed directly to British intelligence.

Curiously, Popov himself had no idea just how good his plan was. From the start of the war, the Abwehr had experienced great difficulty in getting money to the agents it believed to be operating in Britain, particularly since it was a first principle of espionage that spies should work in isolation from one another to avoid mass arrests. The problem was exemplified by the extraordinary capers involved in paying Hans Hansen,[17] a Dane who had parachuted into Cambridgeshire on the night of 19 September 1940. Hansen sprained his ankle on landing and aroused local suspicions when he limped into a nearby village to buy food. He was arrested and found to be in possession of a forged identity card with a number supplied by Alfred George Owens ('Snow') – a document that instead of offering some protection instantly marked him as an Abwehr spy. After intensive interrogation at Latchmere House, Hansen eventually agreed to be turned. He was given the codename 'Tate', because of his slight resemblance to the popular music-hall comedian, Harry Tate.

MI5 was well aware of the Abwehr's difficulty in getting money into England, so it obliged its double agents constantly to demand payment. Hansen was no exception, and early on in the war Lisbon took the risk of ordering Owens to send him £100 by registered post to keep him in business. The Germans then planned to drop a package, containing £500 in notes, from an aeroplane, but the logistics proved insuperable. Subsequently Hansen was ordered to various clandestine meetings in London (one of them, ironically, was at the Tate Gallery) to meet 'a friend' who would hand over cash; inexplicably, none of the rendezvous was kept. The final attempt almost descended into farce when Hansen received a message to wait at Victoria station and follow a Japanese man carrying a copy of *The Times* in his left hand onto a number-eleven bus. Unfortunately, the number-eleven bus did not go to Victoria station. Hansen sent a message back suggesting a number sixteen, which was accepted. On the appointed day and time, under the surveillance of MI5, Hansen followed a Japanese in civilian clothes onto a number-sixteen bus at Victoria station, exchanged prearranged remarks and picked up *The Times*, which he left on the seat. It contained £200. MI5 watchers trailed the Japanese back to the Japanese Embassy, where he turned out to be the assistant naval attaché, with diplomatic immunity.

Popov knew nothing of all this, but he was well aware that von Karsthoff would have difficulty paying Metcalfe after Popov had left for the United States and came up with an original solution. He suggested to MI5 that he should tell von Karsthoff that he had found a businessman in Britain anxious to exchange sterling for dollars and not too bothered about currency exchange regulations. In return for US dollars deposited in a bank account in New York, this businessman was prepared to release an equivalent sum in sterling to a nominated individual in Britain. Robertson was quick to see the potential for draining Abwehr funds and gave the project his blessing.

Plan Midas needed the nominal cooperation of a wealthy individual in Britain who wanted, for one reason or another, to move funds abroad. MI5 came up with Eric Glass, a London theatrical agent and a Jew, who lived in Hampstead. The cover story to be given to the Germans was that Glass was convinced Britain would lose the war and anxious to protect his considerable private fortune. MI5 set up a bogus office for him in Piccadilly House, overlooking Eros, through which to handle the operation.

After long discussions about exactly how the plan would work, it was left to Popov to sell the idea to von Karsthoff. As an incentive to pull it off, Popov was offered 10 per cent of the deal as 'commission'. In the first instance he was to try to exchange a maximum of £20,000 at a minimum exchange rate of $2.25 to the pound. Von Karsthoff would, of course, want confirmation that the sterling was being paid out in Britain, but that was simple enough to arrange – once the dollars had been deposited in the United States, one of MI5's double agents in Britain would send a report to Lisbon confirming that he had received the cash from Glass. In reality, the money would flow directly from New York into the coffers of MI5.

If he was successful in getting von Karsthoff to agree to the plan, Popov would send a cable to Glass, either from Portugal or the United States: 'X had a son/daughter yesterday, weighing Y kilos. Please inform Z.' The first letter of 'X' would inform London of the amount that was exchanged (as a double check, it would be a son if the amount was up to $10,000 and a daughter if it was between $10,000 and $20,000); 'Y' would indicate the exchange rate and 'Z' would be the name of the agent to whom, notionally, the sterling was to be paid and who would be required to contact Lisbon with the glad news.

With the discreet assistance of MI5, Popov was able to acquire a visa for the United States in early June, but before he could leave he needed confirmation from Lisbon that the Germans had obtained a Portuguese transit visa for him. Popov accepted the transformation in his life with remarkable equanimity. Before the war he had enjoyed stability, comfort and wealth; now his world was characterised by risk and uncertainty, forever writing requests for visas and money, never sure of his status, never knowing what challenges might be around the corner. If it bothered him, he certainly never let it show.

When no word was forthcoming about a transit visa, Popov wrote a tetchy letter to von Karsthoff:

I have already lost one seat in aeroplane at the beginning of the month because of delayed visa. Now I am doing all I can to make certain of another seat but the situation is very difficult. If you do not arrange the required visa immediately and if I lose another seat I shall very probably also lose my priority and my return will be in danger.

I have in my possession very good material and several settled questions which I have not sent by post. Please inform me at once of the situation with regard to my visa. At the same time I have not received the money for June. If you do not see the possibility of sending money or visa at once, telegraph the money for I must pay my friends.

I fear that the Portuguese police suspect my activities, if so arrange everything necessary to avoid difficulties from this side until my arrival.

Four days later he wrote again:

I possess information of the first order; fruit of modest efforts of the whole of my organisation. I cannot send it by letter because it would be necessary to write a dozen letters all to the same three addresses. It is clear that I should get caught immediately. I have arranged a possible scheme for laying hands on the plan of the minefields, which is certainly up to date. That has been proved to me.

I am in a position to carry out a very interesting monetary transaction which would settle the question of the payment of my agents.

The 'exit permit' and the USA visa I have obtained after gigantic efforts and on condition that I fulfill certain propaganda missions in the USA (which will open to us a new field of work).

I am running the risk of losing my priority for a seat in the aeroplane if I put off once more the date of my departure. All this for the simple reason that I am unable to have a Portuguese visa. Believe me that I am most astonished and I cannot express my displeasure

at the slowness with which your agents responsible for procuring the visa are working. Please inform me by telegram of the situation.
  Ivan.
PS I am almost without money and I must pay my agents.[18]

When no immediate replies were received, there was a sudden scare that German suspicions had been aroused by the letters' rapid passage through the censors, but eventually the visa came through to the relief of Luke, who was evidently becoming entangled in Popov's complicated commercial activities.

Luke somewhat wearily reported:

Among the complications throughout was the fact that Tricycle's continued delay in London was putting in peril in Lisbon another of those mysterious business deals which appear to follow him from capital to capital; and it was even thought at one time that it might be necessary, in order to obtain his goodwill, for this Department to refund him the losses which he was always on the point of incurring. It seems, however, that this particular danger was satisfactorily averted by his agent in Lisbon . . .
  The question of what reward he should receive from us was again discussed with Tricycle and he again declined to accept any money, but re-emphasised his extreme anxiety to become, after the war, the British consul in Dubrovnik. It will be remembered that the Germans had also offered him the Wolff agency in Yugoslavia and he was not at all unwilling that we should reciprocate by obtaining for him some equally large commercial agency, perhaps that of Shell-Mex. He was also not a little concerned what his position might be with regard to his own country . . . he was most anxious that it should not be thought by his friends and countrymen that he was going to America to escape the war . . .

On the morning of 22 June, Popov turned on the radio in his room at the Savoy and learned that Germany had attacked Russia at dawn along an 1,800-mile border stretching from the Arctic Circle to the Black Sea. One hundred German divisions made huge territorial advances over the next few days as the Russian army – seven million strong, but apparently caught unprepared by the onslaught – regrouped. Popov shared the elation with which the news that Britain was no longer fighting alone was greeted in London. He also hoped that the opening of a second front would stretch the German forces and perhaps provide some relief to his benighted homeland, from where the news was all bad. The German occupiers in Yugoslavia had retaliated with such ferocious brutality against communities suspected of harbouring guerrillas that the Chetniks – the Serbian resistance organisation led by General Mihailovic – had been forced to abandon active operations.

At a final briefing before he left for Lisbon, en route to the United States, Popov was rehearsed on his role in Plan Midas and was urged, once again, to try and convince the Germans of the authenticity and value of Montagu's minefield chart. He was also required to memorise a number of elaborate anecdotes that had been prepared for him by the XX Committee. Written in the first person, with the usual meticulous attention to detail, they were designed to offer the Germans more pieces in the jigsaw being constructed for them by British intelligence.

One involved Popov speaking to an extremely indiscreet naval officer on the subject of the difficulties that would confront England in the Far East if Japan entered the war:

> He did not know the details of the plan but took the attitude, which seemed to be based on a certain knowledge, that the US would take over part of the naval patrolling in the Far East. He then told me that as a precaution against a sudden attack by Japan before the American fleet could take up position, the new King George V class battleship *Anson* had sailed for Singapore, leaving England only a few days ago. I said I thought that only the *King George V* and the *Prince of Wales* were in service and he replied 'Oh, that is what we want you to believe. We want to surprise the Japs if they start anything. Therefore the ship left after the officers had been told that they were going to the Mediterranean to hunt the Italians.' I am sure this is correct because I learned it from someone very important at the Admiralty. The official is well in the know for he meets the representatives of the fighting services in ministerial conferences and soldiers and sailors are not always discreet amongst each other. I am convinced that he believes that this information is correct and not just a story because he said later on in the course of a discussion about the *Hood* being sunk by the *Bismarck* [HMS *Hood* went down in less than ten minutes in May 1941, after a broadside from the German battleship *Bismarck*] that he would bet that the Admiralty regretted having sent the *Anson* so far. I tried to find out how far the *Anson* had got, but I am not sure that he knows and in any case it is a question in which it is rather risky to seem too interested. The impression that I got from him was that

the ship is somewhere in the South Atlantic off the coast of Africa because he intimated that the crew were probably having better weather than we were (it was raining at the time and was rather cold).[19]

Popov was supposed to have picked up another story simply by eavesdropping on a conversation in the bar at the Savoy:

I heard a Merchant Service Officer talking to a Naval Captain at the Savoy. The M.S.O. asked the Naval officer whether it would not be possible to have torpedo nets for use in the areas where submarines are active and prevent the present losses. At the end of the last war they had had a torpedo net which was quite successful but it was no good in this war – not only had the power and size of torpedoes increased, but the speed of ships had also increased. As a result, the nets were either quite useless as they would not stop the torpedo, or they wore out in less than no time owing to the speed of the ship, or they were so heavy that the crew could not handle them and they practically stopped the ship. The M.S.O. asked if they had been dropped altogether, and the Naval Captain replied that they had had another try with a so-called perfected type in the '*Arandora Star* – and you know what happened to her'. [The *Arandora Star* was sunk while carrying Italian internees to Canada in July 1940.] The M.S.O. asked if she had her nets in use at the time and the Naval Captain replied that he did not know but the fact remained that if she had, they were no good, and if she didn't, it was probably because there was too much sea or that she was going too fast or because of some other of the defects; anyhow the Navy had given up the experiments after that. The M.S.O. said that he supposed that they would have to rely on more escorts, and the Naval Captain replied that he supposed that was so, but there were other things we might try; he then lowered his voice and I could not catch any more before they left.[20]

Popov was also given new instructions on how to contact British intelligence in Lisbon. He was to call Lisbon 52346 from a public telephone box and make an appointment for the following day, and then meet at the tennis pavilion at Tapada Ajuda an hour before the time stated. Alternatively, he could pass on a message on the same telephone number. If he mentioned that it was a lovely day and he was enjoying the sunshine, it would mean that the Germans suspected nothing and everything was going well. If he said he thought a storm was brewing and it was likely to rain, it would mean that the Germans suspected something and he was not happy with his position. If he said the party was over, it would mean that he had been found out and that his position was 'completely brûlé' (burned).[21]

Popov left for Lisbon on 28 June. Two days later he called Lisbon 52346 and left a message to say how much he was enjoying the sunshine. Word was immediately passed back to London that Tricycle was safe and well.

Jebsen was in town and the two friends got together as soon as they could, driving out to a remote headland overlooking the Atlantic at the Boca do Inferno cliffs, where they could safely talk without being overheard. Popov was aware that Jebsen had been away on a top-secret mission, but knew none of the details. Jebsen filled him in. He had been working, he said, for the Japanese. Yosuke Matsuoka, the Japanese foreign minister, had made a formal request to Berlin for a full report on the British attack on the Italian fleet at Taranto. The request was passed to the Abwehr, and Jebsen, because of his family's business connections in the Far East, was nominated for the job. The Tokyo offices of Jebsen and Jebsen shipping were used as a cover by the Abwehr.

On 11 November 1940, a large British naval force under Admiral Andrew Cunningham had managed to sail across the Mediterranean without being spotted by the Italian air force. Under the cover of night, from a distance of fifty miles, the aircraft carrier *Illustrious* launched twenty-four aircraft in two waves against six Italian battleships anchored off Taranto, a large naval base on the heel of Italy. Three were seriously damaged and two cruisers were disabled. Thereafter the Italians were forced to move the remainder of their fleet to Naples and were unable to operate in the eastern Mediterranean for the rest of the war.[22]

Jebsen was sent to Taranto with Baron Wolfgang von Gronau, the German air attaché in Tokyo and a former Luftwaffe ace in the First World War. His instructions were to compile a full damage report and an analysis of the effectiveness of Italian defences. Popov asked his friend why the Japanese would be so interested in the operation. Because, Jebsen replied, they must be planning something similar. Baron von Gronau, who was a close friend of Goering, had admitted that he thought it was inevitable that the Japanese would enter the war and it was likely they would do so by attacking the United States. Popov could hardly believe it.

While Jebsen was in Taranto he had heard that the Italians would probably move into Yugoslavia as the occupying force, and he told Popov that he had made arrangements to ensure the continuing safety of Popov's family in Dubrovnik. He also had news of Popov's older brother, Ivo, who was a medical officer with a Yugoslav army unit in Montenegro when the Germans attacked. In the confusion after the surrender Ivo had escaped being taken as a prisoner of war and had walked home to Dubrovnik, stopping at a friend's house on the way to borrow civilian clothes. Jebsen said that one wing of Popov's family house in Belgrade had been destroyed by a bomb that fell on the neighbouring Royal Automobile Club, but by then the family had left for Dubrovnik, so no one was hurt.

Popov was unhappy about the implications of German 'protection' for his family, as he explained in a letter to Tar Robertson written from the Palacio Hotel and sent to London in the diplomatic bag:

> The news from Yugoslavia is very, very bad, millions of people are being persecuted and massacred ... This morning von K has given me a telegram from Berlin in which I am to be informed that Jebsen has himself left for Yugoslavia in order to organise the protection of my family. It appears that things are very black because they did not consult me on the subject. I do not like this 'protection' very much; it obliges me in any case to ask you two things. First of all immense prudence (my own life is much less important to me than that of my family) and then not to forget to arrange to have me decorated in the way we spoke about in London because it is absolutely necessary that I should have something to white-wash the stigma of the German protection.
>
> Say how do you do for me to all our mutual friends, especially to Bill [Luke, whom he knew as Bill Matthews]. I hope to continue to be useful to our common cause and to be able to help within my modest means to bring the victory which alone will bring me happiness.
>
> All the best,
> Dusko.[23]

As a result of this letter, Luke asked Felix Cowgill of MI6's counter-espionage section to arrange for Popov to be advised in Lisbon that British intelligence would 'take every precaution to ensure that the Germans do not discover that he has been working for us, in view of his anxiety regarding the repercussions on his family which such a discovery might entail'. Popov was also to be reassured about being decorated, but was to be warned, in case word leaked out, that 'it would be extremely inadvisable for us to make representations for him to be decorated at the present stage'.[24]

While still waiting to be allocated a seat on a flight to the US, Popov received an urgent summons to von Karsthoff's villa. He found the German sitting under a tree in the garden in unusually good spirits, a manila folder on the bench by his side. With a sly smile, von Karsthoff said he had got something for Popov, took out of the file yet another typewritten questionnaire and handed it over. Popov glanced at it and saw it was the first questionnaire for his trip to the United States and was even longer and more detailed than usual. He groaned, made some quip about having to go back to school and promised he would set about memorising the document that day.

Von Karsthoff's smile grew even broader. 'No, no,' he said, 'no more memorising. Come.' He got up and led Popov into his study, where there was a microscope on a table. Von Karsthoff waved at it: 'Here, take a look.' Popov put his eye to the instrument, fiddled with the focus adjustment and the first page of the questionnaire came into clear view. The German then removed a glass slide from the microscope and showed Popov what he had been looking at – a tiny dot no bigger than a typewritten full stop. It was, he explained, a *Mikropunkt*, which had recently been perfected by German scientists and would be the form in which all documents would be transmitted to Popov in the United States. Stuck onto a letter, it was virtually undetectable. It would, von Karsthoff promised, revolutionise Germany's espionage system. He was so excited that he called on his secretary, Elizabeth, to produce a bottle of champagne, poured three glasses and proposed a toast to Popov's success in the United States.

Later the two men settled down to discuss the questionnaire in detail and Popov quickly realised that a large number of the questions concerned defences at the US naval base in Hawaii – Pearl Harbor:

1. Exact details and sketch about the situation of the state wharf, of the pier installations, workshops, petrol installations, situations of dry dock No. 1 and of the new navy dry dock which is being built.
2. Details about the submarine station (plan of situation). What land installations are in existence?
3. Where is the station for mine search formations? How far has the dredger work progressed at the entrance and in the east and southeast lock? Depths of water?
4. Number of anchorages?
5. Is there a floating dock in Pearl Harbor or is the transfer of such a dock to this place intended?

Popov recalled his conversation with Jebsen and his friend's mission to Taranto on behalf of the Japanese and realised the import. 'At that time,' he said, 'most people thought that Japan was likely to attack Dutch East India. It was only when I saw the questionnaire that I realised they were going to attack the United States.'[25]

When he suggested to von Karsthoff that this information would be of more interest to Germany's 'Asian ally' than to Germany itself, the German was non-committal, but insistent that Popov should go to Hawaii as soon as possible. Popov pointed out that it was way off his beat, but von Karsthoff was not to be deterred; Popov would just have to find some excuse. 'Or he can run off on some amorous escapade,' Elizabeth, who had just walked back into the room, snarled sarcastically, 'then he won't have to pretend.' Popov, who always thought of Elizabeth as a classic 'Gretchen' type, wondered if her obvious dislike of him was rooted in the fact that he had neglected to make a pass at her.

Next day Popov arranged a discreet meeting with Jarvis at the tennis pavilion at Tapada Ajuda and handed over a copy of the questionnaire.[26] He had also made some notes about the development of the *Mikropunkt* system:

> Very often during recent months the Germans do not write any more to their first class agents in secret ink. They employ full stop marks. These are diminutive photographs of letters reduced to about this size. It is possible to read the whole letter with a microscope. I received 6 for my trip to America. I will show them to J. [Jarvis]. I am doing what I can to arrange for the future correspondence with Ivan II with these full stops. The full stops are stuck on to the interior of the envelope. I have marked on this envelope the places where the full stops have been stuck in my presence for one of their agents. Unfortunately I do not know for whom or where, but they do not always stick them onto the same places. My six full stops have been stuck on an old telegram and in the letter which I shall receive at New York they will be inside the envelope.[27]

In London, Robertson and his colleagues were anxiously waiting for news about the fate of Plan Midas. As soon as Popov had arrived in Lisbon, he had told von Karsthoff about his rich theatrical-agent friend who was looking for a safe way to offload sterling and suggested making a deal with him. Von Karsthoff had instantly recognised the merits of Popov's proposal, not only to set up a safe and foolproof system for paying agents in Britain, but also to make some money for himself.

Obtaining authorisation from Martin Töppen, the Abwehr's financial supervisor in Berlin, took several weeks, although Töppen finally approved the plan and sanctioned the full payment of £20,000. But the problems were only just beginning for Popov. First, von Karsthoff demanded a half-share of Popov's 10 per cent commission, then Popov made a foolish, and uncharacteristic, mistake by muddling the name of his so-called friend. On 31 July he sent a telegram to Piccadilly House: 'TILLY HAD YESTERDAY A DAUGHTER WEIGHING 3 KILOS PLEASE INFORM HARRY WHEN YOU MEET HIM. MARIA CONCALVES.' Unfortunately it was addressed to Eric Sand – momentarily distracted, Popov had subconsciously substituted 'Sand' for 'Glass'.

In London, ructions followed. Dick White, assistant director of B Division, complained bitterly that the mistake could have been 'catastrophic' if the Germans had attempted to check on Sand's identity and discovered he did not exist. Bill Luke did his best to pour oil on troubled waters. 'Although Tricycle's mistake about the name of the "cold-footed Jew" in this country who was anxious to change pounds into dollars was serious,' he agreed, 'I do not think that any useful purpose would be served by taxing him unduly on the subject. He has done very well to push through Plan Midas and we would prefer that he should be complimented rather than blamed.'[28] Luke was right: considering the amount of information Popov was obliged to memorise, and the pressure that he was under on every trip to Lisbon, it is surprising he did not make more mistakes.

White was also irritated that Popov had negotiated a lower exchange rate than that authorised. On 2 August he wrote to Felix Cowgill of MI6:

You will see that in addition to giving the wrong name which might have been catastrophic, he has also made another mistake which might also have resulted in disaster, he has given the weight of the child as 3 kilos and according to the plan this would indicate that he had negotiated the deal at a rate of exchange of $2 to the £, which is 25 cents below the minimum we authorised.'[29]

Popov insisted that $2 was the best rate he could get at that time on the open market. In the end, it all worked out. Von Karsthoff gave Popov $40,000 – less his commission – to deposit in an account in New York in the name of 'Erik Sand'. Popov took his remaining half of the commission, and after a few weeks Hans Hansen reported to von Karsthoff that he had been handed £18,000 in cash by 'Mr Sand'.

Plan Midas would eventually work out better than anyone could have anticipated. The Abwehr ultimately laundered the equivalent of about £85,000 through 'Mr Sand' to maintain their agents in Britain – almost enough to pay for the total operating costs of the XX Committee throughout the war – and Plan Midas continued operating until Martin Toeppen was arrested by the Gestapo for embezzling Abwehr foreign-currency reserves.

If, however, Dick White had known just what Popov was doing in Lisbon with the money he had been given by von Karsthoff, he would have been even more angry. That evening Popov headed, as usual, for the casino in Estoril with around $38,000 tucked into the inside pocket of his Savile Row dinner jacket. He had thought it better to keep it on his person rather than raise eyebrows by depositing it in the hotel safe.

A vulgar Lithuanian whom Popov had frequently seen in the casino was playing at the baccarat table. He irritated everyone by calling '*Banque ouverte*' every time he had the bank, indicating that there was no limit on the stakes. It is customary for the banker to set a limit, but the Lithuanian, who was short, fat and extremely wealthy, liked to try and intimidate the other players, which was considered extremely bad form.

As Popov arrived at the table the bank passed to the Lithuanian and, as always, he called '*Banque ouverte*' and the croupier responded, '*Les messieurs debouts peuvent jouer*' (gentlemen standing may play). Fingering the wad of money in his jacket, Popov simply could not resist the temptation. He reached into his pocket, pulled out the money and slowly laid $30,000 on the green baize of the gaming table. Even in those fevered times, it was a fortune to gamble on the turn of a card and an expectant hush fell on the crowd watching the game. The Lithuanian stared at the money with bulging eyes and seemed unwilling to play. Popov innocently enquired of the croupier if the casino was backing the Lithuanian's bet, since no objection was raised to him calling '*Banque ouverte*'. The croupier replied, as Popov knew he would, that the casino never backed any player's stake. With that, Popov swept the money off the table, tucked it back into his pocket, complained loudly that the casino should prohibit such irresponsible play since it was a 'disgrace and annoyance' to serious players, and stalked off, leaving the humiliated Lithuanian standing at the table with his mouth open.

Years after the war, Popov was told that Ian Fleming, a young British naval intelligence officer who had witnessed the entire incident, used it as the inspiration for James Bond's epic baccarat battle in his first book, *Casino Royale*.

6

The Pearl Harbor Questionnaire

ON THE AFTERNOON OF 10 AUGUST 1941, POPOV BOARDED A PAN American Dixie Clipper flying boat at the Cabo Ruiva dock in the Tagus estuary in Portugal for the twenty-two-hour flight to New York, via the Azores and Bermuda. He was fully equipped for espionage: in his briefcase he carried $70,000 in cash; four telegrams containing eleven microdots; a hardback copy of *Night and Day*, a novel by Virginia Woolf, which he was to use for coding radio messages; the torn half of a business card to identify himself to a German agent presenting the other half of the card, who would provide him with a radio; a phial of white crystals to make invisible ink; and a list of ten addresses as mail drops (eight in Lisbon, one in Italy and one in South America). He had also slipped into his case, without von Karsthoff's permission or knowledge, a typewritten copy of the Pearl Harbor questionnaire — a document he fervently believed was a warning to the United States that Japan was planning to attack Pearl Harbor.

Dinner, of excellent fresh fish, was served in the Azores while the big six-engined aeroplane was refuelled and stewards made up bunks for the passengers. Popov slept soundly all the way to Bermuda, where he was met by Hamish Mitchell, an amiable British intelligence officer who was to escort him on the remainder of the journey to New York. In the Clipper bar en route, Mitchell took it upon himself to introduce Popov to 'a great American institution': the dry martini.

Arriving at Pan Am's flying-boat terminal in Port Washington on the north shore of Long Island on 12 August, Mitchell carried Popov's briefcase through passport control while the Yugoslav completed the lengthy immigration formalities. They then shared a taxi downtown to the swank Waldorf Astoria Hotel on Park Avenue, where a room had been booked for Popov. Mitchell walked to his office in the Rockefeller Center and made the necessary arrangements to pass the contents of Popov's briefcase to the FBI.

Popov went up to his room, took a shower, ordered a club sandwich from room service and decided to take a stroll along Park Avenue – it was, after all, his first trip to New York and he was keen to see the sights. Out of habit, before leaving his room he carefully marked the position of his suitcases in the closet and left a hair in the clasp of his Gladstone bag.

Strolling in the warm sunshine through midtown Manhattan, looking up at the skyscrapers and appraising the many pretty women on the street, he sensed he was going to enjoy New York. He crossed Fifth Avenue on 42nd Street and found himself outside a car showroom on Broadway, admiring a new maroon Buick Phaeton convertible with red leather upholstery and white wall tyres. Half an hour later, very pleased with himself, Popov was heading back to the Waldorf Astoria with an agreement in his pocket to buy the car. Back in his room, his sunny mood darkened somewhat when he checked his cases and discovered they had been moved, but he decided that it could have been a maid tidying the room.

Despite assurances from London about Popov's loyalty, the FBI was deeply disinclined to trust him and had made arrangements for him to be kept under constant surveillance, without his knowledge. He was surreptitiously followed everywhere by FBI agents whose orders were to check if he was being tailed by German agents. Every telegram Popov sent or received was read by the Bureau; every contact he made was noted and investigated. The credit manager at the Waldorf Astoria was persuaded to report on every telephone call to and from his room. This last was not particularly productive, since Popov only made two calls in his first few days: one to Billy Rose's Diamond Horseshoe and one to Ben Marden's Riviera, which the FBI dourly noted was 'a well known nightspot and presumably gambling house on the New Jersey side of the Hudson'.[1]

The FBI plan was to keep Popov 'in quarantine' for a couple of days after his arrival to see if any German agents attempted to make contact with him, but confusion ensued when the Yugoslav was visited at the Waldorf Astoria by Agent Stuart Murray from military intelligence and Agent Chambers from naval intelligence, who were running a routine check on new arrivals in the United States. When they introduced themselves to Popov at the hotel, he assumed, not unreasonably, that they were from the FBI and readily explained his business. Within a short time it was all round the hotel that a British spy had arrived.

This dangerous leak was immediately blamed on Popov, as an FBI report noted:

In checking to verify Tricycle's residence at the Waldorf Astoria it was ascertained that he had told an official of the hotel that he was a British agent and had $70,000 with him and asked what arrangements could be made to place it in a safe. It was further ascertained that the fact that Tricycle was a British spy had been disseminated to a considerable extent among the personnel of the hotel, which of course is undesirable and steps were immediately taken to remedy this.[2]

Popov could not have survived as a double agent for more than a few days if he had been so ludicrously indiscreet. Growing up in Dubrovnik, he had learned how gossip spread: whenever he and his brothers had been involved in some mischievous escapade, the news was all round town within hours. Now that he was a double agent, not only his own life but the safety of his family back in Yugoslavia was dependent on his absolute discretion. Since arriving in Britain, he had shuttled back and forth between London and Lisbon and had managed to convince both the British and the Germans of his ability to keep his mouth shut. It is hard to believe that he would arrive in a New York hotel and announce to all and sundry that he was a British spy.

In fact the FBI records indicate that it was Agent Murray, not Popov, who arranged a safe-deposit box with the hotel's assistant manager, and it may be that Murray accidentally let slip the identity of the foreigner recently arrived from Bermuda. Either way, the Bureau was more concerned by the fact that other intelligence agencies were trampling on its turf and a message was sent out that they were to 'lay strictly off', and that the FBI alone was handling the Popov case.

By 1941 the Federal Bureau of Investigation was not only the most powerful law-enforcement agency in US history, but also the personal fiefdom of J. Edgar Hoover, its mercurial, devious and autocratic director. Hoover ran the FBI for nearly fifty years, wielded great influence on the White House and Congress and unquestionably viewed himself as above the law. He was a bigot and a racist, freely abused the civil rights of his fellow citizens, kept secret files on those he perceived to be his enemies, was quite capable of stooping to blackmail and would brook no criticism. After his death in 1972, he was exposed as a closet homosexual and, allegedly, an inveterate cross-dresser in the privacy of his own home. This was the man charged with protecting the internal security of the United States.

When war broke out in Europe, the FBI officially cut its ties with British intelligence for fear of compromising the United States' neutrality, but Winston Churchill, then First Lord of the Admiralty, secretly secured President Roosevelt's approval to set up a clandestine intelligence headquarters in New York under the cover of a trade mission. British Security Coordination (BSC) occupied a small suite of offices in the Rockefeller Plaza and was run by William 'Little Bill' Stephenson, a Canadian First World War flying ace, a pioneer of radio and television and a multi-millionaire businessman, who was given the codename 'Intrepid'. This new organisation absorbed the staff of the MI6 station in New York, headed by Colonel Dick Ellis, a veteran MI6 officer, to whom Popov would report while he was in the United States.

Stephenson had been introduced to Hoover through a mutual friend, Gene Tunney, the former heavyweight boxing champion, and in April 1940 he met the director at his home in Washington to ask for FBI cooperation on intelligence matters. Hoover's response was that he could do nothing without a mandate from the president. What he did not know was that the president was about to be seduced by British intelligence. Churchill had agreed that Stephenson could tell FDR about the sensational capture of an Enigma machine, the key to decoding German communications, and shortly afterwards the president decreed that there should be 'the closest possible marriage' between the FBI and British intelligence. It was a risky political strategy, since America was still not in the war and a powerful 'America First' isolationist movement was intent on keeping the United States out of the conflict. Memories of the horrors of the First World War had not been forgotten, and many mothers did not want their sons to cross the Atlantic again to fight in another European war.

At first the marriage prospered, with the FBI and BSC freely exchanging intelligence garnered by their respective agents, from code-breaking and letter intercepts. The relationship only began to break down when William 'Wild Bill' Donovan, a prominent Republican lawyer, was appointed Coordinator of Strategic Information, the forerunner of the Office of Strategic Services. OSS would work closely with Britain's Special Operations Executive, dropping agents behind enemy lines to cause mayhem and organise local resistance forces.

Hoover viewed Donovan's new organisation as a direct threat to the supremacy of the FBI, furiously denounced his appointment as 'Roosevelt's folly' and became Donovan's implacable enemy. Unsurprisingly, Donovan soon turned against the FBI director and made no secret of the fact that he would do everything in his power to get him fired if the Republicans returned to power. Stephenson, meanwhile, was becoming increasingly disillusioned with Hoover's plodding 'policeman's mentality' and believed he was making poor use of the intelligence he was being given. When it became clear that Stephenson had forged a bond with Donovan, working together to set up a coordinated intelligence-gathering operation, Hoover began to treat the British with ill-concealed hostility.

It was into this maelstrom of jealousy and clashing ambitions that Popov stepped when he arrived in New York. There was almost nothing about him that Hoover could like, despite the enthusiastic endorsements provided by British intelligence in London. First of all, Popov was a spy and therefore intrinsically untrustworthy; the fact that he was a double agent only made him, in Hoover's eyes, doubly untrustworthy. Second, he was a foreigner, and Hoover hated all foreigners. Third, he was a playboy and a womaniser, the kind of man whom Hoover despised, since he (Hoover) presented himself to the American public as a man of almost puritanical morality. The fact that Popov soon became a popular figure at the fashionable Stork Club – one of Hoover's favourite haunts – also did nothing to endear him to the director.

In truth, the FBI had little interest in running Popov as a double agent; as far as Hoover was concerned, his only value to the Bureau was to act as a 'honey-pot' to attract other German agents in the United States, who could then be arrested. Hoover saw his job as catching spies and destroying spy rings, not allowing so-called double agents to create them, and in this area he could claim considerable success. A few months before Popov's arrival, Captain Ulrich von der Osten, the Abwehr's top spymaster in the United States, had been knocked down by a taxi while attempting to cross Broadway near Times Square. He was rushed to hospital with serious internal injuries, but died without regaining consciousness. Another agent, Karl Ludwig, who was with him at the time of the accident, managed to grab his briefcase, but worried about what might be found in his room at the Taft Hotel, where von der Osten was staying under the name of Don Julio. Ludwig telephoned the manager to request that Mr Julio's belongings be packed up for collection, but when the manager asked Ludwig to identify himself, he panicked and put the telephone down. With his suspicions aroused, the manager contacted the New York Police Department, who alerted the FBI. The documents found in von der Osten's room eventually led to thirty-three German agents being arrested and convicted of espionage in a blaze of publicity that was extremely favourable – and welcome – to Hoover, who thoroughly enjoyed being portrayed as America's number-one spycatcher. 'It was', he trumpeted, 'the greatest spy round-up in US history.'

After forty-eight hours 'in quarantine', Popov was summoned to his first meeting with the FBI in the person of Percy J. Foxworth, the agent in charge of the FBI's New York field office, known to everyone as Sam. Popov left a colourful account in his memoirs of the cloak-and-dagger preamble.[3] He was told to ask for Charles Lanman – the agent who would become his case officer – at eleven o'clock sharp in the lobby of the Rockefeller Center, where the FBI maintained an office to liaise with BSC. Popov arrived on time, met Lanman in the lobby and followed him into an elevator up to the twenty-ninth floor, where the agent stepped out, with Popov hard on his heels. They completed a brisk, apparently pointless, tour of the corridors and returned to the elevator bank, where Lanman pressed the 'Up' button and focused his attention on the lights indicating the position of the various elevators. A vacant elevator arrived, but the doors opened and closed without Lanman making a move. When the doors opened on a second elevator, they revealed a man in a suit who nodded, almost imperceptibly, at Lanman, Lanman got in, followed by Popov, and the elevator whirred up to the forty-fourth floor without stopping. As the doors slid open, Lanman and the other man took up a position on each side of Popov and virtually frog-marched him along a corridor, through a secretary's room into a large office, where Percy Foxworth was waiting.

Foxworth got up from behind his desk, shook Popov's hand and said he was pleased to meet him, contriving at the same time to give Popov the strong impression that he was not in the least pleased. After they were all seated, Foxworth reached into a drawer and pulled out the documents that were in the briefcase Mitchell had carried through immigration controls at the airport two days earlier. He sifted through the pile, extracting a typewritten translation of the Pearl Harbor questionnaire, a copy of which, he said, had been forwarded to FBI headquarters in Washington.

During the course of the next hour, Foxworth made little secret of the fact that he viewed the questionnaire with suspicion. It was too pat for his taste, too obviously designed to indicate that an operation was being planned against Pearl Harbor. Foxworth's instincts told him that it was some kind of trap and he wanted to know every detail of the circumstances in which Popov had been given the questionnaire in Lisbon. Popov spelled out his relationship with von Karsthoff and his close friend Jebsen, causing Foxworth's eyebrows to twitch when Popov admitted that Jebsen was a serving Abwehr officer. He explained Jebsen's mission to Taranto with von Gronau, and Jebsen's belief that the Pearl Harbor information was destined for the Japanese.

The longer he talked, the more it seemed Foxworth was convinced it was all a ruse. Exasperated, Popov pointed out that the Abwehr considered him to be one of their top agents and that he had been given a specific mission to set up a spy network in the United States. Foxworth remained sceptical, but Popov was able to restore some credibility when the American turned to a small sheaf of old bills, telegrams and personal letters that had been found in a file in Popov's briefcase and asked if they had been included by mistake. Popov smiled broadly, not without a certain sense of triumph. Far from being included by mistake, he explained, the apparently innocent papers actually contained his detailed instructions from the Abwehr, along with the entire five-page Pearl Harbor questionnaire in German. He challenged the three agents to find the material and each of them examined the papers, turning them backwards and forwards, holding them up to the light, scrutinising them minutely to look for traces of invisible ink. A cryptanalyst who happened to be visiting from Washington was called in to try and identify some mysterious code, but he, too, pronounced himself baffled. How could a questionnaire comprising several thousand words be hidden in documents containing less than half that number of words? Codes used more characters, not fewer.

Popov, by now enjoying himself hugely, asked if there was a microscope in the building. When one had been found, he picked up a telegram and, holding it to the light, demonstrated how one full stop in the text was faintly reflective. Carefully lifting the dot from the paper, he slid it into the microscope and invited the Americans to view the result. To Popov's irritation, Foxworth was obviously much more intrigued by the revelation of the microdot than he had been by the contents of the questionnaire itself – so much so that he decided he should go to Washington to show the microdots personally to Mr Hoover. (In fact he got no further than an assistant director, who obviously wanted the kudos of breaking the news to the director.) Popov left the meeting with an assurance from Foxworth that Hoover himself would be making decisions on exactly how and where he would be used. In the meantime he was to spend his time 'settling in'.[4]

Unquestionably the revelation of the Germans' microdot technology generated a great deal more excitement in Washington than the questionnaire. On 21 August, assistant director Earl Connelley showed the microdots to Hoover, and on 3 September Hoover wrote to Major-General Edwin M. Watson, the secretary to the president, at the White House: 'I thought the President and you might be interested in the attached photographs which show one of the methods used by the German espionage system in transmitting messages to its agents . . .'

The letter included a photograph of one of the cable forms with two microdots attached, an enlargement of the German text they each contained and a translation into English. Crucially, neither of these microdots made any mention of Pearl Harbor – one asked for information about aircraft production and the other requested details of the strength of the Canadian air force and its training facilities. Evidently Hoover attached little importance to the fact that other microdots demanded detailed information about the defences of Pearl Harbor.

The following day General Watson forwarded Hoover's letter to the president, but there was no reason for Roosevelt to consider the information anything other than mildly interesting evidence of Germany's development of microphotography.

Popov assumed he had fulfilled his duty regarding the warning about Pearl Harbor; meanwhile he needed to get on with his duties as a German 'spy'. He had impressed on Foxworth the need to contact Lisbon without delay, both to report his safe arrival and to indicate that he was making some progress with his mission, but Foxworth insisted that the Bureau would have to supervise any communications Popov made with the Germans. The implication was clear: the Bureau was worried that he might try to slip in some unauthorised information.

On 22 August Popov and Charlie Lanman got together to prepare the first of a number of letters in secret ink that would be dispatched to the cover addresses Popov had been given in Lisbon. Von Karsthoff had asked him to report details of the passport control arrangements in Bermuda and New York. They picked out a name, Joseph G. Gabor, from the New York telephone directory and gave him a fictitious return address, 330 East 71st Street, then typed out an innocuous letter that would cause no problems with the censor. The 'ink' was made with a mixture of water and Pyramidon, a headache powder available at any pharmacy. Using a steel-nibbed pen, Popov wrote out the message – which had been cleared by Dick Ellis of BSC – between the typewritten lines. He reported that Bermuda presented no problems, but the immigration authorities in New York were much stricter and had questioned him closely about his connection with the British Ministry of Information and how he was to support himself. He ended on an optimistic note: 'Owing to my semi-official position I am making very good connections here and hope soon to be able to send supplies and material. Ivan.'

Apart from this not very onerous duty, Popov was more or less left to his own devices and devoted himself to settling in, in considerable style. He booked a course of flying lessons at Mitchell Field, took delivery of his new Buick convertible, signed a lease for a penthouse on the twenty-second floor of a new apartment block on the corner of Park Avenue and 61st Street – paying a year's rent, $3,600, in advance since he could supply no references – and hired an interior designer to decorate it. He spent some $12,000 on furniture, first-edition books, a state-of-the-art hi-fi system and hundreds of records. When Lanman warned Popov that Mr Hoover was 'a very virtuous man and would not approve' of his extravagant lifestyle, Popov asserted, perhaps a touch ingenuously, that the Germans viewed him as something of a playboy and he needed to live up to that reputation to maintain their trust and his cover.

On 2 September, Popov moved into his handsome new apartment along with an elderly Chinese manservant, Chen-Yen, whom he had hired after advertising in the *New York Times*. He had suggested to Lanman, a mite sarcastically, that the FBI might like to provide him with domestic staff so that they could keep an even closer check on his activities, but as Connelley explained in a memorandum to the director: 'Other and more satisfactory arrangements are being made which will enable us to obtain complete coverage of informant's activities while he is in his apartment.' What they had in mind was installing microphones to eavesdrop on 'any German agents who might call'. They also proposed arranging a verbal signal so that Popov could alert the FBI if he suspected he was being led into a trap. Popov apparently raised no objection to these arrangements, provided he could have a cut-off switch, as 'there would undoubtedly be certain personal matters in connection with his entertaining in his apartment which he did not feel he would like to have disclosed'.

One of those 'personal matters' was a lively young English woman by the name of Terry Richardson, who would, through no fault of her own, cause the FBI no end of trouble. Popov met her through a mutual friend at a dinner party in New York and they became lovers, within a month of his arrival in America, during a languorous weekend spent on Shelter Island. The Bureau immediately mounted a vigorous investigation into her background and initially concluded there was 'no evidence of espionage or un-American activities'. But then the newspaper baron Cornelius Vanderbilt Junior set alarm bells ringing when he informed the FBI about the activities of two women with 'decidedly pro-Nazi sympathies' – one of them Richardson. According to Vanderbilt, Richardson could speak fluent German, had lived in Paris before the war, had been taken to Cairo by a young Jewish boy who was her lover, and was friends with a Mme Holsether, who had 'photographs of herself with Hitler, Goering, Hess and Goebbels'. Further enquiries established that Richardson, who was twenty-seven, was trying to divorce the husband whom she had claimed to US immigration officials had been killed while fighting with the British army. Richardson would never be entirely cleared of suspicion, but in the end the Bureau decided she was probably no more than a 'gold digger'.

Popov, blissfully unaware of the question mark hanging over Richardson, suggested to Lanman that he should take her to Hawaii for a 'frolic in the sun', which would provide excellent cover for the trip the Germans would be expecting him to make as soon as possible in order to formulate answers to the numerous questions about Pearl Harbor in the questionnaire. Lanman hesitantly agreed and told Popov to start making arrangements while he secured authorisation from his bosses at the FBI.

A few days later Lanman called and asked Popov to meet him, as usual, in a midtown hotel. A routine had been established for such meetings: Lanman called with the name of a hotel, room number and time. Popov was warned to take careful precautions to avoid being followed: never to take a cab directly to the rendezvous, for example, but always to use at least two separate cabs; or to jump out of a subway car as the doors were closing; or to buy a ticket in a movie house, sit down in the dark and then immediately sneak out again.

Popov was hoping that Lanman, whom he had come to like, wanted to see him to give him the go-ahead for his trip to Hawaii. In fact it was the reverse: Lanman abruptly announced that the trip was off. Popov was dismayed. He argued that his relationship with the Germans was based on trust, and that trust would be seriously damaged if he was not allowed to go to Hawaii. The whole operation was being jeopardised for reasons he could not fathom. At the very least, he pleaded, he needed some information about Pearl Harbor to send back to Germany, otherwise his masters would assume he had been compromised.

Lanman, who was far from stupid, was sympathetic, but said there was nothing he could do. He understood there was a communication problem between BSC and the FBI headquarters. He was sure that Mr Hoover would sort it out, but in any case the director was coming to New York in two weeks' time and wanted to see Popov, so Popov could take it up directly with the boss. Lanman's advice was to 'take it easy' until Hoover arrived in town. Popov, furious and frustrated, walked out.

From this moment on, relations between Popov – now known in the Bureau files as 'Confidential Informant ND 63' – and the FBI began to deteriorate. When the Bureau asked him to keep a daily log of his activities, he refused, pointing out that the British had never asked for anything similar and adding sourly that the FBI was watching him so closely that they knew everything he was doing anyway.

Within the FBI opinions about Popov varied. Lanman was supportive, reporting to Washington: 'To date nothing has been determined which would indicate that the informant is anything other than sincere in his desire to cooperate with this Bureau.' But assistant director Connelley remained deeply suspicious. When Popov suggested giving the Germans information about a ship leaving a US port for Britain, but having the letter delayed by the censor in Bermuda so that it did not arrive until after the ship had crossed the Atlantic safely, Connelley offered the view, without any explanation, that the proposal created 'a very serious doubt as to the informant's sincerity'. Connelley's theory was that once Popov had been provided with the information, he might find some way of transmitting it to Lisbon in time for the Germans to intercept the ship and sink it. There was not a scrap of evidence that he could, or would, act with such treachery; nor is it possible to understand, in retrospect, why Popov's suggestion should be interpreted as casting 'very serious doubt' on his sincerity, other than the fact that the Bureau simply did not trust Popov.

On another occasion when Popov complained about the extent to which he was kept under surveillance, the Bureau's instant reaction was to speculate that there must be a reason why he was complaining, which in turn led to a discussion about whether the British really had confidence in him. Paranoia about the motives of British intelligence was a constant theme in the Bureau's dealings with Popov. If he was such an important and successful double agent, why had the British agreed to his mission in the United States, where he could be of little benefit to them? Was there some other reason, an agenda about which the FBI knew nothing? The fact that the British had failed, despite numerous requests, to provide the Bureau with precise details of what Popov had achieved since his recruitment as a British agent only served to increase the Bureau's unease. It was indicative of how little trust existed between the two agencies and how reluctant both were to cooperate with the other.

Popov's mood was not improved by news from Dubrovnik that an uncle and two cousins had been killed by the Ustashe, the pro-Nazi militia that was terrorising the country. Popov gloomily predicted to Lanman that unless he could prove to the Germans that he was working on answers to the questionnaire, they were likely to become suspicious and perhaps retaliate against his family in Belgrade. Dick Ellis of BSC stepped in at Popov's request to see if he could help and arranged a meeting with Foxworth, at which he said that Popov's morale was very low because he thought (quite correctly) that the Americans did not trust him. Foxworth duly reported the meeting in a memorandum to Hoover, who scrawled a reply on the bottom telling him, somewhat obtusely, to 'get this Popov thing settled'.

On 9 September Lanman and Popov met in a room at the Governor Clinton Hotel to compose a second letter to Lisbon, this one claiming that Popov had found someone to work as a radio operator. He had brought with him instructions on how to operate a radio station and it was assumed that the Germans would want a radio link set up as soon as possible. Popov again tried to impress on Lanman the need to keep up a constant stream of information to his German masters and asked if it would be possible to supply economic or political intelligence that they had not even asked for, to convince them of his diligence as an agent. He also said he would need information about defence arrangements in Florida, and when Lanman raised an eyebrow, Popov announced with a wolfish grin that he was taking Terry Richardson to Miami in his car for a short holiday to compensate for not going to Hawaii.

This news apparently caused consternation at the FBI, ostensibly because driving Richardson to Florida would contravene the Mann Act,[5] which made it a federal offence to transport women across state lines for immoral purposes. In reality, the concern was that Richardson had not yet been fully investigated and, if she turned out to be a German agent, the last thing the Bureau wanted was for the two of them to take off together. A flurry of memoranda flew back and forth between Washington and New York. Assistant director Connelley, ordered to make sure that Popov and Richardson did not travel together, deputed Lanman to warn Popov about the laws against transporting women across state lines. Lanman was told to handle the matter very carefully to ensure that 'no embarrassing circumstances arise in connection with this matter'. He was to use 'all his influence, without making Popov angry', to see that he did not go to Florida with Richardson.

To someone like Popov, the notion that an affair could be against the law simply because it was conducted in a different part of the country was utterly absurd. He did not know whether to laugh or cry when Lanman explained the Mann Act to him, but at the same time he absolutely refused to change his plans. While he had been in the United States long enough to recognise the deep strain of puritanism, particularly on sexual matters, that was part of the national psyche, he could hardly imagine being arrested for sharing a hotel room with his lover. However, if it was necessary to avoid arrest, Popov said, he and his new lady friend would take separate rooms.

Lanman was thus obliged to report his failure to his bosses and on Sunday, 14 September, Popov and Richardson headed south out of Manhattan in good spirits, with the top of the Buick down, bound for Florida. The 1,300-mile journey took them three days and they were tailed the whole way by FBI agents. At the Pancoast Hotel on Miami Beach they ostentatiously checked into separate rooms, which fact Lanman, who had flown down earlier to Miami and was staying in the nearby Cromwell Hotel, doggedly reported to Sam Foxworth in New York. Foxworth forwarded the report to Hoover, who was taking a baleful interest in Popov's trip.

All telephone calls made and received by both Popov and Richardson were monitored. Popov made only one call – to his interior decorator, Miss Rosemary Dudley, telling her to fire his manservant, Chen-Yen, because he was too old and half-deaf. Richardson made several calls to Butterfield 8-5018, which FBI agents quickly established was the number of the Stanhope Hotel on Fifth Avenue, where a friend of Richardson, one Baroness de Loqueyssie, was living.

Popov and Richardson spent most of Wednesday lounging by the hotel pool. On Thursday morning Popov went deep-sea fishing while Richardson went out to look for an apartment to rent in order to establish legal residence from which to begin divorce proceedings against her husband. In the afternoon they both went fishing, and in the evening they drove to Jack Dempsey's Club and Bar at the Dempsey Vanderbilt Hotel. The agents shadowing them reported that they stayed for several hours, but did not attempt to make contact with anyone. On Friday they spent the entire day fishing and on Saturday they stayed in the hotel because of bad weather. On Saturday evening, Richardson returned to New York by air, having failed to find a place to stay for the winter. Popov left by car on Sunday, 21 September, arriving back in New York at four o'clock on the morning of Tuesday, 23 September.

In his memoirs, *Spy/Counterspy*, Popov records a rather different, and slightly more colourful, version of events,[6] claiming he knew nothing about the Mann Act until two FBI 'heavies' approached him on the beach and asked for a 'quiet word'. In the beach bar they warned him that since his companion was not his wife, he would be well advised to arrange for her to leave Florida without delay. Popov asked what would happen if he refused and was told that he could be arrested and sentenced to one year and a day in a Florida prison. Popov said he protested vehemently, but felt he had no alternative but to accept their 'advice' and that Terry took the news badly, bursting into tears and accusing him of wanting to get rid of her.[7]

Back in New York, Popov resumed writing letters to Lisbon, but complained constantly that he was not being supplied with sufficiently impressive information. Some, he said, was 'shit' and not worth sending. The only way to maintain his high standing in German eyes, he warned the FBI, was to produce higher-quality intelligence. It was no use just sending material that had already been published, since the Abwehr had set up an efficient system to establish whether information supplied by agents was simply culled from newspapers. 'Confidential Informant ND 63 is inclined', Lanman wearily reported, 'to be rather temperamental.'

On 24 September Dick Ellis sent a note to Tar Robertson in London: 'Tricycle . . . finds the atmosphere [in the United States] a little strange and is inclined to under-estimate the intelligence and imagination of his FBI contacts. The FBI fully appreciate the need for great care and discretion and are anxious to proceed slowly, whereas Tricycle wishes to progress more rapidly.'[8]

In fairness to the FBI, the Bureau was having extreme difficulty in extracting material from the naval and military intelligence agencies, neither of which could see much benefit in voluntarily providing Germany with information about the defence capabilities of the United States. Connelley suggested they could produce disinformation – for example, details of defensive plans they never intended to put into effect – but even this was turned down. At the same time the FBI was getting restless at the total lack of results from running Confidential Informant ND 63, whose claim to 'high standing' with his German masters was looking increasingly thin. Not only had no German agents attempted to make contact with him, but thus far no reply had been received to any of the letters dispatched to cover addresses in Lisbon. Adding to the difficulties was the fact that Popov was still regarded with suspicion. When one of his letters was accidentally destroyed by the British censor in Bermuda, the Bureau took it to mean that the British, too, were possibly sceptical of Popov and 'may actually distrust him'.

If Popov thought these problems could be sorted out in his promised meeting with Hoover, he was wrong, judging by the brief and bitter account of the encounter in his autobiography. He recalled how he was summoned to Foxworth's office to find the director sitting behind Foxworth's desk 'like a sledgehammer in search of an anvil'. There were no introductions and no preliminaries. The director, 'with an expression of disgust on his face', ordered Popov to sit down and immediately began to rant, pounding the desk with his fist as he recounted Popov's various transgressions: chasing women, renting penthouses, breaking morality laws, attempting to corrupt FBI agents and generally besmirching the agency's record as 'the cleanest police organisation in the world' – all very much in keeping with Hoover's self-image as guardian of public and private probity. At the end of it, purple with rage, Hoover turned to Foxworth, as if he could not bear to address Popov directly, and said, 'He may leave now.'

But Popov had no intention of leaving. According to his account, he coolly lit a cigarette and began a spirited defence of his position, asserting that he had not come to the United States to break the laws or to corrupt the FBI, but rather to help with the war effort. He had brought with him a serious warning that Japan was likely to attack Pearl Harbor and had handed over 'on a silver salver' evidence that the enemy had developed microdot technology, a new and dangerous espionage weapon that could have done a great deal of harm, had it not been discovered at this early stage. He added that he could also have organised a spy network in the United States that would have been entirely under the Bureau's control, if he had been afforded some cooperation.

Hoover muttered something about being able catch spies without help from anyone, least of all Popov. He accused Popov of being a 'bogus spy', citing the fact that not a single German agent had attempted to make contact with him since he arrived in the United States.

Popov countered by pointing out that he needed to produce results in order to satisfy his German masters, and that he had had precious little assistance from the FBI. 'You're like all double agents,' Hoover interjected, 'you're begging for information to sell to your German friends so you can make a lot of money and be a playboy.'

Barely able to control his temper, Popov denied that he was in the business for money. He had always lived well, he said, and one of the reasons he had been recruited by the Germans was that he mixed in the kind of social circles they wanted to penetrate. If he suddenly cut his standards and lived like a monk, just to please the director of the FBI, the Germans would immediately become suspicious. If he was begging for information, it was only because he wanted to do a good job, not because he wanted money.

Hoover had had enough. He turned to Foxworth and sneered: 'This man is trying to teach me my job.'

'I don't think anyone could teach you anything,' Popov snapped as he got to his feet and stalked out of the office, slamming the door behind him.[9]

Not long afterwards Popov discovered, to his fury, that the 'cut-off' switch installed by the FBI on the bugging devices in his apartment was a dummy and that the Bureau was able to listen in continuously to everything going on. His first instinct was to rip out all the microphones, race over to Lanman's office and wrap the wires round his neck, but common sense prevailed and he sat down to think it through. He was aware that his handlers in London were trying hard to bring pressure on the FBI to make proper use of him; it would be stupid to do anything precipitate that might jeopardise the negotiations. He decided, for the time being, to say nothing, but he had no intention of allowing the FBI to listen in to his every movement, particularly as Terry Richardson was not the only young lady he entertained in his bedroom. He carefully wrapped each microphone with several layers of cotton wadding and sat back to await developments.

Next morning Lanman telephoned, apparently for no other reason than to make small talk. Popov guessed correctly that he wanted to find out what had gone wrong with the bugs and was simply checking if he was home, so he broke off the conversation, saying that he had to go out for a lunch date. He took the elevator to the ground floor, asked the doorman to call him a cab and loudly gave the driver the address of a restaurant in Greenwich Village. As soon as the cab had turned off Park Avenue, Popov told the driver to double back to the service entrance on 61st Street. He took the service elevator up to the twenty-second floor, quietly let himself into his apartment and took a chair in the sitting room, from where he could see the front door reflected in a mirror. He did not have long to wait before he heard a key sliding into the lock and the door opened a few inches. He coughed gently and the door silently closed. He thought he could hear the footfalls of at least two people hurrying away in the corridor outside.

At a subsequent meeting with Lanman, Popov asked him if he did not want to know why all the microphones in his apartment had gone dead. The FBI man did not bother to deny anything, nor did he apologise, but he had the grace to look shame-faced. Popov also talked to Dick Ellis and told him the whole story. Ellis was sympathetic, but cautioned Popov not to cause any trouble. His best course of action would be to rise above the irritation he felt about the FBI's behaviour and keep trying persuade them of the benefits that could accrue from the agency's cooperation. Even if he was not the kind of man that Mr Hoover could like or even respect, Popov was the person selected by the Abwehr for the operation and the Bureau was stuck with him. If he failed in his mission, the Germans would send over another agent who would not be secretly working for British intelligence, so the FBI had every reason to help him.

Around this time new fears were raised about Terry Richardson. Investigation into her finances revealed that the large property portfolio she claimed to own, along with a major investment in Suez Canal stocks, were non-existent. The FBI immediately jumped to the conclusion that she was being financed by Germany to spy on Popov. When Lanman raised this possibility with Popov, he calmly replied that if it could be proved that Richardson was a spy, he would kill her. Lanman hastily warned him that if he did such a thing, he would be arrested, tried for murder and probably sentenced to death. Popov was unabashed. 'Okay,' he said, 'I'll take her to South America and kill her there.'

Once again Popov was questioned about the circumstances in which they had met. He explained that he had been playing cards in his apartment with an Austrian friend, Otto Stephan Feldman, who had arrived in New York from Lisbon in May. Feldman had another engagement uptown with the Baroness Cyrena de Loqueyssie. He had called to say he would be a little late and the baroness had said she had a woman friend with her, so perhaps Feldman would like to bring Popov along? The woman friend was Richardson. All three − Feldman, the Baroness and Richardson − had been under surveillance for weeks without arousing suspicion, but Lanman now asked Popov if he would host a dinner party at his apartment for the baroness and Richardson. The third guest would be Special Agent George Starr, who would pose as an indiscreet army colonel. Popov agreed.

The plan was for the conversation, over coffee, to turn to conditions in Europe and the 'marvellous way' Hitler's armies had been able to go through various countries. The 'colonel', in response to questions by Popov, would innocently give information about forces in various countries and start a discussion about the relative merits of US tanks as against Axis tanks.

Starr reported that the dinner went off very well and that Richardson definitely appeared interested when the dicussion turned to tanks. Starr said he had got the impression she was a very mercenary person and certainly the type who might engage in espionage. 'The two women did not join in the conversation but the Baroness tried to continue talking to Richardson who did not respond very readily and simply sat seemingly listening to the conversation between agent Starr and informant.' Starr got the impression that Richardson grew more nervous as the conversation went on. The baroness was younger and prettier and Popov was paying her court, perhaps causing Richardson concern. Starr definitely concluded that Richardson was under some kind of nervous strain, although 'whether this is due to espionage activity or merely the strain under which a fortune hunter operates I am unable to say'.

Popov could not have been too worried about Richardson being a spy because the day after the dinner party he helped her move into an apartment in his building and agreed to pay her first month's rent, $200, having swallowed her sob story about not being paid huge sums owed to her. When, however, she showed signs of expecting Popov to continue subsidising her, he began to look for ways of breaking up his relationship with her. The question of whether she was a spy was never definitely resolved, although Popov made it clear to the Bureau that he would have no hesitation in exposing her, if she let slip to him that she was working for Germany.

Meanwhile, the unfortunate Lanman was ordered to run a background check on Popov's new butler, a man called Marshall Davidson Baldwin, who, for reasons best known to himself, went by the professional name of Brooks. The agency that had placed him said he was a 'very superior type of person' and the only minor stain on his character was fabricating a couple of bills when temporarily short of cash in a previous employment.

While 'Brooks' was being checked out, Popov was becoming increasingly concerned at the total lack of response from Lisbon to his letters. On 7 October, he sent a personal letter, written in secret ink in French, to von Karsthoff, in an attempt to find out what was going on:

> Dear Friend,
>
> I am using French this time so as to be able to communicate with you directly. I have at my disposal a trustworthy man to handle the radio set. A very safe and capable man. I have made arrangement with him following your personal instructions. I am busy trying to find a house outside NYC for installation. Please have the set sent at once so as to begin direct contact, because communications by letter rather risky. I have already started very good and important relations. I hope to be able to solve the majority of the questions with relatively short delay . . . Since my arrival I have been completely without news of you. Have you forgotten me? So long, Ivan.

When there was still no reply, Popov suggested to Lanman that he should try to provoke the Germans into making some kind of personal contact by claiming to have acquired documents too lengthy and complicated to copy out in secret ink. The Abwehr had asked for 'TOs' (tables of army organisation) in its original questionnaire. Popov now persuaded Lanman that if he could be provided with some TOs, he felt certain of getting a reaction from Lisbon. Somewhat to Popov's surprise, given the FBI's obvious disaffection with him, the plan was approved. In fact this was the kind of operation the Bureau wanted to set up all along – using Popov as the bait to catch other German agents.

On 15 October Popov wrote to Lisbon to say he was in possession of TOs:

> It would be impossible to send you by letter all of them because it would take nearly a month to write them all down. Arranging to photograph them. Suggest following solutions:

(a) You tell me to whom to deliver the films or you send somebody very sure to take them from me. In that case the password would be your secretary's first name.

(b) I could fly to a Central or South American capital, taking films with me. I could arrange trip under cover of diplomatic courier there and back. This solution is more convenient because it would enable me to take out other material I have. In case you take solution (b) send at once a cable . . . because I should take steps to obtain my diplomatic visa as soon as possible. Insert in a cable city to which I should go. Immediately after my arrival in designated city, I will send you my address by cable so your man can contact me. I should use same password as in solution (a).

> In case you take solution (b) send me at once the expenses for my trip or have man who contacts me reimburse me . . . Why don't you communicate with me? Have heard nothing from you since my arrival here.
>
> Ivan.
>
> How is Ivan II getting along? Greetings.

Popov added a postscript for good measure: 'The amounts appropriated for Naval excise during 1942 and 1941 − 1942 − $945,411,100. 1941 − $982,320,200. What about sending me money? When will receive a radio? Ivan.'

A week later he wrote again with details of pilot training and new armoured vehicles being introduced, adding another plea for communication: 'For God's sake what is the matter with you? Has the owner of Ivan III [Popov had given a dog called Ivan III to von Karsthoff's secretary, Elizabeth] forgotten me? Ivan.'

On 25 October, to Popov's great relief, Lisbon at last responded. A postcard in Elizabeth's handwriting was delivered to his Park Avenue apartment, couched in hurt, but affectionate, terms and indicating that Lisbon had so far only received one of his letters:

> My dearest Dusan,
> I am really sorry that you don't write me any more. You promised me so much before your departure, and up to the present I only received one letter which I cannot quite understand. You know how I am longing to have any detail of your life now you are abroad, and to hear how you accustom yourself to the new atmosphere. Your dog is all right and has become very tall. It is really a beauty and I doubt

whether I will ever give him back. Please write to me as soon as possible and don't keep me waiting too long. Yours affectionately, Mady.

Popov replied immediately in secret ink:

Received your letter. Can't understand why you have not received my letters. Have sent till now 14 [actually, he had only sent eight] with some very important and complete material. If you are not yet in possession of these letters let me know at once so that I can send them again. Wonder what has happened to the radio? Have retained my radio man nearly a month ago and must sign the lease for a house outside New York. I could avoid a lot of trouble if you would act with more speed. It is now clear that communication by letter is too dangerous and shows bad results. What about my suggestions with regard to Tables of Organisation? You should have that letter now. Have not yet received any money and I am beginning to be short. Please don't delay it any more. I am afraid to write any more if my letters are not reaching you. For that reason I wait impatiently the radio and your instructions. Greetings, Ivan.

On 30 October, Popov received a succinct cablegram from Lisbon: 'Elizabeth departed for Rio. Francisco.' This was a coded instruction from von Karsthoff ('Francisco') that he should make his way to Rio de Janeiro to deliver the TOs in person, as he had suggested earlier.

With the prospect of face-to-face contact with German agents at last in sight, the FBI moved quickly to facilitate Popov's trip. To avoid the risk of just being required to hand over the TOs and then told to leave, he was provided with a mass of extra information, which he would insist on dictating in order to play for time and perhaps discover more about the Abwehr network in South America. He made longhand notes of War Department appropriation figures, characteristics of armoured vehicles, training of army pilots, monthly production figures of tanks and aircraft scaled down by 15 per cent, and details of new torpedo nets, provided by the Office of Naval Intelligence, which were inaccurate but plausible. Popov used the camera given to him by the Germans to photograph the Tables of Organisation.

A few days after he had visited Washington to obtain diplomatic courier status and the necessary visas, he received another communication from Elizabeth Sahrbach, written as a love letter and dated Lisbon, 24 October 1941:

Darling,

I'm so happy that I finally received some news from you. O, darling, you don't know how delighted I was to get your three letters and I thank you very much. You are always the same dear old darling who cannot stay in one place for a long time, because as you write, you have now again some intentions to travelling abroad. But you are quite right, take a good look at the whole of beautiful America, so that you can tell me a lot about it . . .

There is not much to tell about myself. I am quite all right. We still have a lovely sunshine weather here, but I am condemned to go bathing quite alone because you are so far away. Your pretty dog is a darling and is very attached to us. He also sends hearty greetings. I already told you in my last letter that he is awfully tall and nice. My dear uncle has now a marvellous time. He has been travelling abroad for some time, but has returned now. He too sends you a lot of greetings, because as you well know, he is very fond of you. I was very anxious about Dicky, but he is really a nice chap. I got a letter from him some days ago. I would be so glad, if we could arrange to meet us all together in some nice place.

Well, darling, enough for today. Please write me as soon as possible, as I'm always thinking of you.

A lot of love and kisses,

Your

Mady.

Popov was easily able to read between the lines. Sahrbach reported that Lisbon had now received three of his letters, and the reference to travelling abroad confirmed his instructions to go to Rio. 'Uncle' was von Karsthoff and 'Dicky' was Ivan II – Popov's sub-agent, still operating in Britain and apparently doing well after a shaky start.

On 12 November another cablegram indicated that Popov would be paid when he got to Rio: 'Objects sold as remittance according to my instructions impossible. Sum paid to Elizabeth. Francisco.'

At a final briefing with Lanman and Foxworth, Popov was given a 'shopping list' of the intelligence he was to try and obtain during his trip. Top priority was any information regarding the names and identities of German agents in the United States. After that he was to find out all he could about the German espionage operations in South and Central America. If he was given microdots to deliver to other agents in the United States, he was to send a cable to a cover address in New York giving details of his departure and adding, 'Looking forward to seeing you. Love Dusko.' If he was ordered simply to carry the microdots back to the United States, he was to omit his name. If he had no microdots, he was to cable only his departure details.

Popov left New York at two o'clock on 14 November on an Eastern Airlines flight for Miami. As always in such situations, he was exceptionally calm, trusting his safety to luck and native cunning. He had no idea, of course, what might await him in Rio, but he was confident that he would be able to handle whatever situation arose and that he would be returning safely to New York. He certainly never dwelt on the real possibility that his cover had been blown and the Germans were only enticing him to Rio to capture him. In Miami he transferred to a Pan American Clipper bound for Rio de Janeiro, via an overnight stop in Belém, a steamy port in the Amazon delta where he was appalled to discover a thriving slave market, with men, women, girls and boys penned in wooden cages and on sale for a few dollars a head. He was relieved, on day three, to arrive in Rio and check into the sumptuous Copacabana Palace Hotel, facing Rio's famous beach.

A cablegram was already waiting for him: 'Elizabeth will visit you there. Francisco.' Popov found it no hardship at all to divide his time between the beach and the hotel, but after five days he had still not been contacted, so he sent a cablegram to Lisbon: 'Having to leave Rio soon. Wonder if will be able to contact Elizabeth.' The reply was almost immediate, but incomprehensible: 'Received your cablegram. Everything possible is ordered. Francisco.'

After a full week kicking his heels in Rio, Popov took matters into his own hands and called, unannounced, on the German Embassy, where he asked to see one of the military attachés. After a number of whispered telephone conversations he was eventually shown into the office of the assistant naval attaché, Herman Bohny, who was known by the FBI to head a big espionage network in Brazil. Bohny's demeanour was stiff and formal and he immediately demanded a password. When Popov said 'Elizabeth', Bohny visibly relaxed, shook Popov's hand and said he knew the agent was in town, but Lisbon had neglected to let them know where he was staying. Bohny shook his head as if in despair at the hopeless inefficiency of the Lisbon station, although Popov privately thought that it could not have been too difficult to find him, if anyone was interested. Bohny asked for the material Popov had brought with him and said he had instructions to pay him $10,000. Popov handed over the photographs, but said he would need to dictate the remaining material from his scribbled notes.

Popov returned to the embassy the following day and spent the morning dictating his notes to a male secretary. At the end of the morning he was given a message saying that when 'Number One' (Bohny) wanted to see him again, a Mrs Dubois (actually, Bohny's wife) would call his hotel posing as a friend and give him the time, date and place. On Wednesday, 26 November, he got a telephone call from Mrs Dubois telling him to go to apartment number eighty-four at the Edificio Manhattan that evening. But when Popov arrived, he was told that 'Number One' could not make it and he was to go to another address – 91 Rua Bulhoes de Carvalho – in Ipanema the next day. He was instructed not to take a cab, but to walk.

In Ipanema the following evening Bohny introduced Popov to 'Number Two' – Albrecht Gustav Engels, a dyed-in-the-wool Nazi whose cover was a directorship in the South American division of AEG, the German electrical conglomerate. Operating under the codename of 'Alfredo', Engels ran a powerful short-wave clandestine transmitter through which the majority of the Abwehr radio traffic to and from the Americas was channelled.

Popov explained the frustration he was having in setting up a radio link from New York. He said he had hired a radio operator, but Lisbon had so far not supplied him with a transmitter. In the meantime he had learned it was possible to buy all the necessary parts needed to build one, without the US authorities ever knowing about it. Engels thought this was the obvious solution to the problem and sent a coded message to Berlin suggesting that 'Ivan' should build his own set. A few days later Berlin agreed, but instructed Popov to maintain communication through letters to mail drops in Lisbon until the radio was set up and running.

Engels had a special job for Popov. Representatives of three major US companies had been combing South America for supplies of uranium ore. He wanted Popov to discover how the ore was being processed, to what degree of purity and how much had been stockpiled. Mystified, Popov said he would do his best. He wondered if he was being downgraded as an agent to handle commercial espionage, being completely ignorant (like most of the world) of the Manhattan Project, the scientific race to produce an atomic bomb. If Engels knew what it was all about, he gave no indication to Popov, but he did talk freely about Abwehr operations in the Americas – information Popov was able to pass on to the FBI back in New York.

On 1 December, Popov had a final meeting with Bohny and Engels in an apartment at Nacimento Silver 13. He was given the $10,000 he had been promised and additional instructions on two microdots attached to a blank hotel message form. Engels said further instructions would be sent by microdot from Lisbon under the inside flap of envelopes.

Popov had decided to return to the United States by sea and booked a passage on the SS *Uruguay*, which, by happy coincidence, also accommodated a famous ballet company – Colonel de Basil's Ballet Russe de Monte Carlo – returning from a successful South American tour. Popov could not have been more pleased to find himself on a ship with a score or more of unattached and exotic young women, and by the time they arrived in Trinidad he was paying diligent court to a beautiful ballerina by the name of Dora. They had planned to explore the island together and, as the ship dropped anchor in the harbour at Port of Spain, they stood idly at the rails watching a pilot cutter cutting a creamy swathe through the blue water towards them. The cutter manoeuvred alongside and a short, red-haired man, very obviously British, climbed up a ladder onto the ship. He had a brief, whispered conversation with one of the ship's officers, who pointed to where Popov was standing. Smiling broadly, the man marched up to Popov, offered his hand, cheerily introduced himself as a Major Wren and asked if he could have a 'quiet word'.

Reluctantly detaching himself from the lovely Dora, Popov joined Wren and moved to an area of open deck. Walter 'Freckles' Wren was MI6 head of station in Trinidad. He had orders to conduct a thorough debriefing of Popov, as London wanted a full account of his trip to Rio. Wren apologised and said it was likely to take all day. Following Popov's eyes to where a puzzled Dora was still standing at the rail looking at them, Wren whispered, 'Sorry, old boy, you'll have to leave your lady friend behind.'

Popov sighed, went off to explain to Dora that some unexpected urgent business had suddenly cropped up, and left the ship with Wren on the pilot cutter. Actually, the day turned out much more agreeably than he had expected. Wren lived in a charming house overlooking the harbour and served an excellent Creole lunch, after which he called in his secretary Jane, a long-legged classic English beauty, to dictate a report to London. Popov could barely take his eyes off her. Wren had to drive to his office in town to encode the report, leaving Jane to look after Popov as 'compensation for your ballerina'. Ballerina? In the delightful company of Jane, Popov had forgotten all about Dora.

Wren returned in good spirits and insisted that Popov join him in a 'sundowner' on the terrace before returning to the ship; he could not leave Trinidad without sampling a local speciality – a planter's punch. Several drinks later, Popov climbed unsteadily into the car that was to take him back to the ship. By the time the SS *Uruguay* sailed, Popov was, true to form, busy re-establishing relations with Dora, who was sulking because he had abandoned her for the entire day.

On Sunday, 7 December, three days from New York, incredible rumours began to circulate that Japanese aircraft had attacked American ships. An hour or so later the captain's voice boomed over the ship's Tannoy, asking all passengers to assemble in the first-class lounge. When everyone was present, the captain, looking very grave, announced the news that the Japanese had mounted a surprise attack on Pearl Harbor; as a consequence, the United States had entered the war. Information was still sketchy, but since the ship was now vulnerable to torpedoes from enemy submarines, the captain ordered an immediate lifeboat drill and requested everyone to be alert until they reached the safety of New York.

Alone among those on board, Popov was neither surprised nor dismayed by the news. He was certain his questionnaire had been forwarded to US military intelligence, probably to President Roosevelt himself, and that adequate precautions had been taken to defend Pearl Harbor. Indeed, his first reaction to the news was that the operation had probably left Japan with a very bloody nose. 'Most of my co-passengers had long faces,' he said, 'but I was happy because it now meant that it was no longer a question of "if" we were going to win the war, but "when".'[10]

Rarely in history has a surprise attack caused such devastating losses. By the time the Japanese strike force finally withdrew from Pearl Harbor, some 2,400 people, most of them US navy personnel, had been killed; eighteen vessels, including eight battleships, had been sunk or seriously damaged; 188 aircraft had been destroyed and 159 damaged. The Japanese lost just twenty-nine aircraft out of a raiding force of 353 planes.

Only when the grim details began to emerge, as passengers gathered round crackling radio sets all around the ship, did incredulity and anger set in. 'I was flabbergasted,' said Popov. 'I knew they had been warned. I couldn't believe it.'

7

Radio Games

UNTIL THE END OF HIS LIFE POPOV WAS CONVINCED THAT HOOVER, motivated by personal animosity, was responsible for ignoring the clear warning that he had brought with him to the United States that Japan was going to attack Pearl Harbor. He was, unsurprisingly, in a state of considerable agitation when he arrived back in New York on 15 December 1941. Charlie Lanman was waiting to meet him when his ship docked and, as soon as they were alone in a car heading for Manhattan, Popov angrily demanded to know what had gone wrong. Lanman, perhaps out of embarrassment, affected not to understand what he was talking about. Later Sam Foxworth was similarly obtuse, refusing to answer Popov's persistent questions and advising him not to search for 'truth beyond his reach'. He suggested, with no little menace, that Popov had better learn 'to walk in step'.

If either man believed that the Bureau bore some blame for the Pearl Harbor disaster by ignoring the questionnaire that Popov had delivered a few months earlier, neither was prepared to discuss it. What they wanted to talk about was butterfly trays. Popov had reported from Rio that one afternoon, when he was leaving the German Embassy by a side door, he had passed a large room where a number of men were working on what looked like glass trays containing pressed butterflies. When he returned the next day to dictate notes to a male secretary, he had seen them again. Hoover, it seems, was obsessed by the notion that the trays were being used to conceal microdots with secret messages for agents in the United States. In a report about Popov's trip to Rio he had underlined the mention of butterfly trays and scrawled in the margin: 'This is vitally important. Get copies of "dots" so I may see them. See that no more butterfly trays are allowed to enter US.'

Five hundred butterfly trays were taken off the ship on which Popov returned to the United States and carted off to the FBI laboratory for examination. For almost a year afterwards, the Bureau would relentlessly track down all butterfly trays entering the United States from Brazil marked with a black and gold label inscribed 'Industra Brasileira Atelier Elizabeth, R. B. Gerardo 44-10, Rio de Janeiro'. Thousands of trays were minutely examined, but not a single microdot – or any other incriminating evidence – was discovered. All were returned to the US Customs Service.

Despite his frustration with the FBI, there was some good news for Popov when he returned to New York: his friend, Ewen Montagu, from the XX Committee, was in town. They met in Popov's Park Avenue apartment and Popov wasted no time venting his feelings. 'For the only time in our friendship,' Montagu noted, 'I found him depressed and worried, with all that gaiety which exudes from him completely gone.'[1] Popov complained bitterly about the way the Pearl Harbor questionnaire had been ignored and the constant surveillance he had been under. 'I'm no fool,' he told his friend. 'I understand that just because the British say I am OK it does not necessarily mean they can trust me, but they are such fools. There are microphones everywhere. When I bend over to smell flowers in a vase I scratch my nose on a microphone!'[2]

Montagu had been sent to the United States to try and build bridges with the FBI. Both Stewart Menzies, head of MI6, and Bill Stephenson of BSC had expressed concern to Hoover that unless Popov was more active as a German agent, his cover would be jeopardised. 'We in the XX Committee were naturally confident that Tricycle would be welcomed on reaching America,' Montagu wrote after the war:

> When the offer of Tricycle's services had been made to Hoover, 'C'
> [Menzies] had briefed him fully and given him a complete picture
> of Dusko Popov's background, character and way of life, and how he
> would have to continue to live a 'playboy' type of life if the Germans
> were not to deduce immediately that he had been caught and was
> operating under control.
>
>   To our horror, we learned that Hoover's management of Tricycle
> could not have been more calculated to blow him if Hoover had sat
> down to devise and plan a method of doing so . . . Hoover, the
> policeman, obviously only regarded Tricycle as potential fly-paper
> which other agents would approach and so get caught and impris-
> oned, with all possible publicity.[3]

After five months of US intransigence and procrastination, MI5 was determined to try and safeguard one of its top agents. Montagu's brief was to keep Popov 'alive' in the eyes of the Germans, while continuing efforts were made to persuade Hoover to cooperate. To this end Montagu was to establish a 'mini' XX Committee in Washington, comprising selected officers from each of the British service missions, to provide reasonably high-grade intelligence for Popov to transmit to his German masters, if the FBI would agree. A cover story was devised under which Popov would explain to the Germans that, despite his supposed position with the Ministry of Information advising the Yugoslav expatriate community in the United States, he had found it difficult to make worth-while contacts, but had now met a British officer who might open doors for him.

Neither Montagu nor Popov was optimistic:

> I explained to him what I had been able to fix up, but he realised as well as I did that it was pretty futile unless Hoover could be persuaded to play, which did not seem likely. But I think that my mission and visit to him were really worthwhile – when one has regards to Tricycle's service in the rest of the war – because of the boost that they gave to his morale. It persuaded him that there were people who still believed in him, that we were ready to go to real trouble to keep him 'alive' as a double agent, that we still wanted to use him and, from his point of view, to enable him to continue his work against the Nazis for which he had risked his life on each visit to Lisbon, as he was to risk it again, more than once.
>
> Nothing would move Hoover – it is hard to know why. He couldn't, or wouldn't, see the value of deception of the enemy. I suppose it was because he was really just a policeman and just good at catching people. There was also, of course, his reported patholog-ical jealousy of, and reluctance to share [intelligence] with other services – and double-cross deception can only be done with some form of XX Committee bringing complete co-operation of all Services.[4]

After Montagu had left for home with nothing achieved in terms of changing the attitude of the FBI, Popov, thoroughly disillusioned, took himself off on a skiing holiday to Sun Valley, Idaho. He had seen a Sonja Henie movie, *Sun Valley Serenade*, featuring the resort and thought a break on the slopes would cheer him up. Sun Valley had only opened in 1936 and was instantly taken up by Hollywood celebrities: Bing Crosby, Clark Gable, Errol Flynn, Claudette Colbert and Lucille Ball were among the regular visitors. Popov, who liked nothing more than a party, soon got swept up in the social whirl, which was perhaps even more frenetic now that the country was at war. He skied from dawn to dusk and his nights passed in a 'blur of alcohol and sex'.[5]

But even while distracted by the heady pleasures on offer in Sun Valley, he was rarely able to escape a nagging guilt about what he was doing. His family was living under brutal Nazi occupation; his intelligence colleagues in London were enduring nightly bombing raids; his best friend, Johnny, was risking his neck apparently playing a double game in the Abwehr – and he was kicking his heels in the United States, neutralised by the hated Hoover, a man he later chose to characterise as 'a despotic bureaucrat'.[6]

Popov spent Christmas 1941 and New Year at Sun Valley, skiing, drinking and womanising. On New Year's Eve he reminded London of his existence by sending a Western Union telegram to Professor Masterman at the United University Club: 'Wishing you and all our friends a Happy New Year – Popov.'[7] The XX Committee was acutely aware, of course, that its star agent was languishing in the United States, and was similarly aware that Hoover was showing no inclination to cooperate with the 'mini' committee set up in Washington by Ewen Montagu. But Masterman and his colleagues could hardly have anticipated what was about to happen.

A few days after New Year's Eve, Popov received a telephone call from Charlie Lanman asking him to return to New York. He had surprising news: the FBI was going to attempt to set up a direct link with Germany. A transmitter had been installed in a so-called 'safe house' in Long Island and the FBI was ready to start sending messages to Germany on Popov's behalf. Popov's spirits suddenly soared: at last, he thought, he could get back to work. Clearly the Bureau was ready to run him properly. Once direct contact had been initiated, he could convince the Germans that he was finally building a network and re-establish himself in their eyes as a valuable agent.

Popov caught the first available flight back to New York and took a cab direct from the airport to the Bureau's field office, anxious to waste no time. Lanman was at his desk, but did not look particularly pleased to see him. Popov had a thousand questions to ask: where was the radio; when was he going to start transmitting; had they got a good operator standing by; had the first messages been prepared and encoded . . .?

Lanman wearily held up a hand to stop him. It might not be quite as he thought, he said carefully, for the radio was going to be a Bureau operation. Of course, Popov replied, he completely understood that, but . . . Again Lanman held up his hand. It was going to be an *exclusive* Bureau operation. It had been decided, at the highest level, he said, that Popov was not only to have no input on the traffic, but was not even to be shown the traffic. The orders from Washington were unequivocal, an embarrassed Lanman admitted. Popov was not to be allowed near the transmitter; he was not even to be told where it had been set up; and he was to have no contact with the operator.

Popov was stunned. Didn't Lanman realise what this meant? His career as a double agent would be finished when he left the United States. How could he meet his controller if he had no idea what information he was supposed to have transmitted in the previous months? The Germans would smell a rat, would soon realise that the reports were not emanating from him, and then the whole operation would be compromised. It was madness. What if the Germans asked personal questions about him – how were they going to be answered?

Lanman, shame-faced, said that Washington was confident Popov would cooperate since his entire family was still in Yugoslavia. He could not afford, for their sake, to 'let things go bust'.[8]

Infuriated by this implied threat, Popov walked out and went straight round to the BSC office in the Rockefeller Center to see his case officer. Dick Ellis was appalled by what Popov had to say and sent an urgent report to London, where it was greeted with dismay, particularly as no one held out any hope of being able to persuade Hoover to change his mind. The fact was that the Bureau did not necessarily need Popov to be involved in the transmissions to Germany. Popov had explained how to encode and decode messages – so long as the Germans believed it was Popov sending the information, that was all that mattered. As for the implications for Popov's continuing career as a double agent, the Bureau could not have been less interested.

Popov himself was under no illusions as to who had given the orders to cut him out of the loop – his nemesis, Hoover. The director's loathing of the Yugoslav was unquestionably based to some extent on Popov's success with women. To Hoover, Popov's lifestyle was tantamount to a personal affront, and during the time he spent in the United States, FBI agents wasted hundreds of man-hours investigating Popov's bedroom adventures, ostensibly for security reasons, but perhaps as much to stoke the director's disgust. Coincidentally, around the time the radio station was being set up, the Bureau was interrogating a female passenger who had arrived in New York on board the SS *Cabo de Buena Esperanza* and told immigration officers that she was hoping to marry Dusko Popov, a 'Yugoslav government officer' whom she had met in Estoril, in January the previous year. Andrée Renée Deyris, a thirty-five-year-old French divorcée, said she thought Popov was some kind of courier as he made several trips to London during the six months she knew him in Lisbon. 'Deyris is a smart type with certain attractions,' the report noted ungallantly, 'which she is undoubtedly willing to exploit to the utmost and she has almost certainly been supplementing her income in this way.'[9] The report only served to prove to Hoover, if he needed further proof, that Popov was a *boulevardier* of the worst kind.

The FBI could have set up a transmitter in their New York office in Foley Square, but in order to maintain the charade that Popov was running the show, a small house was rented in Wading River, on the north shore of Long Island. Sam Foxworth had asked the Office of Naval Intelligence and the Army's G2 department to supply answers, 'not necessarily accurate, but which cannot be checked', to a questionnaire about armament production and shipbuilding that Popov had brought back from Rio concealed in two microdots.

The original plan was to attempt a first transmission on 15 January, allowing sufficient time to make it look as if Popov had bought all the parts needed for the radio and got it constructed, but technical difficulties caused some delay. It was 20 January before a coded message – 'Sorry have been ill unable to write' – was sent to a Francisco Barros dos Santos at a cover address in Lisbon, indicating that the station would be up and running in eight days' time, ready to transmit and receive between 2200 and 2230 GMT. Special agent D. D. Johnson was assigned the duty of operating the radio key, and Lanman was put in charge of coding and decoding, using Popov's copy of *Night and Day*. On 29 January a cable arrived from Lisbon: 'Best wishes for recovery. Hope to get cable news soon. Francisco Barros.' This indicated that Lisbon was listening out for Popov's radio.

Two days later there was still no contact. A message was sent from Wading River: 'I have been trying to reach you, results negative. Can you suggest other times? Ivan.' It was decided that if this did not produce results, Popov would be asked to write a letter in secret ink suggesting that his radio operator believed 1500 to 1530 was a better time to transmit. Although Popov was not to be told where the radio station was located or what was being transmitted, the Bureau still required his help as the 'middle man' to send and receive letters in secret writing and to interpret the real meaning of messages received from Lisbon.

At 7.52 p.m. on 31 January Special Agent Johnson at last picked up, faintly, the European station call sign on 6950 kilocycles. Lisbon advised that they had received the earlier messages, although they recognised their own messages were not getting through, and asked Ivan to stand by until the next day. The problem, it transpired, was that Wading River could only be heard on 13150 kcs and Lisbon could only be heard on 6950 kcs.

On 1 February, Johnson tapped out, in code: 'Because of situation here have to be very careful. Can only transmit for short time so I won't be discovered. Advise me of time to listen for you. Ivan.'

When this message was acknowledged, the Bureau wasted no time in trying to set up a trap for other German agents operating in the United States. As far as the FBI was concerned, this was the primary objective of setting up the radio link and the only useful service that Popov's presence could still render to the United States. On 2 February, a message was sent to Lisbon dangling the prospect of juicy information, but only if the Germans would send someone to collect it: 'It is very difficult to obtain material and I have to be cautious for my safety . . . am in possession of most important conference notes regarding naval state of production, condition of readiness and data on logistic situation too long to transmit by radio. This is ready for delivery. Ivan.'

Lisbon ignored the temptation and replied: 'In future call for your safety only if there are important messages. We are listening each day at 22 GMT. Please intensify your work because of utmost interest.' Foxworth was obliged to ask Popov what the Germans meant by asking him to 'intensify' his work. Under the circumstances, it would not have been surprising if Popov had decided to withhold all further cooperation with the FBI, but to his credit he did not. He once again explained that the Germans were always demanding better-quality information – the kind, he added bitterly, that they were accustomed to receiving from him before he had arrived in the United States. Popov laid out the continuing risks, both to him and his family. The least-bad scenario, he said, was that if he were reduced, in German eyes, to a purveyor of petty gossip, he was likely to be demoted 'with a corresponding cut in salary'.

'Should this occur,' Foxworth reported in a memorandum to Hoover, 'there is little doubt that the Informant will become greatly incensed with the Bureau.' Hoover was unlikely to have been worried about incensing the man he dismissed as a 'Balkan playboy', but he might have been more concerned by the remainder of Foxworth's memo:

Informant naturally fears that if his work in the United States appears to be of such an inferior quality as compared to his work in England, the Germans will check on his activities here and uncover his connections with the Bureau. Should this happen the Informant states that the Germans would undoubtedly take steps to dispose of his family who are presently under the protection of the German government . . .

Foxworth, one of Popov's few supporters, appealed for the Bureau to give 'preferred attention' to obtaining a steady flow of information to be transmitted to Lisbon of sufficient quality to convince the Germans that Popov had established good contacts in the United States and was ready to undertake more assignments on their behalf. He added that if this could be accomplished, it was 'highly probable' that other German agents would come forward to make use of the Wading River station.

Hoover remained unimpressed and did nothing to persuade the military to provide more information. When Popov realised there was nothing he could say or do to influence events, he more or less gave up. Since he was not going to be allowed to work effectively in the United States as a double agent, he decided he might as well devote himself to pleasure and enjoy life as the licentious hedonist Hoover believed him to be. With more time on his hands, he took it into his head that he needed a weekend retreat. He signed a lease on a large cottage in Locust Valley, in the heart of Long Island's fashionable Gold Coast, and hired a gardener and domestic staff, regardless of expense.

At around this time he was also able to resurrect a passionate affair with a gorgeous French movie star, Simone Simon, whom he had first met in Paris before the war. Simon was working as a fashion model when she was 'discovered' by Marc Allegret, the man who launched the film career of Brigitte Bardot. She had the same girl/woman sensuality and soon caught the eye of Darryl F. Zanuck, who offered her a contract with Twentieth Century Fox in Hollywood. She starred with Tyrone Power in a film called *Girls' Dormitory*, but was unhappy in Hollywood and returned to Paris in 1938, where she embarked on a love affair with Popov while playing the beautiful but predatory female lead in Jean Renoir's fatalistic masterpiece *La Bête Humaine*. The international success of this film re-invigorated her career and she returned to Hollywood in 1940 to work for RKO Studios. She was filming a horror B-movie called *The Devil and Daniel Webster* when she got a telephone call from Popov to say that he was in New York and wanted to see her.

Simon was soon flying to New York every weekend, telling her friends that nothing was too much trouble to be with her 'darling Dusko'. And when shooting finished, she moved into an apartment on Park Avenue – in the same block as her lover. They became familiar faces at opening nights and the best parties, regulars at El Morocco and the Stork Club, where a blue-uniformed doorman with a whistle in his mouth tried to keep photographers and autograph seekers at bay as celebrities stepped out of their limousines and swept inside through a huge bronze door. Hoover, who loved rubbing shoulders with the likes of Ernest

Hemingway, Charlie Chaplin and the Duke and Duchess of Windsor in the Stork Club, was enraged when photographs of Simone Simon, hanging on Popov's arm, appeared in gossip columns listing who was at the Stork Club the previous night and omitting to mention *his* name.

Coincidentally, the FBI already held a file on Simon, which had been opened after she was rumoured to be having an affair with the composer George Gershwin – just the kind of gossip guaranteed to attract the prurient attention of Hoover. After Gershwin's death in 1937, a gold-plated key to Simon's Hollywood apartment was said to have been found among his possessions.

Popov, too, remained under close surveillance, with a tap on the telephone, Regent 4-1175, in his Park Avenue apartment. When Popov instructed his valet, Brooks, to contact the Ace Detective Bureau in the hope of tracking down Eleanor Roven, an old girlfriend in Phoenix, Arizona, the Bureau knew about it immediately, called at her address and established that she was now married, to an officer in the United States army. At one point the Bureau considered hiring Brooks to spy on his employer, but abandoned the idea when they discovered he had lied about having been a captain in the US Army Intelligence Service in the First World War.

Although Popov had finally broken off with Terry Richardson, the Bureau also maintained 'continuous mail cover' on her, reporting on 6 March: 'To date this mail cover has proved entirely unproductive. Popov gets occasional telephone calls from her but otherwise no contact and he believes she is only interested in finding a man with enough money to support her.' In an earlier report, the Bureau had concluded that she had started associating with other men soon after her marriage and was regarded as no more than 'an expensive type of prostitute'.

With a champagne lifestyle, two properties to maintain, domestic wages to pay and expensive girlfriends to entertain, it was as inevitable as night follows day that Popov would, sooner or later, run out of money. It happened sooner. Although he had arrived in the United States with $70,000 (a small fortune in those days, and worth about $500,000 today), $38,000 had gone straight back to MI5 via the fictional bank account of Mr Sands and the remaining $32,000 had slipped through his fingers with remarkable ease.

At the end of February, Popov asked Lanman to send a radio message to Lisbon demanding money. Since this was entirely in character and could only reinforce the Abwehr's belief that 'Ivan' was operating the radio, there could be no objection and Lanman encoded the following message, sent on 25 February: 'Please remember to send for first of March money for next three months. A. Me and Ralph [alleged radio operator] six thousand. B. Me, [for] special American [alleged informant], three thousand. C. Radio operator and house, three thousand. D. Radio equipment six hundred. Being out of resources need urgently. Thank you.'

Lisbon initially ignored his request and instead, on 11 March, demanded more information: 'Keep main attention on preparation for action of expeditionary corps and shipping of troops. Give exact details of embarkation, destination and kind of troops.' In the same message it was suggested that Popov might make a trip to Lisbon. The Bureau immediately saw another opportunity to ensnare a Nazi sympathiser and replied: 'Difficult to obtain diplomatic courier status and difficult to secure passage on Clipper due to war. Could you help me?' This last was added in the hope of flushing out anyone in the United States who might intervene on Popov's behalf. It was similarly ignored.

Meanwhile, serious trouble was brewing in Berlin. On 22 March, British intelligence intercepted an Abwehr radio message from Berlin recommending 'extreme caution' in dealing with Popov since there was a suspicion he was 'working for both sides'. William Stott of British Security Coordination immediately informed the FBI in a guarded note to Sam Foxworth: 'We have been informed by our friends in London that they have good evidence that Tricycle's German employers suspect that he is playing a double game.'

In London, MI5 began an immediate investigation into what might have gone wrong. After a great deal of soul-searching and second-guessing, it was decided that two factors had put Popov at risk. First, the poor quality of the information being supplied from the United States might reasonably have led his German controllers to conclude that something was amiss. How else to explain Popov's metamorphosis from super-spy in Britain to lacklustre second-grade agent in the United States, other than that his output was being controlled by US intelligence? Second, Alfredo Engels was among a large number of German spies recently arrested in South America and it was possible that the Abwehr concluded he had been fingered by Popov. As it happens, Popov's visit to Rio did not precipitate Engel's arrest – the security services had been waiting for some time to round up the Abwehr network in Brazil.

BSC asked the FBI for its agreement to take up the matter directly with Popov to deal with this 'serious crisis'. At the same time Stott sent a testy memorandum to Sam Foxworth complaining forcefully about the lack of cooperation from the FBI in the handling of the Popov case. 'Before he left England in the summer of last year,' he wrote, 'Popov was regarded, as he still is by my colleagues in London, as an agent of supreme importance and the very highest of value. The work which he did in England was of the utmost consequence in the revelation of the enemy espionage network in that country.'

Stott pointed out that all the papers and background information about Popov had been handed over on the understanding that BSC would be kept fully informed and that the results of Popov's efforts in the United States would be pooled with the British. It had not happened:

From that date until the present time we have not received, with one single exception [microdots from Rio], any communication from you on the subject . . . Furthermore we have never been informed by you what members of your staff are handling the case, nor any suggestion has ever come from you that your agents in charge of the case should consult with us; nor have we received copies of any messages dispatched or received since the W/T station commenced operation. This state of affairs does not, to my mind, reflect at all favourably on the spirit of mutual co-operation in which it was understood from the beginning, and is still understood both by our friends in London and ourselves, that the case should be handled . . .

I have every reason to believe that Popov is by no means satisfied himself as to the manner in which he is and has been handled. It is only natural that Popov should have felt a little bewildered and unhappy when he first arrived in what was for him a totally strange country; and I cannot help feeling that if consultation between us had been more frequent and more close this feeling would have disappeared instead of becoming, as it evidently has, more accentuated . . . Incidentally, Popov stated the other day that he had not been taken by you to see the W/T station and had no idea of its location, although he had asked to see it. I feel there is very real danger here such as might arise if he were suddenly asked by one of his friends to transmit a message rapidly.

Stott concluded, somewhat apologetically, that he had been obliged to write 'in this strain' because of the 'very great store' which London had set by Popov. It was BSC's last roll of the dice in an effort to salvage Popov's mission.

Foxworth forwarded the memorandum to Hoover with a note which laconically underlined the fact that the Bureau was only interested in Popov for one reason: 'To date Popov has not been contacted by any member of the German espionage system in the United States.' Hoover completely ignored BSC's complaints and by way of reply ordered Foxworth to obtain from BSC, as soon as possible, information about the way Popov's network in Britain was operating and the results of its activities, in terms of numbers of German agents uncovered and the type of information supplied.

If the Abwehr in Lisbon suspected that Popov had been 'blown', it certainly did not diminish its voracious appetite for information from the United States. On 26 March, the radio station at Wading River received the following:

> First, please inform number launchings and production merchant ships January, February, March forty-two. Second, total production front and training planes each month. Third, name and place of factory of thirty-five hundred horsepower motor. Fourth, rubber importations December forty one, January, February, March. Fifth, delivery war materials to Great Britain, Africa, Near East, India, Australia, Russia.

This was in addition to two letters, one with four microdots and the other with three, containing more detailed questions.

Lisbon also sent messages to Wading River regarding Popov's sub-agents, Ivan II and Yvonne ('Balloon' and 'Gelatine' to MI5), but neither Popov nor MI5 was informed until weeks later, considerably increasing the risk of Popov's cover being blown. On 21 March, for example, Lisbon sent Yvonne a new cover address, but MI5 was not told about it until 30 April, long after she should have started writing to the new address. This new level of recklessness by the FBI infuriated British intelligence.

By the beginning of April, with no money forthcoming from Germany, Popov was broke and asked the FBI for a loan. Lanman, who was the luckless intermediary, was obliged to point out to his bosses that Popov needed the money to cover his 'obligations to his servants, to his grocer, tailor, florist and other individuals who must be paid immediately'. Since few FBI agents had servants, let alone accounts with tailors and florists, their reaction to Popov's 'plight' can easily be imagined. Nevertheless, a loan of $2,500 was reluctantly approved. Popov's extravagant lifestyle and spendthrift habits would soon become a major issue – he was spending $2,500 a month on entertaining, over and above the expense of running his apartment and Long Island cottage – and the cause of deep resentment in the higher echelons of the Bureau, particularly when, three weeks later and blithely unchastened, he asked for another

$2,000 to make a payment on his summer cottage and to buy a birthday present for Simone Simon. This last was probably added by Popov to make mischief and rile the FBI, in which he certainly succeeded, as a vexed note in his file pointed out: 'If buying a birthday present for Simone was such an important item in the informant's life, he might have given it some consideration before today.'

On 8 April, Popov received by letter eleven microdots which, when developed, contained a daunting list of extraordinarily complex and demanding questions about aircraft production, the development of rocket-aeroplanes, exports of iron and steel, armament production, the shipping of foodstuffs and raw materials and the disposition of army and naval units. Popov was told to try and recruit informers in various government offices and was warned: 'It is absolutely necessary to give the correspondent dates of each information, for instance, the dates of dislocation or formation of a new unit, date of delivery of aircraft material to any of the above mentioned ports, date of the manufacturing contract given to any firm. At least the date, as well as the source of each obtained information should be given.'

Buried among the questions was one that set alarm bells ringing in London and Washington at a time when atomic research was a closely guarded secret:

Decay of Uran [uranium]. According to some information obtained, there is reason to believe that the scientific works for the utilisation of the atomic-kernel energy are being driven forward into a certain direction in the US partly by use of helium. Continuous information about the tests made on this subject are required and particularly:

(1) What process is being practised in the US for the sending of heavy uran?
(2) Where are being made tests with more important qualities of uran? (Universities, industrial laboratories, etc)
(3) Which other raw materials are being used at these tests? It is to be recommended to entrust only best experts with this test, and if not available, to abstain from it.[10]

To give him his due, Sam Foxworth was doing his best to provide answers to the stream of enquiries from Lisbon. After the spy round-up in South America, Foxworth had come round to the idea that it might be possible to develop the Wading River station to the point where it could become as important to the German espionage system in the United States as Engels was in South America. 'In order for our informant to assume this role of importance,' he argued in a note to Hoover:

> It is vital that he furnish to the German authorities information which on its face is genuine . . . His value to us is dependent upon their estimate of the information which he supplies. For these reasons we should endeavour to see that he supplies as authentic information as possible, so long as it will not be to the detriment of our own war effort. The supplying of inaccurate information or information generally circulated through the medium of the press would of course weaken his value.

In mid-April Popov finally got a payment from Lisbon: 250,000 escudos ($10,250) were transferred to the Manufacturers Trust Company on his behalf, for the 'part sale of jewels'. The FBI requested the US Treasury Department to authorise the clearance of the funds without delay, but Popov made no effort to repay what he owed the FBI. He 'showed unreasonable reluctance in repaying the FBI', an MI5 report noted later, 'on the specious grounds that they had run his case in such a way as to prevent him earning as much from the Germans as he should have done'.[11]

Popov was also irritated that the Germans had not sent him the full amount he had claimed and were paying him in escudos. He drafted a hectoring message to Lisbon to complain: 'Having big difficulty selling escudos. How do you imagine I and my V-men [sub-agents] can work and live without money? Why don't you send the full amount? Why don't you send it in dollars? Shall I have the same difficulty with the next remittance on the first of June?'

On 30 April, the Wading River station sent a message to Lisbon correcting an earlier message about shipping production figures and intended to indicate that Popov was alert and anxious at all times to furnish the Germans with accurate information. However, it was clear from intercepts that Berlin still harboured grave doubts about him. Felix Cowgill of MI6 reported on 8 May:

> We have heard from another source that Berlin definitely decided on May 5 that both Tricycle and Balloon have been under control since the former arrived in America. They have ordered Lisbon to send to Berlin all questionnaires issued to Tricycle and Balloon. While this investigation is proceeding no further air questionnaires are to be sent to either. We do not know the reasons for this deci-

sion but we do know that the Germans in Berlin think them sound.

MI5 began drawing up damage-limitation plans in a memorandum circulated by Robertson: 'Evidence is now available to us that the Germans do not trust this organisation [the Tricycle network] and we are led to believe that they place the date when Tricycle came under control as being his arrival in America. In these circumstances it appears desirable that we should salve what we can from the wreck . . .' A complicated game plan was drawn up attempting to second-guess how much the Germans knew or suspected, then devising various scenarios either to divert them from their suspicions or turn those suspicions to Allied advantage.

To convince the Germans that Tricycle had not been controlled before going to America (and thus putting at jeopardy validity of all his radio traffic up to that date), it might be quite a good thing if the FBI, when the time comes when they have to cease using Tricycle as a controlled agent, were to boast how much better they had shown themselves in this case than the British Secret Service, e.g. how it was the FBI who caught Tricycle and ran him when he went to America, although he had successfully fooled the British . . .[12]

In May plans were made for Popov to attend the Inter Allied Air Conference in Ottawa, ostensibly to gather intelligence as a German spy. William Stott persuaded the FBI it would be a good idea for Popov to be seen there, in case the Germans had someone checking up on him. Popov, being Popov, also resolved to utilise the trip to visit Simone Simon, who was filming in Montreal and staying at the Mount Royal Hotel. As a precautionary measure, BSC asked the Royal Canadian Mounted Police to keep an eye on them:

We are most anxious, repeat most anxious, not to attract the slightest attention to Popov but it would be helpful if Simon's contacts, particularly during the time Popov is in Montreal, could be watched. We have nothing against her but in view of her association with Popov wish to keep track of any contact she may innocently or otherwise have with any suspects. A note of telephone calls made and received would be helpful.

In the end, Popov never made it to the conference – he was barred from entry into Canada because of some problem with the exit permit the FBI had obtained for him. Inevitably he believed that the Bureau had deliberately sabotaged his trip. It was by now clear that he had reached the endgame of his relationship with the FBI.

On 20 May, Lisbon responded to Popov's constant complaining about lack of money with a surprising offer. A message was received at Wading River: 'Have you any cover address to which our courier can deliver dollars for you? Your name must not be mentioned. Greetings.' Foxworth and Lanman were ecstatic – here at last was an opportunity to start making arrests. BSC was informed and was immediately suspicious. William Stott felt the message was a trap – another test of Popov's trustworthiness – and advised that the reply should be in the negative. Popov disagreed: thoroughly fed up with the inactivity, and not averse, incidentally, to picking up some cash, he argued that a meeting should be set up. The Bureau was, for the first time in their tortured relationship, wholeheartedly behind him. Once BSC accepted that the FBI was intent on arranging a rendezvous, it tried, in vain, to dissuade the Bureau from rushing in and making arrests, arguing that a courier was an unimportant functionary and unlikely to be able to tell them much; furthermore, such action would irrevocably blow Popov's cover.

But the Bureau had been waiting for close on nine months for Popov to lead them to other German agents in the United States and it was not about to pass up this opportunity. A reply was sent to Lisbon: 'Have no cover address but can arrange to register at any hotel, preferably New Yorker, using cover name Eric Brown where your courier may deliver dollars to me. Advise me of date. Greetings.' The Bureau drew up detailed plans for how they would keep the hotel under surveillance when the Germans came up with a time and date for a meeting, but Lisbon fell silent for three weeks.

On 13 June, the FBI tried to prod Lisbon into action, sending a plaintive message: 'Position about money is very urgent. Why don't you reply?' Two days later Lisbon replied. The plan to deliver money by courier was apparently forgotten; now Lisbon suggested that money could be transferred to Popov through Ivan II (Dickie Metcalfe, Popov's supposed sub-agent in Britain). William Stott was certain, this time, that it was a trap. If Popov accepted the arrangement, the Germans would guess that he could call on help from the British authorities – presumably through intelligence contacts – since strict currency control regulations would have made it very difficult for Metcalfe to transfer the money to the United States. (Plan Midas only worked because 'Mr Glass' was unable to move his funds abroad himself.) This arrangement would also be of absolutely no benefit to the FBI, so there was no argument about rejecting the suggestion. On 22 June, Lanman encoded a reply at Wading River: 'Your message about money. No justification for transfer from Ivan Two's country. I don't care how you pay me but it is necessary you pay me at once as I am practically without funds ... Hurry as last information cost very much. Greetings.'

When Lisbon replied – along with a long list of questions about the new 155mm Howitzer guns – that it would 'do its best' to transfer a paltry $3,000, Popov was furious and suggested it must be a mistake. He asked Lanman to send a very strong message back explaining his position and the absolute necessity to receive sufficient funds with which to operate.

In truth, as the FBI was all too aware, Popov did not need funds to operate as a German spy; he needed funds to finance the extravagant lifestyle that he insisted was necessary for his cover. It should perhaps be pointed out that both the FBI and MI5 were getting his services for free, since he was being paid by the Germans, and that he had every right to do what he liked with his own money. Nevertheless, the Bureau had become heartily sick of its spendthrift double agent:

> Popov apparently has no concept of the value of money. He presently owes $1,500 for his summer house, which he contracted for previously, and also owes considerable money to his servants ... To date Popov's services have been of no value so far as developing information relative to the operation of German agents in the United States ... No information has been received as a result of his services pertaining to the identities or activities of any other German agents in the United States ... I asked McSwain [Special Agent in Charge, George McSwain, of the New York field office] whether the continued services of Popov are considered valuable and he advised that so far as his opinion in the matter is concerned he feels that as an informant Popov is of no value whatsoever.

Popov was bluntly informed that the Bureau would advance no further loans to him and that he should ask the British if he wanted more money.

When BSC representatives met Sam Foxworth in an attempt to sort out Popov's financial problems (he was in debt to the tune of $17,500 and the telephone company was threatening to cut off his telephone for non-payment of a $200 bill), they found him deeply unsympathetic. The FBI had already loaned Popov a considerable sum, he said; his presence in the United States had achieved little; and Foxworth certainly did not feel he could recommend to the Bureau that 'large sums should be advanced to Tricycle to maintain him in his present state of living'.[13] If Popov was to continue in the United States he was going to have to modify his lifestyle, something that Foxworth doubted Popov would agree to.

Although the British were unaware of it, the Bureau was making firm plans to get rid of their troublesome double agent, as an internal memorandum written by an aide to the director made clear:

> In view of the fact that Popov has been here since August of 1941, has been totally unproductive so far as developing any German espionage or other subversive activities in the United States is concerned, and has been a continuous source of annoyance in connection with his lavish expenditures and difficulties in obtaining funds from his principals, it is believed that his services are of no value in connection with the Bureau's counterespionage work ... It is therefore recommended ... that he be turned back to the British for use by them in London or such other part of the United Kingdom as they might desire.

Popov was called to a joint meeting with FBI and BSC representatives, at which he was given a 'talking to' about his extravagance. He protested, as usual, that his lifestyle was an essential part of his cover and that his financial difficulties were largely a result of funds not being received from Germany. This latter point could not be denied, but he was on shaky ground when attempting to justify his expenditure as being necessary to his work as a double agent. The fact was that the Germans initially supplied him with generous funds and he saw no reason at all why he should not enjoy himself.

It was decided that Popov should send one last demand for money to Lisbon and, if that failed to produce an answer, the Wading River transmitter would be shut down. The Bureau approved the following message on 6 July:

> Due to the absence of funds from you, I am subjected to great risks from my V-men and informers, some who are unpaid for last months for information. If money not received within next few days will have to give up my house and radio, as regular income far below needs. My contacts social and otherwise which I have worked hard to develop will be lost. Please tell me frankly what is the matter, as I am upset with the treatment of me. I cannot continue on present basis. Your message of June 25, 1942, mentions $3,000. This sum would be absurdly insufficient. I want advice at once as to what you expect to do. My radio man is getting nervous and I must pay him

a bonus. You should have a better understanding of my obligations to those working with me during present critical circumstances. Ivan.[14]

No response was forthcoming and on 24 July Hoover approved a recommendation that Popov be 'turned back' to British intelligence.

In London, preparations were already being made to extricate Popov. Ian Wilson, a young solicitor seconded to Tar Robertson's section, was sent to New York to see what could be salvaged from the mess and to make the necessary arrangements for his departure. The big question was: could Popov continue as a double agent or was he hopelessly compromised? If the latter, then his life and those of his family would be worth nothing if the Abwehr could get their hands on him. Either way, the risks of continuing were formidable, particularly in the light of the frequent intercepts indicating that the Germans were suspicious of his true allegiance.

'Colonel Robertson put the problem to Tricycle,' Ewen Montagu wrote after the war.

> He could end his double agent work with our gratitude or he could come back via Lisbon and try to explain away his failure in America and rehabilitate himself with his Abwehr masters. Tar Robertson warned him that his chances were nothing like even money. How was he to explain his complete failure in America, in spite of having spent the large sum that they had given him? Even more difficult – how to explain his complete failure to do any of the things that he had been told to do? Worst of all, how to cover up his complete ignorance of anything that he had sent on the radio? The odds must be at least two to one that he was blown. And, if he was, it was pretty certain that he would be tortured to squeeze him dry of information about our system, and there was equally probable death awaiting him at the end.[15]

To Montagu's astonishment and admiration, Popov made it clear that he wanted to continue as a double agent and return to Lisbon. He was confident, or at least he said he was confident, that he could beat the odds and convince the Germans that he was still on their side. 'It remains for me', Montagu noted, 'the greatest instance of cold-blooded courage that I have ever been in contact with.'[16]

8

Hoover on the Rampage

MI5 WAS DELIGHTED THAT ITS STAR AGENT WAS PREPARED TO STAY IN business, but acutely aware of the difficulties involved in explaining away the previous twelve months. Not only had Popov been largely excluded from the bogus 'espionage' carried out in his name after the FBI had set up the Wading River radio station, but the Germans would certainly want to question him about his sources, and no thought had been given as to where and how he might have obtained the information that had been transmitted. As if that was not bad enough, in the Bureau's continuing and fruitless attempts to flush out other enemy agents, a dozen or more messages had claimed that Popov was in possession of important and valuable intelligence that, for one reason or another, he could only hand over personally. Now the Germans would expect him to bring it with him to Lisbon. The problem was that it did not exist.

If Popov was to have any hope of staying alive, all this – and more – needed to be resolved. It was for this reason that Ian Wilson had been sent to New York. Wilson's brief was to prepare the Yugoslav in every way possible to answer all the tricky questions he was likely to face when he arrived in Lisbon and was confronted by his controller, von Karsthoff, once again. Before leaving for the United States, Wilson had had a meeting in London with an FBI Supervisor, Harry Kimball, who had been sent from Washington to assist. Wilson handed over extensive notes setting out exactly what Popov needed for his cover story, including details of how he had supposedly obtained a radio set and operator, and a complete record of the intelligence that had been transmitted to Lisbon on his behalf. Wilson stressed that suitable sources would have to be attributed to everything and that they needed to be real people, preferably people whom Popov had met and could describe. Kimball promised to see what he could do.

When Wilson arrived in New York he expected that the FBI would have already prepared much of what was required. In fact the Bureau had done nothing. Wilson was appalled to discover that no one – not the FBI, BSC or MI5 – had made any attempt to provide Popov with cover to explain his presence and activities in the United States. He had been sent, ostensibly, on a mission for the British government to report on the effect of propaganda on the Yugoslav community, but that had been quietly forgotten. The British Ministry of Information in New York knew nothing about him and had thus made no move to keep up the pretence. The Yugoslav community recognised he was working for someone, but was unsure whether he was on the side of the Allies or the Axis, and thus treated Popov with deep suspicion, bordering on hostility.

No progress had been made in persuading the FBI to release the radio traffic or to provide Popov with intelligence to take to Lisbon. The Germans had been told via the radio that Popov had written more letters in secret ink than he actually had, but the FBI had failed to produce any information that might have been included in the missing letters. Wilson had asked, in particular, for Popov to be equipped with up-to-date statistics of the kind that had been transmitted from Wading River, arguing that the Germans would immediately smell a rat if Popov was suddenly unable, after the shutting down of the transmitter, to keep up the flow of intelligence he had achieved while the radio link was in opera-tion. 'I would be lacking in frankness,' Wilson reported to Tar Robertson, 'if I did not record I was deeply shocked by the failure of the FBI to obtain for Popov information deemed to have been acquired by him between June and Oct 1942 comparable in quality and quantity to that sent by radio and letter. Only two answers were supplied, one a negative and the other a re-hash of an item submitted by another agent.'[1]

Although there was supposed to be close cooperation between MI5 and the higher echelons of the FBI, the reality was that each regarded the other with something less than warmth. Fundamental to their differences was the fact that MI5 was a secret service, operating murkily in the shadows, often beyond the law. Lies, subterfuge and deception were its stock in trade. It was possible for British intelligence to round up a network of spies without a word leaking out. When the FBI rounded up a spy network in the United States, it made front-page headlines. In Britain individuals suspected of espionage could be detained without trial, or sentenced after a trial in which all the evidence was heard *in camera*. No such powers were available to the FBI.

Adding to the problems was the fact that each organisation had entirely different objectives with regard to Popov. To British intelligence, the value of a double agent was not always tangible. It involved the slow accretion of information about Axis intelligence methods, analysing questionnaires to deduce enemy intentions and, most importantly, feeding disinformation to confuse and deceive. 'A double agent is a long term investment,' Ewen Montagu explained. 'The strategy is to provide enough information so that he is trusted when it comes to the big pay off.'[2]

It was of vital importance to the British to ensure that Popov was not blown, partly to protect other agents – certainly 'Balloon' and 'Gelatine', and probably 'Tate', who was likely to be compromised because of his involvement in Plan Midas. To the FBI it was of no importance whether or not Popov was blown. The first priority for the British was to keep its double agents 'alive'; the last priority was to use them to entrap other enemy agents. For the FBI the priorities were precisely reversed.

Wilson was obviously aware of Popov's rapidly deteriorating relationship with the FBI, but he was perhaps unprepared for another problem – the total hash the Yugoslav had contrived to make of his financial affairs. 'While I do not for a moment doubt Tricycle's patriotism,' he remarked in an early report to London, 'his financial conduct cannot be justified.' Wilson calculated that Popov had spent all the money he had received from the Germans, that he still owed the FBI $3,200 and had also spent $8,500 entrusted to him by the Bailoni family in Lisbon. 'I cannot distinguish the handling of this money from embezzlement,' Wilson wrote:

> He is trusting to get sufficient from the Germans to repay [Mrs Bailoni] in Lisbon. His excuse for his expenditure – over $5,000 a month – is that it was necessary to provide himself with the right social background, but as he obtained no information whatever for himself in the USA and had no contacts of use from a double agent point of view, his excuse cannot be accepted.[3]

'Freckles' Wren was given the deeply unenviable task of sorting out the mess, but was finding the FBI less than cooperative, perhaps because he had blundered in with an uncharacteristic lack of tact. At a meeting with ASAC (Assistant Special Agent in Charge) Donegan in New York, Wren explained that Popov had outstanding debts of $18,500, which had to be cleared up before he could leave, and asked what steps the Bureau intended to take to resolve the situation. Donegan was flabbergasted. In a memorandum to Washington he said Wren's request was 'absolutely atrocious'. Popov's total indebtedness, as far as the Bureau was concerned, was $3,200 (in the end he had borrowed $5,700 from the FBI, but had paid back $2,500), and the additional $15,300 was the result of Popov's 'careless spending for social entertainment with such persons as actress

Simone Simon and others which was absolutely without the authority or knowledge of the New York office'.

Fortunately tempers had cooled at a subsequent meeting between the two men, perhaps because Wren exercised a deal more delicacy. When Donegan asserted that the Bureau felt under no further financial obligation to Popov, as he was about to be terminated, Wren asked Donegan to reconsider, pointing out the need to liquidate Popov's debts to enable him to leave as soon as possible and continue his work in Europe. He proposed setting aside the $8,500 that Popov owed Mrs Bailoni as entirely his private responsibility and splitting the remaining $10,000 debt – if MI5 paid half, would the Bureau liquidate the other half? In the end, the Bureau reluctantly agreed, writing off the cost to an 'informant' who had been an 'unreliable investment'.

Wilson, meanwhile, devised a strategy to make use of Popov's financial woes to explain why his performance for the Germans had been so lacklustre in the United States and why he had been forced to close down the operation. He briefly considered a hypothesis attributing responsibility to Popov's 'radio operator' getting cold feet; but blaming the Germans for not providing him with sufficient finance seemed to cover all the options, as well as giving Popov an opportunity to bluster and assume the role of injured party – a dedicated agent neutered in a strange country by a simple lack of funds.

This case was bolstered by Popov's increasingly irritable demands for money during the final weeks of transmissions from Wading River:

> For God's sake what is happening about money? My radio man has refused to send messages except this present one. In last months I have worked bad but I cannot be myself if I have to avoid contacts and creditors. Reply me at once to prove radio man you intend keeping last promise to send money so he will start again and so I could send good information in my possession . . .

And later:

> No money has yet come. Will probably be able arrange journey London over Lisbon as courier but my situation regarding money desperate. Leaving here without regulating main debts put in danger my return. All material I possess will bring with me because radio man refuses send long messages. Could I meet Johnny in Lisbon? Advise what to do about radio man. He will continue work if he is paid. Do you want to deal directly with him?[4]

This last was added by the FBI – even at the end, it was hoping to persuade the Germans to reveal other agents in the United States.

On 3 August, Popov was formally 'turned back' to British control, to the undisguised relief of Sam Foxworth, who had sent a memo to Washington recommending that the Bureau have 'nothing further to do with him'. When Foxworth ran into Stott, from BSC, he could barely conceal his pleasure in announcing that Popov was, from that moment onwards, BSC's 'problem'.

While arrangements were being made for Popov's return to London, via Lisbon, Wilson and Wren were burning the midnight oil putting together, for the benefit of the Germans, an extraordinarily detailed, and almost entirely fictional, account of Popov's activities in the United States. They began by devising a colourful story explaining how he had managed to obtain a radio.

Their yarn alleged that it had been built by an Indian, Mohamed Ali Khan, whom Popov had met, by chance, in the reading room of the British Library in New York. They had got into conversation and become friends, and Popov had learned Khan's whole story. A Muslim from Rawalpindi in the Punjab, Khan spent time in Calcutta, where he became involved in Bengali revolutionary circles. In 1932 he took an active part in the civil-disobedience campaign and terrorist movement, was arrested and suffered 'corporal punishment'. As a result he harboured an intense hatred of the British. He succeeded in getting on a ship to Rangoon, then worked his way across the Pacific, arriving in California during the Depression.

Hard-working and resourceful, Khan had saved enough money to study electrical engineering and radio at the University of Illinois, but had to abandon his studies when he failed to obtain a scholarship. He drifted to New York, where he had a succession of jobs in radio factories and became expert at radio construction. He began to take an interest in politics again and wanted to form a group to enlist US sympathies for the liberation of India from British rule. To bring himself up to date with news from India he started visiting the India section of the British Library, which was where he had supposedly met Popov.

Subsequently Khan let it be known that he was really anti-British, even though he was a regular visitor to the British Library. When Popov learned that his new friend was a radio expert, he asked if Khan would be able and willing to construct a radio; Khan agreed, for a fee of $600. He deposited the set in suitcases in the left-luggage offices at Grand Central and Penn stations, giving the counterfoils to Popov, who handed them on to a Yugoslav friend who was to be the wireless operator. The Yugoslav

Dusko and Ivo at home with their parents in Dubrovnik, early 1920s.

Dusko, arms resolutely crossed, posing for a family photograph as a young man.

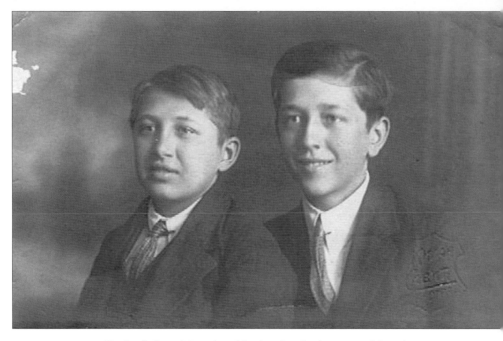

Dusko, left, and Ivo, the older brother he hero-worshipped.

Popov in uniform as a reserve
officer in the Yugoslav army
shortly before the outbreak of war.

Dusko in his element, with a girl on each side.

Dusko and Ivo at the Café Gradska in Dubrovnik before the war.

Dusko's alien's registration card, issued soon after his arrival in Britain.

Posing, second left, in London with an unidentified woman friend and two Yugoslav colleagues.

Johann 'Johnny' Jebsen, Dusko's best friend, sacrificed by MI5 to save the D-Day deception plans.

J. Edgar Hoover, director of the FBI, detested Popov and ignored his warnings of the attack on Pearl Harbor.

Simone Simon,
the glamorous French film
star with whom Popov had
a passionate affair in 1942.

A picture from MI5 files of
Maria Elera, one of Popov's
wartime women friends.

Skiing in Sun Valley, Idaho, in 1942, at a time of maximum disillusionment with the FBI.

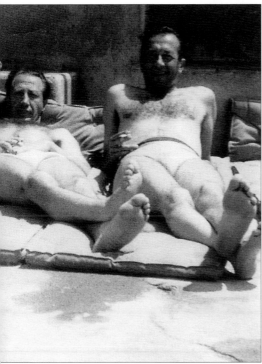

The three Popov brothers, Ivo, Dusko and Vlado, relaxing in the south of France after the war.

Dusko, grinning wolfishly at his wife, Jill, at a party at Chateau Castellaras, in the early 1960s.

Dusko's stunning young wife prompted media comparisons with James Bond.

Relaxing in the Bahamas in 1974, during a break from the promotional tour for his book, *Spy/Counterspy*.

collected the set in a second-hand Ford that Popov had bought for him and set the radio up, locked in an upstairs room, in a house at Oyster Bay, Long Island. When assembled, the set was five feet high and eighteen inches deep, with an aerial hidden in nearby trees.

Popov was allegedly present on the first occasion that a message was sent. The general procedure was that the operator would telephone, usually from a call box, to say he was coming into town, to warn Popov to stay close to the telephone. On arrival in the city, the operator would check into a hotel, call from a public call box in the lobby and give Popov the name of the hotel and the room number. (This was clearly cribbed from the procedure adopted by the FBI in setting up meetings with Popov.) Popov then met the radio operator in his hotel room, received incoming messages and handed over coded messages to be transmitted. The operator, said to be a Croat by the name of Nicolas Polic, never knew the code.

When he knew he was leaving the United States, Popov had supposedly instructed the operator to dismantle the set and hide it in a tool shed in the garden of the Oyster Bay house, as he was uncertain about his future. He did not want to see the set destroyed, in case he should return to the United States. If the operator received a letter posted in London, saying that Mary wanted his car and please get it ready by such-and-such a date, it would mean that Popov was returning; if the letter said that Mary did not want the car and he should sell it, it would mean that Popov would not be returning and the radio set should be destroyed.

In this fictional scenario Wren and Wilson were not concerned about creating imaginary collaborators, but were determined that Popov would produce, for von Karsthoff, real names of real people as his principal informants. It was standard MI5 operating procedure to use actual people as the supposed source of information for double agents, so that he or she could 'live the part' of a real agent in the enemy's eyes and talk convincingly about his or her contacts. Crucially, no information was ever used by MI5 without prior consideration of how the agent could have obtained it.

They asked George McSwain and Charlie Lanman to help them come up with names, possibly giving the FBI men the impression that their proposals would be formally cleared with the Bureau. Later, when Hoover was on the rampage, firing off angry memos in all directions, the two MI5 officers would protest, perhaps disingenuously, that they 'naturally' assumed that McSwain and Lanman had obtained permission before giving them any names and they were thus free to use them in any way they saw fit.

Trouble might have been avoided if Wilson and Wren had simply picked names out of the New York telephone directory. But they did not. They involved in their scurrilous 'scenario' senior politicians, bureaucrats and businessmen, some of them with close connections to the White House, and made them look devious, naïve or downright treacherous.

To provide Popov with a source for aviation intelligence, for example, Wren had put together an especially fanciful story. While Popov was taking flying lessons at Mitchell Field soon after he arrived in the United States, he was said to have met a 'Mr A', who conveniently worked at the Aeronautical Chamber of Commerce at the Rockefeller Center. Popov told Mr A that he, too, was working in the same building, at the British Library, and went to some lengths to contrive a meeting. One day, visiting the library, he came across an empty office with a telephone and seized his opportunity. He slipped inside, picked up the telephone, called Mr A, invited him to lunch and suggested that he drop by Popov's 'office'. He then went out to the receptionist and told her that he was working temporarily in the empty office and was expecting a visitor. Would she direct him when he arrived? In Wren's story, the plan, naturally, worked perfectly and enabled Popov to establish a friendship with Mr A, who was married and lived in Washington, DC, but commuted to New York every week.

One night Popov invited a couple of chorus girls to join him and Mr A for dinner at his apartment and, with Popov's encouragement, Mr A began an affair with one of them, borrowing Popov's apartment for afternoon sex and occasional illicit weekends. Popov told him that while he was working for the British Library he also had an unofficial second job for the Yugoslav minister in New York. Although the British gave the Yugoslavs a good deal of information, the latter felt they were not given the whole picture and Popov explained that he had been asked to get details of US war production so that the figures could be checked against information provided by the British. Mr A was by no means anti-British, but regarded them as 'stuffed shirts' and thought it was typical to treat their Allies in such a high-handed way, so he was supposed to have offered to provide Popov with the information.

Wren pressed McSwain for a name to be given to Mr A, mentioning that the Germans had specifically urged Popov to find an informant in the Aeronautical Chamber of Commerce. McSwain checked through Bureau files and came up with Edward L. Bacher, who seemed to fit the bill and was in charge of the Chamber's National Defense Committee. McSwain would later claim that he had only put up the name to be considered for possible use; crucially, he was told nothing of the rackety background story dreamed up by Wren.

Mr Bacher was never told that his name was being used as an informant or that his reputation as a married man was being casually traduced
by MI5. There was little risk to MI5, or to Popov, in giving the Germans
real names. (Even if it had been possible to check that these people really
were providing information to Popov, it was to be expected that they
would deny it.) But there was a considerable risk to the unfortunate Mr
Bacher's future if, after the war, German files suggested that he had been
passing information to a spy.

All the other individuals named as Popov's informants were similarly
ignorant of their inclusion. Igor Cassini, a Russian–American journalist
who wrote a column for the *Washington Times Herald*, was alleged to have
sold him confidential information about guns, planes and tanks, obtained
from the War Production Board. According to the MI5 scenario, Cassini,
who was openly anti-British, was prepared to sell on the material to
Popov, who he knew was spying for Germany.

Sol Bloom, the staunchly pro-British chairman of the House of
Representatives Foreign Affairs Committee, was alleged to have given
Popov War Department appropriation figures before Pearl Harbor, in the
belief that Popov was connected to the British government and that the
figures would support Bloom's contention that the United States was
making preparations to enter the war.

A Mr Robbins, the former business partner of Secretary of War, Henry
Stimson, was said to have provided Popov with some of the information
he took with him to Rio, while intelligence about tanks and armoured
cars came from Major George Starr, the 'officer' (actually, an FBI special
agent) who was invited to dinner with Popov to check up on Terry
Richardson the previous year.

Finally, Wren wanted a source for one of the very few items – naval
conference notes – produced by the FBI for Popov to take to Lisbon.
Wren asked McSwain if he could obtain the name of a US navy officer
who had been assigned to the New York area (and thus could have met
Popov), but who had later been transferred to active duty and conveniently killed in action. McSwain called the Office of Naval Intelligence,
which said it was unable to help but mentioned a story in the current *Life*
magazine, which referred to a Lieutenant Commander Frank Waldron,
recently killed in the Pacific. McSwain drew Wren's attention to the
article, but pointed out that he had no authorisation to use the name.
Wren was undeterred and concocted a thoroughly slanderous story about
how Popov had used Simone Simon as a lure to obtain an introduction
to Commander Waldron. He then supposedly invited the officer to dinner
when he was returning from the naval conference, provided him with a

girl and, while the officer was occupied in the bedroom, took photographs of the conference notes.

On 29 September, Popov moved out of his Park Avenue apartment, back to the Waldorf Astoria, in preparation for his departure. The Bureau ordered the tap on the telephone in his apartment to be removed, but listened in to all his calls from the hotel, diligently noting for the files that he had been talking to Simone Simon in Los Angeles about his money problems and that she had immediately offered to let him have $20,000 if he needed it. He had not taken up her offer.

As the day of Popov's departure grew closer, Wren and Wilson spent hour after hour closeted with Tricycle going over and over his story, testing him on every detail until he was word perfect. Popov thought the scenario depicted him perfectly – an ingenious playboy spy prepared to go to any lengths to get what he wanted. He particularly liked the telephone scam in the Rockefeller Center and the idea of procuring chorus girls for wayward naval officers.

At this stage, Hoover knew nothing of what the British were doing. Indeed, he was still apparently under the impression that the names Popov was going to give the Germans as his contacts would be fictitious. Plans had been drawn for FBI agents to assume the identities of these supposed informants in the forlorn hope, even this late in the day, that other German spies in the United States might try to contact them.

A few days before Popov was due to leave, Wilson produced a summary of his instructions, in the form of a memorandum that Popov would use in Lisbon as a basis for his story (see Appendix 2). Popov had been consulted on every aspect, since both Wilson and Wren agreed that he was the best judge of what he could get away with. The memo began: 'Your objective in passing through Lisbon is to satisfy the Germans that you have been genuinely acting as an agent for them and that any faults they may have to find with your information or activities since you have been in the USA are solely due to their failure to keep you supplied with funds . . .'[5]

The ten-page briefing document dealt, point by point, with every question the Germans could be expected to ask during Popov's stay, which was to be kept deliberately short to limit the opportunities to interrogate him. While in Lisbon, he was to have no contact whatsoever with the British authorities except in the case of 'extreme personal danger'. Popov was to tell the Germans he could not stay longer than three or four days without arousing British suspicion, that his job in the United States was finished and that he was ready to resume work for the Germans in Britain. He was to insist on the Germans paying him what they owed him and making proper provision for his payment in future. He had received no funds in the United States since June and thus had been unable either to pay informants or make useful contacts.

The biggest problem, still unresolved, was that Popov was going to arrive in Lisbon with virtually empty hands. Despite wheedling, cajoling and pleading in every quarter, Wilson and Wren had only been able to come up with meagre pickings – nothing like the substantial intelligence that had been promised in radio transmissions, and which they hoped would convince the Germans of both Popov's merit and his *bona fides*. Wilson and Wren were particularly worried that the FBI had refused to supply war production figures. The Wading River station had transmitted production figures, suitably adjusted for intelligence purposes, every month until June, shortly before it was shut down. The British argued that as Popov had seemingly been able to obtain the figures while the station was on air, the Germans would expect him to bring recent figures with him. The Bureau disagreed and refused to help.

'It is obvious that the FBI have lost all interest in Tricycle,' Wilson reported to London:

> and that their headquarters in Washington were not, in spite of their assurances to the contrary, willing to take any trouble to help his case ... The FBI in Washington was, either through incompetence, lack of power, lack of interest or lack of goodwill, of no assistance and let us down badly by their failure to provide the traffic on which we were relying up to the last minute. Whatever instructions Tricycle may be given in Lisbon, it is in my view unthinkable that he or any other agent who has ties with other British double agents should be permitted to come to the USA.[6]

After long discussions with Popov, it was agreed that he should try and explain away his lack of up-to-date intelligence by adopting a defiant attitude. He had always made it clear to the Germans that he only worked for them for money, and for no other motive, and as the money had ceased to arrive, he had ceased to work. As a result all he had picked up in the last three months were dinner-table indiscretions. He was to say that his references to forthcoming good information in his traffic were inserted merely to spur the Germans on to pay him.

If Popov was worried about what lay ahead, he was certainly not showing it. 'Tricycle showed great confidence in his ability to survive his meetings in Lisbon,' Wilson noted. 'His story is thin and cannot be expected to survive searching interrogation, but he is satisfied his personal relations with Johnny Jebsen and von Karsthoff will pull him through.'[7]

Von Karsthoff was unquestionably the key to Popov's survival and here there was reason to be optimistic. First, von Karsthoff and Popov were on good terms; they liked each other. More importantly, it was very much in von Karsthoff's interests that Popov not be exposed as a double agent. Such exposure would reflect badly on the Abwehr and very badly on von Karsthoff, who was likely to find himself on the Russian front in short order, if not facing a court martial. Lastly, British intelligence was certain that von Karsthoff was on the take, creaming off a slice of the money channelled from Berlin for payments to agents in Britain under Plan Midas. Thus there was every reason why von Karsthoff should believe Popov, providing he was able to present a reasonably credible, word-perfect cover story and convince the German that his poor performance in the United States was entirely due to lack of funds. If he started making mistakes or contradicting himself, he was in trouble; if the Germans brought in an expert interrogator, his story was likely to fall apart.

While Wilson and Wren had warned Popov of the grave risks entailed, neither man had mentioned the fact that numerous signals had been intercepted indicating that the Germans no longer trusted him. To do so would have revealed the Ultra secret – the very last thing MI5 wanted Popov to know. MI5 accepted there was a strong possibility that he would be arrested, and if he knew that British intelligence had cracked the Enigma code, he could not be expected to keep this information secret under torture by the Gestapo.

Whether Popov would have made a different decision had he known of the intercepts is doubtful. The truth was that he was thoroughly sick of working under the aegis of the FBI and had tired of the inactivity and the frustration of being a spy in name alone. He wanted to get back into the game, what he called 'the duel of wits, the aura of unrefined danger'.[8] Tar Robertson made no secret of the fact that he thought the odds were probably stacked against Popov, but Robertson was not a gambler; Popov was. 'If you are in a game,' he said in an interview after the war, 'you don't quit in the middle.'[9] He was also supremely confident of his raffish charm and of his ability to talk his way out of trouble. He had, after all, been doing so for much of his life.

So it was that Popov was in a positively jaunty frame of mind as he made his round of farewells in New York – an emotion shared by most of his FBI colleagues, who could barely conceal their impatience to be rid of him. If he had a regret, it was that the lovely Simone Simon was not on hand to see him off, for she was still filming in Hollywood. On 9 October, he sent a grammatically tortured cable to her room at the

Beverly Hills Hotel: 'Missing you darling more than I thought I will. Love Dusko.'

On the same day Wren wrote to an FBI official in Washington, appealing for a last-minute attempt to be made to furnish Popov with more information to take to Lisbon:

> I am sure you appreciate that its absence will gravely imperil him in Lisbon and if he fails he will bring down several other important units in our set-up in the United Kingdom. Popov has stated in a message to Germans that he will be bringing good information with him and the story we have built up for him to tell in Lisbon will break down very easily in the event he does not produce information of some kind.[10]

In the event it was too late, since Popov's departure was brought forward by more than a week because of travel complications. Tar Robertson had sent a cable from London suggesting that Popov should travel with State Department officials, as if he had official business to conduct, in order to limit the time he was able to spend with the Germans in Lisbon. 'In general,' Robertson advised, 'concentrate on getting past history straight and simple as possible and leave it to Germans to make suggestions for future activities.'[11] But the FBI proved reluctant to involve any American officials and failed, despite a number of promises, to supply a passenger list from which MI5 might have selected someone to assist. As there were no British officials travelling and it was too dangerous to send someone without sufficient cover, this plan had to be abandoned, but Popov warned Lisbon by cable that his visit would be brief: 'Might only stay between planes. Please arrange Elizabeth's boss [von Karsthoff] will be available. Will telephone office on arrival. Hope Johnny will be waiting for me. Will have material with me.'

It was the 'material' that was the problem. When Popov left the Waldorf Astoria by taxi for the airport on 12 October he carried a Yugoslav diplomatic bag. Concealed under a false bottom was the very best intelligence that Wilson and Wren had been able to put together, but it was still not much. 'The last-minute failure of the FBI to produce any traffic,' Wilson reported, 'in spite of their repeated assurances to us and to the Germans (even in the last wireless message) that good information would be forthcoming, produced a most critical situation. The failure only became apparent after Tricycle was fully committed to visit Lisbon and his passage was fixed.'[12]

In the secret compartment of the diplomatic bag were photographs of the doctored naval conference notes (taken with a camera supplied by the Germans, allegedly while the owner was occupied in a bedroom in Popov's penthouse), which had been cleaned so that only Popov's finger-prints appeared on them. In addition there were copies of field-service regulations; a basic field manual allegedly stolen by Popov from the office of the Yugoslav military attaché; Popov's own notes of indiscretions supposedly dropped by well-placed social contacts; and copies of maga-zines requested by the Germans: *Air Progress*, *Air Tech*, *Field Artillery Journal*, *Army Ordnance* and *Canadian Engineering Journal*. Finally, included at Popov's insistence, there were some silk stockings for von Karsthoff's secretary, Elizabeth. In the genuine diplomatic bag he was to carry personal letters to members of the Yugoslav Legation staff, asking them to send food to prisoners of war. The verbal information he was given to pass over was similarly sparse, mostly aircraft production figures supplied by London and 'two not very satisfactory answers which were all that the FBI produced'.[13]

Irritating bureaucratic difficulties with the US Revenue caused consid-erable delay when Popov arrived to check in for his flight. He was notionally on the payroll of the British Ministry of Information in New York, but an over-zealous Revenue official discovered that his name was not on the list of staff supplied by the State Department. Several frantic telephone calls to Washington failed to clear up the confusion, and Popov was given clearance only after Wren agreed to pay the tax ($480) on the notional salary Popov had never received, thus proving to the satisfaction of the US Revenue that Popov had, indeed, worked for the Ministry of Information. There was another scare when, because of a mistake at the British Embassy in Washington, his address was listed as c/o British Passport Control Office. The FBI got this deleted at the last minute and managed to ensure that he appeared on the passenger list, anonymously, as an 'official'.

After Popov's Clipper had lumbered into the skies over Manhattan, Wren and Wilson were struck by an uncharacteristic pang of guilt at the thought that they might be sending him to his doom. They briefly discussed having him removed from the flight in Bermuda, thereby letting the Germans believe he had been arrested as a spy, but the brutal reality of espionage *modus operandi* prevailed. If he was notionally 'arrested', not only would his services as a double agent be lost for ever, but other agents in Britain would be compromised. If he was allowed to continue, there was a chance – a slim chance – that he could dispel German suspicions and continue his work for the Allies. If he failed . . . Well, as far as MI5 was concerned, the effect would be no worse than staging his 'arrest'.

There was little room for sentiment or friendship in the espionage business, as Wren and Wilson well knew. Calculations were made coldly and if one agent had to be sacrificed to protect others, then the sacrifice was made. It was the dark side of the great game. Both Wren and Wilson like Popov enormously, and thought he was great fun and good company, as well as being a first-class agent. But their affection for him was not allowed to taint their judgement, and it did not.

On the day after Popov's departure, when it was too late for anyone to do anything about it, Wren delivered a copy of Popov's final instructions, which included brief details of the names mentioned in the scenario, to the FBI's field office in New York. There was no apology for its late arrival, only a sly dig at the problems caused by the Bureau's failure to provide sufficient information:

> Popov was in good spirits when he departed and with reasonable luck we believe he has a good chance. What I fear most is that the Germans may send someone down from Berlin to put him through a severe cross examination. The absence of any information – particularly air – proved an embarrassment at the last minute, and we had to revamp our story accordingly.[14]

Later Wilson would claim that it had not been possible to deliver the document before Popov left, because his flight had unexpectedly been brought forward. It was much more likely that Wilson deliberately delayed handing it over to forestall what he correctly anticipated would be furious objections to much of its content. MI5 records show that Popov had been given a copy of the document several days before his departure, since he was not going to be allowed to take it with him and was required to memorise it. Thus there was plenty of time to give it to the FBI. But Wilson and Wren had agreed that there was no point in confusing Popov by getting him to learn one story and then asking him to forget it, because it had not been approved. If Popov had been given the summary and told to memorise it, it meant that MI5 did not intend it to be amended in any way.

In this way the scene was set for a bitter row that would seriously damage relations between the FBI on one side and British Security Coordination and MI5 on the other.

When George McSwain and Charlie Lanman realised, to their horror, that not only real names, but prominent names, had been given to Popov as his informants in the United States, they were in no doubt that the director would throw a fit. They were right. A furious Hoover ordered

Supervisor Kimball to conduct an immediate internal investigation into how this embarrassment for the Bureau had occurred. Hoover made it clear that he considered the unauthorised use of real names in Popov's story to be 'most objectionable'. Suggesting that rubber production figures, for example, had come from the former business partner of the Secretary of State for War implied that this eminently respectable businessman was taking bribes; Sol Bloom, a revered elder statesman, was accused of passing confidential information to unauthorised individuals; and the mention of George Starr could easily compromise future counter-espionage operations, if the Germans decided to check up on him and discovered that he was in reality an FBI agent.

All the New York staff involved were questioned and all disclaimed responsibility. ASAC Donegan swore that the story was never 'cleared' through the New York field office. McSwain and Lanman, who had had a number of meetings with Wren, Wilson and Popov (together and individually) to discuss Popov's cover story, both insisted that they believed their discussions were informal and off the record – a preliminary attempt to start putting the story together – and that whatever the British finally came up with would be formally cleared by the Bureau. Both believed, with some justification, that they had been shamelessly tricked by MI5. There had been talk, for example, of one source being a newspaper correspondent, but both men categorically denied that the name of Igor Cassini had ever been mentioned in their presence.

McSwain similarly claimed that Robbins' name had never come up in his discussions with the British, and Lanman insisted that the only time he had heard Robbins' name mentioned was when Popov remarked that he had met Robbins several times when he was staying at his cottage on Long Island. Wren later raised the idea of Robbins being an informant, but subsequently told Lanman that it would not be feasible and that he had definitely dropped the idea. As for Edward Bacher, Wilson asked McSwain who would have access to the aviation information that had been sent to Lisbon in Popov's name; McSwain replied that Bacher was such a person, but gave no authorisation for his name to be used.

Lanman admitted that Sol Bloom's name had been discussed as someone who would have access to War Production Board appropriation figures through his office in the normal course of business, but said he warned Wren that he would have to make sure that Bloom was in no way involved.

Neither Lanman nor McSwain was particularly worried by cooperating with MI5, they explained, as Wren had promised that in the first instance a draft of the scenario would be cleared with the New York field office. It never was. 'It is apparent', Supervisor Kimball reported to Hoover, 'that Colonel Wren has failed to keep his promise to furnish the Bureau with a copy of his proposed statement for clearance.'

On 22 October, Hoover fired off a 'Personal and Confidential' letter to Bill Stephenson, boss of British Security Coordination, forcefully expressing his displeasure at the behaviour of MI5:

> I am advised that the information contained [in Popov's final orders], which for the most part is extremely objectionable to this Bureau, was not cleared through Mr Foxworth and in turn our Washington headquarters which, as you are well aware, has long been the established procedure . . . I am given to understand by our New York office that your Colonel Wren had promised that the final draft of the story to be used by Popov would be cleared by this Bureau before the instruction of Popov in this regard was undertaken. I am surprised and greatly disappointed that this promise was not kept. I would welcome a statement from you as to what action will be taken to see that a situation of this kind does not occur again . . . Sincerely yours, Edgar J Hoover.[15]

The following day Wren and Gavin Young, from BSC, called on Harry Kimball in Washington to try and make peace. Kimball coldly stuck to the Bureau's outraged position, repeating the view that certain portions of Popov's orders were 'extremely objectionable' and pointing out that they would definitely not have been passed by the FBI had the British, as promised, submitted the material before Popov was on his way to Europe. Wren dissembled furiously, blaming its late delivery to the Bureau on Popov's early departure and the need to enable him to thoroughly digest the story. He admitted that he had not got clearance for using Igor Cassini's name and, while he could not specifically 'recall' getting clearance to use Robbins', he 'thought' he remembered discussing it with Agents McSwain and Lanman. As for Bloom, Waldron and Bacher, Wren claimed he got clearance for each name from either Lanman or McSwain. Pressed by Kimball, Wren said he 'presumed' that Lanman and McSwain had obtained clearance for using the names, but later admitted, embarrassingly, that some names had simply been raised over a dinner table. Kimball closed the meeting by baldly stating his view that there was 'frankly, little excuse' for MI5 failing to obtain formal clearance from the FBI.

'It is quite apparent from my conversation with Colonel Wren', Kimball reported to Hoover, 'that the alleged clearances which he claims he obtained from SAs McSwain and Lanman were obtained during more or less off-the-record conversations at which times he was asking for suggestions as to the type of persons who would have such information available to them . . .'Wren's excuse about lack of time was 'very weak and generally unbelievable'. Hoover was clearly still angry and scrawled in the margin:'Until we have some satisfactory explanation no further information is to be given and contact N.Y. specifically as to this. Let Stephenson know how serious we consider this breach of faith. H.'[16]

Meanwhile, after receiving Hoover's letter, the British were conducting their own urgent investigation and Ian Wilson was called upon to make a full report. He wrote:

> From the moment it was decided that Popov should return, the closest personal contact was maintained with McSwain and Lanman . . . [it was] clear [Popov] would be closely questioned and vital he should have a foolproof story and full details of his sources . . . In Popov's case, almost all sources had to be invented and introduced during preparation for his meeting with the Germans as no sources, real or notional, had previously been provided. The procedure was to decide the type of source which could have provided information and then seek help of the Bureau to provide a name.[17]

Wilson categorically denied any knowledge of an agreement to obtain the FBI's prior approval of the 'scenario' and provided details of how the names were chosen. His account differed subtly from that given by McSwain and Lanman, and contrived to give the impression that the two FBI special agents were eagerly suggesting names. 'All the names, except Cassini,' he said, 'were either supplied by FBI, or known to them at a very early stage in discussions.' He added that both he and Wren had considerable difficulty restraining themselves from 'setting out the very numerous instances in which the FBI had mishandled the case, or had failed to give the co-operation which in our view was called for'.

The report concluded:

> As will be seen from the foregoing, each step in the building up of the story was taken in conjunction with the officers of the Bureau, with whom I have been dealing on this matter, and I assumed they had taken whatever steps were necessary inside their organisation to obtain clearance for names and policy . . . I am distressed that there should have arisen any misunderstanding between us. I can only reiterate my view – which Mr Wilson shares – that we understood

that as each step was taken, it had been approved by the responsible officers concerned.[18]

Bill Stephenson attached the report to his reply to Hoover on 30 October:

I think you will agree after reading this memorandum that, in view of the close co-operation with which our respective officers have worked together on this very delicate case, it was not unreasonable to assume on our part that no names or information would have been furnished or indicated unless prior approval had been obtained. Col Wren agrees he did undertake to provide the Bureau, in writing, with the full story Popov was to take to Lisbon, but he was at no time under the impression that this document would be required for prior approval since the story itself was built up step by step in discussion with your officers. As it was, Col Wren personally handed the final story to your New York office a few hours after Popov had left the city. It is regrettable that there appears to have been a completely honest misunderstanding between our respective officers concerned, but I think we may both rest assured that such an incident will not arise in the future. Yours sincerely . . .'[19]

If Stephenson imagined that his letter would mollify the director, he was wrong. Hoover scribbled a note at the bottom: 'If Stephenson is telling the truth then our NY office talked entirely too much and too freely. I want it stopped AT ONCE and I want no one to deal with any representative of this outfit except where specifically approved by me.'

On 5 November, Stephenson again wrote to Hoover with what he imagined to be good news from London: Popov had got back safely from Lisbon and reported that the Germans seemed disinterested in the names of his contacts. Popov had been instructed not to volunteer any information about sources and would only do so under heavy pressure, but in the event the only names he had to mention were those of Robbins and Cassini and the Germans paid them no attention. Stephenson said he was of the firm belief that no difficulties or embarrassment would arise from the use of these names and that the 'Popov affair', so far as his activities in the United States were concerned, had been successfully terminated.

But Hoover continued to smart. 'I cannot help but feel', he wrote to Foxworth on 24 November, 'that Special Agents Lanman and McSwain were outsmarted and outmaneuvered by Colonel Wren . . . I want it definitely understood that there are [*sic*] to be no such free and easy discussion between individual agents and Stephenson's organisation in the future.'

The British remained resolutely unrepentant. 'None of the instructions to Popov to which the FBI take exception need have been given to him,' Wilson pointed out to Tar Robertson, 'had arrangements been made whereby the FBI took part in his instruction and provided sources of information which they, in his name, had transmitted to the Germans.'[20] This was undoubtedly true, yet it was also clear that Wilson and Wren behaved in an underhand manner hardly fitting the image of officers and gentlemen. They could certainly have arranged FBI clearance if they had so wished. They did not do so because they knew there would be trouble. As far as they were concerned, their primary duty was to protect Popov and, if a few American reputations were ruined in the process, it was a small price to pay.

To Popov it was all entirely personal: 'Hoover didn't approve of me having a film star girl friend. He didn't approve of me having a penthouse on Park Avenue. He didn't approve of my staying in luxurious hotels. He didn't approve of me.'[21]

9

Back in the Game

POPOV, BLITHELY UNAWARE OF THE TROUBLE HE HAD LEFT BEHIND, arrived in Lisbon in the early evening of Wednesday, 14 October 1942, in the company, coincidentally, of three amiable State Department officials he had met on the plane. They all shared a taxi to the Palacio Hotel in Estoril, where Popov was gratified to be greeted effusively by the manager, who was able to find him a suite overlooking the garden, despite the shortage of rooms.

He was delighted to be back in Europe, back in the game again, and seemed unconcerned by the prospect of confronting von Karsthoff in a few hours' time and presenting him with a complicated pack of lies, masquerading as the truth, about what he had been doing in the United States. In no hurry to make contact with von Karsthoff, Popov had agreed to join his new friends for dinner, after which, naturally, they drifted across to the Casino, where Popov introduced the Americans to the intricacies of casino gaming tables.

It was midnight before he put in a call to his controller. As he wrote later in his report to MI5:

I was supposed to ring up the Germany Embassy at once, but as I was with those people I could not do it until after dinner when we all went to the casino. About midnight I slipped out of the casino, telephoned the Embassy from a public call box and asked for von Karsthoff. A man answered and said that Elizabeth wanted to speak to me and told me to call another number. I did this and Elizabeth answered and asked how I was and how long I was staying. I told her I did not know yet, but perhaps until the day after tomorrow and that I would have to see the British Air Attaché [to arrange a flight to London]. She said: 'Do you remember where I gave you once a little packet on the Rossio? I will meet you there tomorrow.'[1]

Elizabeth did not seem particularly friendly, but then she never made her dislike of Popov a secret, and he had no reason to guess from her brusque tone that anything was amiss.

At eleven o'clock the next day Popov was waiting outside the Chiava d'Aura café on the Rossio when Elizabeth arrived in a chauffeur-driven car in the company of a man in civilian clothes who introduced himself as Lieutenant Kammler. His real name was Otto Kürer. He was an officer in Abwehr I, the espionage branch, and he was to assist in debriefing Popov. For a fleeting moment Popov wondered if he was Gestapo, but just as quickly rejected the idea – if he was going to be arrested, there would certainly be more than one man in the car. This, as always, was the moment of truth for Popov. If his cover had been blown, this was the moment when he would be taken away. The fact that Portugal was a neutral country would offer him no protection; he could be drugged and bundled onto an aircraft bound for Germany in a matter of hours and there would be nothing anyone could do to save him. Popov got into the car and it pulled swiftly away – but not in the familiar direction of von Karsthoff's villa. With his heart thumping, Popov asked Elizabeth where they were going. 'Avenida de Berna,' she grunted in reply, which left Popov none the wiser and wondering if he had been over-confident about his ability to survive.

To his great relief, 8 Avenida de Berna turned out to be von Karsthoff's new apartment, on the second floor of a modern block near the bullring in the Campo Pequeño area of the city. The German was waiting for him, with a reassuring smile and a handshake, when Elizabeth ushered him into the study. Popov immediately apologised for not telephoning sooner the previous evening and began to explain how he had been detained by the three State Department officials he had met on the plane, but von Karsthoff cut him short, saying he knew what had happened. Popov realised he must have been under surveillance from the moment he arrived.

Popov was not, of course, aware that von Karsthoff had been ordered by Berlin to handle 'Ivan' with great care and to break off contact with him immediately if he was unable to give a satisfactory account of his activities in the United States. Breaking contact would certainly have led to Popov's arrest.

Von Karsthoff showed little interest in the photographs, documents and magazines that Popov had brought with him, although Elizabeth, despite herself, flushed with pleasure when he produced the silk stockings, then an almost unknown commodity in wartime Europe. She was positively girlish as she tripped from the room to make coffee.

Though perfectly friendly, von Karsthoff quickly made it clear that Berlin was deeply disappointed with Popov's performance in the United States. He read a telegram from Berlin evaluating Popov's work: excellent in England, good in the United States up until his trip to Rio, medium for the next three months, then terribly bad. 'At least you know what Berlin thinks of you,' von Karsthoff said, then paused for a moment and added: 'Some people suspect you have been turned.' Popov took it in his stride and laughed derisively at such a ridiculous notion, in an attempt to conceal his shock. Von Karsthoff gave no indication whether he included himself in 'some people', but he insisted on knowing what had gone wrong in the United States and getting an explanation of why one of their best agents had turned into a virtual sleeper.

With Kammler listening quietly in the corner and Elizabeth taking notes, Popov was careful to stick to the script he had rehearsed in New York with Wren and Wilson, and immediately went on the offensive, indignantly asserting that Berlin was responsible for many of his problems by failing to provide adequate funds. He complained bitterly about the way he had been treated and put into financial straits, which not only prevented him doing useful work for them but, he lied, had forced him into the humiliating position of having to borrow from a girlfriend. 'I started to make a scene about the money saying that they had put me in a spot leaving me without any money,' Popov wrote in his report, 'and Karsthoff said at once, "Please do not say anything. We did all we could. It is Berlin's fault".'[2]

'Karsthoff is a very good friend of yours,' Kammler interjected. 'Berlin are stupid fellows, they are sitting at desks making statistics and cannot put themselves into your, or my, position and don't realise the difficulties of being without money. Therefore please work hard in future or we shall all have trouble here. And you'll see we will be able to give you big bonuses.'

Popov said he would like to send a very rude message to Berlin and went on to give an example of how his shortage of money had hampered his work, further casually trashing the reputation of the unfortunate Edward L. Bacher, the alleged source of his aviation intelligence:

I told them the story of how I got that man to work for me. He usually lived a pretty retired life and was very shy. I met him and won his confidence. I entertained him and introduced him to a chorus girl. He spent the little money he had on this girl and then borrowed money from me. About April he bought her a gold and ruby bracelet for $700. He paid $350 down and was supposed to pay the rest later. He then started ringing me up asking me to lend him some money. I could not give him any as I had not got it. How was I expected to get information when I had to try and avoid meeting this man? Karsthoff agreed that that was reasonable.[3]

Carried away by his burning sense of grievance, Popov suddenly departed from the script and announced that he was no longer willing to work for Germany as he had been so badly treated. This madness probably derived in part from his instincts as a gambler and in part from his talents as an actor. Popov was ready to gamble with his life as a double agent by coolly calculating the odds on his survival; betting that the Germans would not accept his resignation was not likely to cause him much concern. But he was also required to play the part of a disgruntled German agent to perfection and might well have decided that he was performing entirely in character. Nonetheless, if Wren and Wilson had been listening in, they would have been appalled by their protégé's over-confidence. Popov's gamble paid off: von Karsthoff brushed his complaints aside, warning him darkly that once involved in 'this kind of work' there was no turning back.

Over the next few hours Popov contrived, with a subtle combination of frustration and fury, to convince von Karsthoff that he, Popov, was the genuinely aggrieved party in his relationship with German intelligence. When von Karsthoff said that Berlin thought he spent too much time with film stars (photographs of Popov with Simone Simon in American newspaper gossip columns had obviously not gone unnoticed) and not enough time on the job, Popov protested that no one had ever complained about the time he spent mixing with high society in London. Improvising rapidly, he suggested that film stars were the equivalent high society of the United States and just as valuable as contacts. Von Karsthoff smirked, well aware of the Yugoslav's primary motivation for mixing with beautiful actresses, but let it pass.

Fortunately for Popov, von Karsthoff seemed not to want to ask any of the questions he was dreading – why, for example, he had failed to produce any statistics after the radio station was shut down, or what was in the missing letters sent from the United States. It was possible that the German was more interested in rehabilitating his top agent to enhance his own reputation. Instead von Karsthoff questioned him closely about how and where he had recruited his 'radio operator'. This was a story Popov had rehearsed many times in New York. He explained that he had met him in a bar on West 45th Street, a place where many expatriate Yugoslavs tended to gather. The man's work was fine as long as he was well paid, Popov explained, but he tended to be very difficult about money . . . Von

Karsthoff raised his eyebrows at this, perhaps thinking that one Yugoslav was very much like another, then asked if the operator knew the code. Popov shook his head. The German seemed worried by the radio operator and kept pressing Popov to provide more details about his work and character, in particular whether Popov thought he would work for anyone else. Eventually von Karsthoff came to the point and said they feared that the operator had been caught and might have been working under American control. It was not possible, Popov replied categorically, since he did not know the code. He forbore to add that it was not possible as the radio operator did not exist.

At this point, to Popov's surprise, even Elizabeth chipped in to support him, pointing out that 'Ivan would not be here' if his radio operator had been caught and turned, as it would certainly have led to 'Ivan's' arrest. Remarkable, Popov thought, what a few pairs of silk stockings could do.

After Popov had gone through the arrangements he had made to hide the radio and recommission it later if need be, von Karsthoff asked when he would be returning to the United States. Popov replied that he was unsure if he would ever be able to return, since he no longer had a job there with the British Ministry of Information. At this Von Karsthoff frowned. 'For us,' he said, 'the main thing is that you go back to America because the radio you have there is of inestimable value. But if you do not succeed to go back to America you must try for any other English-speaking place, that is to say under British control. It would not interest us at all if you went to South America, for instance, but all places under English or American control are of interest.'[4]

Popov manoeuvred the conversation back to money and insisted that he needed $8,500 straight away to repay the Bailoni family, whom he was going to see that evening. He explained that the Bailonis were old family friends from Belgrade. Mrs Radmila Bailoni had entrusted the money to him before he left for the United States, but he had been forced to spend it because of Berlin's reluctance to pay him. At one point Kammler had blurted out: 'For heaven's sake don't make difficulties about money arrangements, for if it does not work well I shall be taken away from here and sent to the Russian front.'

It was past three o'clock in the afternoon before the meeting ended and Popov thought it had gone well. 'It is definitely sure that Karsthoff does not think it is me that is wrong now in the organisation,' he claimed in his report to London. He left 8 Avenida de Berna with the promise that the Bailonis' $8,500 would be forthcoming within the hour. He was to be at the Chiava d'Aura on the Rossio at four o'clock. Kammler would be sitting at a table. Popov was to walk past Kammler without giving any sign of recognition, go into the lavatory, put his briefcase on the floor and wash his hands. Kammler would come in, pretend to wash his hands at an adjoining basin, slip an envelope with the money into Popov's briefcase and leave. The transfer went off without a hitch.

Much encouraged by this expression of confidence in him, Popov paid a courtesy call on the chargé d'affaires at the Yugoslav Legation, then hailed a taxi to take him to the Quinta dos Grillos, the farmhouse that had been rented by the Bailoni family:

> I noticed on the road that a car was keeping pretty close behind me. You have to go through a village. From the village there is a road going off on the right about three quarters of a mile long and leading nowhere but to the farm where the Bailonis live. When we got to the village I did not see the car that followed me. But from the terrace of the house I again saw this car, it was turning in the narrow road to the farm. This was about 6.30 p.m.[5]

At midday the following day, Popov again met Elizabeth on the Rossio. There followed another meeting at Avenida de Berna with von Karsthoff and Kammler, this time of two hours' duration, almost entirely devoted to wrangling about money:

> Money was discussed every time – and it was only settled at the end. I drew some conclusions from this. My impression was that they have been in a spot with Berlin and that they had quite differ-ent instructions from Berlin about paying me. As they probably cheated and gave me less than Berlin gave them, they were afraid I might make a scene with Berlin. They kept insisting on an arrange-ment with a round sum and I wanted to go into the details as to what they owed me but they did not want to do that. Karsthoff said that I had been living like a Prince and I said that I had to have money to work and we fixed certain amounts but Karsthoff again was evasive.[6]

On 17 October, just three days after Popov had arrived back in Lisbon from the United States, von Karsthoff reported to Berlin that despite 'severe precautions', no suspicious circumstances pointing to Popov being involved in 'double work' had arisen. The message was intercepted by London, where it was received with jubilation and astonishment. Had Popov disappeared, it would have surprised no one; that he was able to convince the Germans so quickly of the authenticity of his 'thin story' was a tribute to his courage, his acting ability and his infectious charm. Von Karsthoff's willingness to believe in his top agent was also undoubtedly a factor.

The remaining meetings with von Karsthoff and Kammler were largely devoted to his future duties. Berlin was no longer interested in statistics or political appreciation, von Karsthoff explained, but now needed intelligence of immediate value for operational purposes. If he was to remain on the Abwehr payroll, he would have to guarantee being able to deliver, by radio or secret writing, 'precise reports of military importance'. Popov was to concentrate on digging up intelligence about the Allies' invasion plans. He was told to contact as many people as possible who might have information; to check what kind of training was going on and what orders had been issued; to ascertain if exercises were taking place, staging mock-attacks against special fortifications; to find out what the fortifications looked like; and to discover what kind of beaches were being used for training. From such intelligence, von Karsthoff observed, 'We may be able to draw our own conclusions.'

Popov was given five 'matches', a new development by German scientists for invisible writing. Previously agents had to melt crystals onto the end of a match; now the matchstick pens, much improved, were ready-made. Popov was told each of them was capable of writing 200 letters in secret ink, and given careful instructions on how to use them. He was advised to write on very smooth airmail paper; if the paper was not smooth enough, he had to rub it for several minutes with cotton wool. He was to attach the match to a pencil and write very lightly with even pressure, in block letters, on one side of the paper only, before writing the open letter with pen and ink. He was warned to be very careful about leaving fingerprints or making scratches if the match-head broke; even if the writing was not visible at the time, it might be by the time the letter reached the censor. Each of the five matches was wrapped carefully in cotton wool, then a secretary sewed them into the shoulders of Popov's overcoat for the journey to England.

At a final meeting with Kammler on his last day in Lisbon there was another furious row about money. Kammler announced that $10,000 had been sent to Popov at a cover address in Massachusetts and, although he had not collected it, it would be deducted from the amount he was owed. Popov flatly refused to accept this arrangement and swore he would not leave Lisbon until he was paid in full. In the end he settled for $25,000 in cash (he claimed he was owed $26,000), plus 6,000 escudos to cover his expenses while he was in Lisbon, and the promise of $2,500 a month in the future if he performed well. 'I had the very strong impression', Popov stated in his report to MI5, 'that Berlin was sending them more money than they gave me.'

At this same meeting Kammler told Popov he would be receiving instructions in London by microdots and suggested that he bought a microscope with 200–300 times magnification in order to read them. He handed over an envelope with three microdots containing naval and military questionnaires. But Popov, who was in no mood to be cooperative, held the envelope up to the light to check the microdots and said they were too obvious. He refused to take it. Kammler examined it and reluctantly agreed. As there was no time to rephotograph the questionnaires, he said he would post them to Popov at the Savoy Hotel. Popov left for England early the next day, 21 October.

After his long absence, Popov noticed a marked change in the national mood when got back to London and checked in, as usual, at the Savoy. When he had first arrived, in December 1940, London was under nightly attack from the Luftwaffe and there was a grim expectation that Germany would invade at any time. No one knew what the future held, only that there were tough times ahead. Now, less than two years later, Popov was impressed by the cheerfulness and optimism of Londoners, despite the battering the city had endured, which had left many of the best-loved landmarks in ruins and unexpected gaps in many streets. There was not much to eat, restaurants were restricted to offering a single course; many commodities were impossible to come by; and people in civilian clothes looked shabby after years of rationing – but there was a discernible lightening of the atmosphere. After months of setbacks in the face of apparently invincible German might, the tide at last seemed to be turning: Allied bombers were pounding Germany every night, the Russians had beaten back the Nazis' summer offensive, the United States had forced the Japanese navy to withdraw from Midway Island in the Pacific and the Eighth Army had halted the German advance in North Africa. All fears of an invasion had been swept away and there was a widespread confidence that the war would be won. That confidence was soon to be bolstered by news of the German retreat from Stalingrad and Montgomery's triumph at El Alamein, which set church bells ringing across the country for the first time since 1940.

The day after his return, Popov was debriefed at Imperial House. J. C. Masterman, chairman of the XX Committee, led the debriefing team, assisted by Ian Wilson, newly returned from the United States, and Tar Robertson. All he had brought back with him, Popov explained, were the match-heads for secret writing sewn into the seams of his coat and money – his instructions would be arriving soon in microdots on letters addressed to him at the hotel. Masterman recalled asking Popov what he

had done with the money. Popov first replied that he 'thought' he might
have left it in a coat in his hotel bedroom, then that he 'might' have it with
him. Watched by the appalled MI5 officers, he casually searched through
one pocket after another until he finally produced a crumpled bundle of
dollar bills totalling $25,000 – a staggering amount of money in those
days, worth around £180,000 today. Masterman wanted to try and trace
the numbers of the larger notes, so he took possession of twenty $1,000-
bills and offered Popov a receipt for them. Popov shrugged and said it was
not necessary, but Masterman insisted on drawing up an official receipt,
which Popov never bothered to pick up. 'His extraordinary casualness
with money is, I think, a danger,' Masterman observed, 'for it is quite
probable that he would have lost or been robbed of this large sum of
money without worrying very much about it.'[7]

Popov reported his view that German morale was 'pretty bad'; all the
Germans he had met seemed tired, gloomy and dispirited. Von Karsthoff
seemed to worry a lot about a possible revolution in Portugal, a pro-
British *coup d'état*, and an Allied invasion of mainland Europe. Popov got
the impression that relations between the Abwehr and the Gestapo were
deteriorating – every time von Karsthoff mentioned his opposite number
in the Gestapo, he could barely conceal his hatred. MI5 had not heard of
Kammler before and Popov was able to provide a description in his
report: '6ft tall, aged about 28, dark hair, brown eyes, slim, clean shaven.
Wears civilian clothes, well dressed, stiff in manner, goes a lot to casino,
speaks English and French.'

In the early afternoon, Popov took time off to visit his legation and
on his return the MI5 debriefing continued for the rest of the day.
'Throughout both interviews Tricycle was extremely voluble and rather
confused,' Wilson reported. 'It appeared to me right to allow him to talk
at will, since he was clearly anxious to disburden himself of a great deal
of vague feelings of grievance with regard to his American visit, and also
with regard to the treatment of his friends, the Bailonis, and also the plans
for the future.'[8]

Popov was extremely impatient for news of his older brother, Ivo, in
Belgrade. All he had been told thus far was that Ivo was working for the
Allies in rather the same way that he was, but MI5 was reluctant to go into
more detail. In fact, although there had been no contact between Ivo and
British officials, he was considered by MI5 to be an 'accredited and reliable
agent'[9] and had been given the codename 'Dreadnought'. It was a fundamental principle of British intelligence tradecraft that all agents should be
kept in isolation from one another, even if they were brothers, and so
Popov was told nothing of all this. Likewise, in Belgrade, Ivo knew

virtually nothing about what Dusko was doing. Jebsen had told Ivo that Dusko was an agent for the Abwehr, but Ivo knew his brother well enough to be confident that he would almost certainly be working for the Allies.

On 1 November, Popov sent his first letter to Lisbon. He could never resist the temptation of creating little dramas in the cover letter, which was always purported to come from a name and address picked at random from the London telephone book. Thus he would write, to Jordão Pinto at Rua S. Mamede 50/10, Lisbon:

Dear Jordão, I think you are utterly wrong in your last letter and only looking at it from your sister's point of view. It is very painful for a man to explain the little misunderstandings that women have between them. I will try my best and I am hoping you will understand me even if you do not approve. Before I say anything, please understand that your sister was not 'thrown out of the house'. She went to live somewhere else after a very calm and dispassionate talk with Rosemarie and myself . . .

Underneath, scrawled laboriously with a match-head, was the real message for von Karsthoff:

Arrived here safely. Address still the same. Shortly might change it but won't do it without advising you. Have not yet received your letter. Hope will get it soon because very anxious to start work and must have questions to start it properly. Now my time is used mostly: 1. re-establishing contacts, which is pretty easy seeing that most of them are still in London; 2. trying to fix my future job. I pulled several ropes. Don't know yet definite result, but I am doing my best to obtain one which would be of best use to you and which would leave me mostly free to move about. As soon as anything will be definite will inform you. It seems very unlikely that I will be able to obtain something to go back to the US but would have much more chance for Canada. Please don't forget sending me the more possible addresses because I hope to be very active and don't want to expose myself too much on the same address. London has not changed much since my last sojourn, except that it is full of Americans. Rationing practically the same as before, but clothes rationing is more severe and some things are very difficult to get even with coupons . . . Please let me know if anything is wrong with my writing. Greetings, Ivan.[10]

In due course Popov received a reply at the Savoy with a microdot – the British called them 'duffs' – attached. As well as providing Popov with a number of new cover addresses (all of them known to MI5) to which he could write, it included a long list of questions about the effect of bombing attacks on England, asking for details about searchlights, the number and deployment of US merchant ships converted into auxiliary air carriers, and much else. There was also a note confirming that Lisbon had received Popov's first two letters in secret writing: 'Your writing is wonderful, I congratulate you heartily. We are all enthusiastic, how quickly you have learnt. We can read every word.'[11] The XX Committee got to work preparing answers for Popov to send back without delay.

At the end of November, Popov moved out of the Savoy into a 'delightful furnished cottage', which he rented for twelve guineas a week. He obtained the services of a Czech maid and lived, MI5 somewhat sourly reported, 'as always, in a state of considerable comfort'. Clock House, in Rutland Gate, was in the best part of Knightsbridge, just south of Hyde Park, and was one of only a handful of houses in the street undamaged by bombs. Some months after he moved in, Lillian Gregg, a beautiful English actress engaged to Prince Bertil of Sweden, rented the house next door, Box Cottage. Popov was tickled by the fact that Prince Bertil's predecessor as Swedish naval attaché in London had been wrongly accused of spying for the Germans. In reality a German spy had been obtaining his daily reports to Stockholm through a contact at the Swedish Ministry of Defence and claimed, after his arrest, that he had got the information direct from the naval attaché in London.

Not long after moving into Clock House, Popov received a passionate billet-doux from Lisbon. The Germans believed that love letters stood a better chance of passing through the censors and Popov was always amused at the thought of Elizabeth, von Karsthoff's dour secretary and mistress, gritting her teeth to compose flowery missives to him:

> My dearest, Christmas is coming and Dusi, my little Dusi, you have not yet returned. It is making me miserable. Eric has invited me to spend Christmas in the country, near to Porto, so I will not return to the capital until the evening of 6th January. It is very sad not to have you with me these days. We will make some amusing trips and I think that I will also have the chance to see a little of the snow. Dusi, my little one, when will you return to hold me in your arms? I am so in love and embrace you tenderly, Your little Jacqui.

Popov ignored the contents of the letter and prised from the surface five microdots. The fifth, to his pleasure and surprise, contained a letter from Ivo, forwarded by Jebsen:

My dear brother,

I am seizing the chance that Johnny gives me to write to you with the probability that you will read it in a short time. It is already a long time since you left and we are without news of you. I have learnt through Bube [Countess Bube Marinovic, a family friend in Dubrovnik] that you are in Europe once more and when she gave us this news we had a real family celebration. First of all I am going to give you our news. Tata [Serbo-Croat for 'father'] is at Dubrovnik to look after his property there. The winter was very hard for him because he did not have the means to buy anything to eat. The situation is now much better from every point of view. Besides I can send him enough money and he says he is very happy. Vladan [Popov's younger brother] was in Germany up to this summer (at Freiburg and Vienna) and since then he has been at Bologna. He does very well. Johnny pays all his expenses and does not dispute the accounts which Vladan sends him, so you can imagine that he takes full advantage of it. I myself, with Mam, Dragica [Ivo's wife] and Misha [their child], are at Belgrade. At first the situation was rather difficult, but one fine day Johnny came along like *deus ex machina*. After that everything went well. Thanks to him I have bought a factory for polishes which supplies me with enough to live on, without thinking of the expenses which today are enormous. All prices have risen to 20–80 times as much as before the war. Theoretically there is nothing at all; in practice, thanks to the black market, one can have nearly everything. Everyone's mentality is directed to one thing, one only thinks of eating and keeping warm, and if it is possible to do business which lets one eat better and be warmer. I have a practice which goes well enough, but now no doctor can earn sufficient. Thank God from time to time Johnny appears and helps me with his contacts and advice, and then all goes well again. In him you have truly a good friend and I do not know how I shall be able to repay him for all the services that he has done for me (don't think that I write this because he will transmit this letter). Maman is in good health except for her feet, which still give her difficulty. Dragica and Misha do marvellously . . . When I think of all I want to tell you I would need to write you a book. I shall keep it for the fine evenings at Lapad, when, with a glass of *Bevande*, we will talk for hours and will never have enough time. Be careful, and God bless you, with every good wish, Ivo.

Popov was delighted to get news from home and more than ever determined to try and see his brothers. He was never averse to asking favours from MI5, and so it was that Tar Robertson and Ian Wilson found themselves invited round to Clock House, where Popov proposed that he should be sent to a neutral country to make contact with Ivo and explore ways in which they could work together. Popov assured his MI5 colleagues that Ivo was utterly loyal to the Allied cause (neither Robertson nor Wilson needed convincing, since Ivo was already on MI5's books as 'Dreadnought'). He also wanted MI5's help to try and get Vladan out of Italy. A friend in Split had written to tell Popov that Vladan was suffering the same 'illness' that had afflicted Popov when he was studying in Freiburg. Popov had not been ill in Freiburg and assumed that Vladan was in trouble for speaking out against the Fascist regime of Mussolini. Popov thought it would be feasible to arrange Vladan's escape without blowing his own cover.

Popov again raised the possibility of recruiting Jebsen as a British agent. He felt that as soon as Jebsen, who was now spending most of his time in the Balkans, realised that Germany was going to lose the war, he would be willing to come over to the Allies. He could ask Johnny to set up a meeting with Ivo and Vladan in some neutral country, at which time Popov would suggest that Jebsen could 'insure' himself against Germany losing the war by being ready to switch sides. His friend was amoral, he said, was never pro-Nazi and had no loyalty to anyone except himself. He was only helping the Abwehr for material gain, and now circumstances were changing, Popov could suggest that Jebsen start collating intelligence so that he would have something to offer the British when the time came.

MI5 viewed Popov's proposal about working directly with his brother as constructive and discussed the possibility of finding him a cover job in connection with propaganda and sending him to Turkey, notionally to interview Yugoslav refugees about the effect of British propaganda and conditions in Yugoslavia. In the end it proved impractical for bureaucratic reasons, and so Popov remained marooned in London, making ever-increasing demands on his MI5 handlers.

It was fortunate for Popov that he was considered to be an extremely valuable agent, since one way or another he was causing MI5 many problems, not least because of the continuing chaotic state of his finances. Despite the cloak-and-dagger shenanigans in the lavatory at the Chiava d'Aura bar, the luckless Bailoni family had still not been paid in full the money Popov owed them. He still owed $10,000 to British Security Coordination and $3,200 to the FBI, which he was extremely reluctant to repay. A debt-collection agency in New York was chasing him for $215.85 – an unpaid bill for 'horticultural supplies' delivered to his cottage in Long Island – and he owed his New York tailor, Wetheralls, a further $549.28. 'Tricycle is never very coherent at the best of times,' John Marriott, secretary of the XX Committee, recorded, 'but he gets particularly obscure when he is discussing problems of international finance.'[12]

MI5 was concerned that the debt-collection agency was sending frequent letters to Popov at the Ministry of Information, where his cover was weak, and it was decided to settle this bill immediately in order to avoid the risk of his exposure as a British agent. Popov naturally thought this was an excellent proposal and suggested that they should also pay his tailor's bill, but he was informed that MI5 was 'rather tired of having to spend time on these personal matters'[13] and told to settle the bill in sterling at the tailor's London office, which he did. BSC in New York was instructed to pay the FBI, and complicated arrangements were made at government level to clear Popov's remaining debt to the Bailonis. Popov consented to repay British intelligence from the dollars advanced to him in Lisbon and signed an agreement with MI5 to put aside two-thirds of all future payments from the Germans into a separate bank account to be used for his living expenses. In return for his cooperation, MI5 promised to do its best to look after Popov when the war ended:

> It is understood that after the war we will do our best to ensure that you receive a suitable British decoration for your services. We will also do our best to assist you in obtaining good commercial relationships with some important British firm and will take up with the Foreign Office the possibility of your receiving some post such as that of British consul in Dubrovnik.[14]

Popov remained serenely unbothered by matters of finance and was soon in debt again. He was also, evidently, disinclined to change his habits. When he was told that the clothes and personal possessions he had left behind in his Park Avenue penthouse were being sent back to him by sea, he immediately asked for $100 worth of chocolates and $100 worth of nylon stockings to be included in the consignment, intimating that Tar Robertson had approved the expenditure, which he had not. Wilson was furious when he heard about it and made it clear to the insouciant Yugoslav that the 'practice of requesting personal favours was unwelcome in wartime'.[15] Even so, MI5 still tried to accommodate him. 'As regards

Tricycle's request for chocolates and stockings,' a BSC representative wrote to Robertson from New York:

> it is probable that the chocolates are intended to delight the interiors of those same exteriors which Tricycle wishes to decorate with stockings. However, please tell him that Mr Thomas [the name by which Popov knew Wren] will include a reasonable package of chocolates. As for nylons, these are now as rare here as they are with you and it is doubtful if Tricycle would favour handing on rayon to his 9, $9\frac{1}{2}$ and 10 lovelies. But we will see what can be done.[16]

On the subject of one particular 'lovely', Popov was fretting that the telegrams and letters he was sending to Simone Simon were not getting through to her and suspected that they were being intercepted by the FBI. Tar Robertson took up the issue on his behalf and persuaded Bill Stephenson of BSC to raise the matter with Hoover. On 25 November, Stephenson wrote to Hoover, enclosing a report about Popov's visit to Lisbon, hastening to assure the director that references to Popov returning to the United States were only 'notional' and that it was 'clearly understood' no such return was intended. 'One final point,' he added, 'Popov says that he has cabled Simone Simon several times but he has the impression that his cables are being held by the censor. If this is in fact what has happened, I can well understand it, but I would be grateful to know if Popov's assumption is correct and whether you will permit communications from Popov to reach Simone Simon . . .'[17]

Hoover, disinclined in any way to accommodate the man he regarded as a loathsome Balkan playboy, prevaricated. In the end, no action was necessary. MI5 noted that while Popov and Simon seemed genuinely attached to each other and he clearly missed her greatly by coming to England, 'he was not long in seeking to console himself elsewhere'.[18]

Popov continued writing frequently to Lisbon, although he quickly discovered that the match-heads he had been given were certainly not good for 200 letters – after writing just fifteen letters the match was already too worn to write without scratching the paper. The XX Committee provided a mass of information (some true, some false) for Popov to transmit to Lisbon in order to maintain his status as a top agent. At his desk in Clock House, laboriously writing invisibly on thin airmail paper with a match-head, he told the Germans about a new and powerful anti-tank gun with high muzzle velocity; a scheme to train a large number of aerodrome defence troops as infantry; a new secret weapon, a flame-thrower, being developed by Canadian forces; information from an

RAF pilot that the Mustang had lateral, elevator and rudder controls in the cockpit and was a 'delight to fly'; reports that between 150,000 and 170,000 Canadian troops – five divisions and a brigade equipped with Churchill tanks – were posted south of London, and a similar number was due to leave Canada shortly for Britain; a list of divisional signs seen on the streets of London; about the organisation and arming of the Home Guard; how, on a railway journey to Bournemouth, he had over-heard Northamptonshire Yeomanry officers talking about delays in the delivery of special tanks in which armour had been sacrificed for speed and lightness . . .

Much of this information was laying the groundwork for Operation Fortitude, the culmination of the XX Committee's labours and its primary *raison d'être*. Fortitude was to be the final trump hand in the great game, a massive deception operation on which the success of D-Day would hinge, by convincing the Germans that the Normandy landings were no more than a feint and that the real thrust of the invasion was planned elsewhere.

By March 1943 Popov had sent, or was supposed to have sent (some letters were assumed to be lost or stopped by the censor), twenty-five letters to Lisbon, but he was becoming distinctly restless in his passive role as a letter writer and wanted MI5 to make better use of his good relations with the Germans. His opportunity arose, entirely by chance, when a Yugoslav refugee arrived in London. What he had to say would lead, co-incidentally, to the Popov brothers working closely together on behalf of British intelligence, while remaining hundreds of miles apart.

10

The Yugoslav Escape Route

ALTHOUGH ONLY TWO YEARS SEPARATED IVO AND DUSKO POPOV AND they would be close all their lives, no one would have marked them out immediately as brothers. Ivo was significantly taller and quite different in appearance – more handsome in a classical sense, with a resemblance to the actor Gary Cooper. Both had been expensively educated abroad, but whereas Dusko slipped naturally into the role of a bon vivant, Ivo was a much more serious student, dedicated to becoming a doctor. At the time he was called up as a reserve officer in the Yugoslav army he was running a successful private practice in Dubrovnik, was deeply involved in medical research, and his wife Dragica was expecting their first child.

Ivo was serving near the Albanian frontier in March 1941 when, to his great delight, a *coup d'état* ousted Yugoslavia's pro-Axis government. Then as now, the Balkans had long been a cauldron of political, religious and ethnic strife, with the Serbs and Croats at each other's throats, Muslims demanding an autonomous Bosnia, and the Slovenes and Montenegrins espousing federalism. Portents of war shored up a tenuous national unity under a government that strengthened the country's ties with Germany, its main trading partner, but ignored public opinion, which was staunchly pro-Allies.

Yugoslavia struggled against the odds to maintain its neutrality, resisting mounting pressure from Berlin to sign the Tripartite Pact aligning itself with the Axis powers – Germany, Italy and Japan. In the end, virtually surrounded by enemies and convinced that the country's military situation was hopeless, the government succumbed and signed a 'protocol of adherence' to the pact. In return, Hitler guaranteed that Germany would not press Yugoslavia for military assistance or violate Yugoslav sovereignty.

Two days later, a group of army officers overthrew the Cabinet, installed a new government under General Dusan Simovic and restored the monarchy, proclaiming the sixteen-year-old son of King Alexander, who had been assassinated by a Bulgarian in Marseilles in 1934, as the new king. A wave of anti-German euphoria swept the country. People took to the streets waving British, French and American flags, shouting anti-Tripartite slogans and 'Down with Hitler'. Germany responded with a ferocious blitzkrieg, bombing Belgrade and pouring thousands of troops into Yugoslavia to crush the 'revolt'. Within ten days the hopelessly outnumbered Yugoslav army had been forced to surrender unconditionally.

Germany, Italy, Hungary and Bulgaria dismembered Yugoslavia. Germany occupied a rump Serbia and created a puppet Independent State of Croatia under Ante Pavelic, leader of the Ustashe (Insurrection) movement, which included Croatia, Bosnia and Hercegovina. Italy won southern Slovenia, much of Dalmatia and Montenegro. Hungary occupied parts of Vojvodina and Slovenia and the Croatian border regions, while Bulgaria took Macedonia and part of southern Serbia. Pavelic, a psychopath and a fervent admirer of Hitler, instituted a reign of terror aimed primarily at Serbs and ethnic minorities: the Ustashe would slaughter some 300,000 Serbs in its first year in power. About one million of the 1.7 million Yugoslavs who lost their lives in the Second World War were killed by other Yugoslavs.

Resistance to the occupation began immediately, divided into two factions: the nationalist, and fiercely anti-Communist, Chetniks, and the Communist-led Partisans. It was a recipe for disaster. Germany warned that it would execute 100 Serbs for every German soldier killed by the resistance. The Partisans, under Josip Tito, the son of a Croatian-Slovenian peasant family, reasoned that such action would only result in more recruits to their cause and continued to conduct guerrilla warfare. Colonel Draza Mihailovic, leader of the Chetniks, feared that German reprisals would result in a Serbian holocaust and ordered his forces not to engage the Germans. Inevitably, by the end of 1941, the Chetniks and the Partisans were fighting each other as well as the Germans.

After the surrender of the Yugoslav army, Ivo fled into the mountains, but was unable to remain in hiding and gave himself up to the Italians as a prisoner of war, promptly escaped and made his way back to Dubrovnik, disguised as a monk. As a Serb and a prominent member of the community, he found his name on the Ustashe Black List, marked out for execution. After much agonising among the family, it was decided that he had no alternative but to flee once more. At that time wives and children were not included on the Black List, but an exception was made in the case of Dr Ivo Popov; after the Ustashe discovered he had gone, the names of his wife Dragica, and of his baby son Misha, were added to the list. Not long afterwards an informer warned the family that they were about to be rounded up the following morning. Ivo's parents, Milorad and Zora, his wife and three-month-old son made an attempt to catch a train for Belgrade that night, but the Ustashe were waiting for them at the railway station. Luckily there was an Italian military presence in Dubrovnik. The Italians were shocked by Ustashe atrocities and a dispute arose between Italian soldiers and Ustashe officials about the fate of the family. The train left without the Popovs, who were given temporary safe haven in the Italian Consulate, which was promptly surrounded by Ustashe thugs.

Four nights later, under the cover of a heavy storm, the Popovs slipped out of the consulate and made their way to the harbour, where a small boat was waiting to take them, and other escapees, to safety. But the boat's engine refused to start. In desperation they began rowing, even though they knew they could not get far enough away to avoid being caught by the Ustashe when dawn broke. Fortunately a family friend, Mirko Ucovic, had been alerted to their plight and arranged for a powerful motor launch to pick them up before first light. The Popovs were taken to the island of Mljet, two hours from Dubrovnik, where they were marooned for six weeks. Dragica's breast-milk dried up because of the stress, and her mother-in-law kept the baby alive by chewing boiled fish and feeding it to him through her lips.

Ivo, who was by then in Belgrade, heard that his brother's friend in the Abwehr, Johnny Jebsen, was also in the city and appealed to him for help. Jebsen eventually arranged for the family to be brought to relative safety in German-occupied Belgrade, where (courtesy of Jebsen) they would enjoy some protection. Ivo's uncle was not so lucky. He refused to leave Dubrovnik and was publicly hanged by the Ustashe, with one of his two sons, in the courtyard of his own home. A second son, a world champion in water polo, was crucified on a barn door and took four days to die. His mother was scheduled for transportation to a concentration camp, but again Ivo asked Jebsen to intervene and he was able to have her removed from the train.

At that stage Ivo knew little of Jebsen, other than that he had been a close friend of Dusko in their student days and that they had had business dealings together. At first, despite all the help he had given the family, Ivo was wary of Jebsen – he was, after all, an officer in the Abwehr – but the more he got to know him, the more he relaxed. Jebsen made no secret of his strong anti-Nazi views and would talk at length about the dangers the Nazi party represented to the future of Germany. When there was a risk that Jebsen would be called up for military service, he asked Ivo, as a doctor, how he could avoid it on medical grounds: Ivo told him how to simulate the symptoms of jaundice.

Stricken with 'jaundice', Jebsen was obliged to stay in Belgrade for several weeks and during this time the two men formed a close friendship, even though they were ostensibly on opposite sides. It was Jebsen who told Ivo that his younger brother was in Britain working as an Abwehr agent. Ivo did not believe it, but kept his opinions to himself.

One evening, when they were sitting together over a drink in the garden of the Popov family home in Belgrade, Jebsen asked Ivo what his plans for the future were. Ivo hesitated, wondering if he could really trust this German. His first priority, he said at last, was to safeguard his family; once that was accomplished, he intended to join the Chetniks, the mountain guerrilla movement led by General Draza Mihailovic. Jebsen nodded, as if that was what he expected to hear, then leaned forward and whispered urgently into Ivo's ear.

There was a better way of fighting the Nazis than going into the mountains, he said. Jebsen explained that he belonged to a loose-knit group of young men with substantial business and financial interests in Germany and pronounced anti-Nazi views. They identified each other using a password, 'Seni'. Their object was to disrupt the centralised economic system which the Nazis planned to set up, by assisting each other in transactions that would keep industry and finance in private hands. 'You, as a Serb, are fighting Nazism,' he whispered. 'I and my friends, who know that a controlled economy is the ruin of Germany, are also fighting Nazism. With your business interests and with our advice you can sabotage the Nazi control of industry in Europe and by so doing you can help in the fight against Nazism much more effectively than as a single soldier fighting in the mountains.'[1]

Ivo recognised the truth in what Jebsen was saying. Overt acts of sabotage against the German occupying forces always led, through the doctrine of collective responsibility, to fearsome reprisals against the local populace. Economic sabotage would be much harder to track down and could, as Jebsen said, be much more damaging. Ivo began his underground activities by asking Slavo Vasic, his brother-in-law, who was a chemist, if it would be possible to change the formula of the boot polish manufactured in the factory owned by his family, so that instead of preserving the leather, it rotted it. There was a simple reason for Ivo's enquiry – the factory's entire output went to the Wehrmacht. Vasic experimented with various formulae and came up with a solution that looked exactly like conventional boot polish, but caused the leather to crack over time. It was said later that the poor condition of the leather boots worn by German soldiers on the Russian front in winter greatly increased their suffering.

This was the start of Ivo's activities as an economic saboteur and he quickly developed his underground skills. The Germans brought to Belgrade, for sorting, all the factory machinery and raw materials that they had been able to seize after occupying Yugoslavia and Greece. Ivo made it his business to ensure that as little as possible of this loot reached Germany, by bribing officials to certify the machinery as useless and sell it on the black market. False samples of raw materials were drawn for the benefit of German inspectors so that high-grade lubricating oil was downgraded and sold off for curing leather. Goods sent by rail were listed by weight rather than being itemised individually, enabling railway workers to replace valuable machinery in transit with relatively useless material.

In time almost all railway employees in Belgrade, from the station-master down to the youngest apprentice, were recruited to work for Mihailovic. Theft from wagons was organised systematically on a huge scale, and hidden sabotage – putting sand in axle boxes and damaging brakes – was rife. To avoid reprisals, direct sabotage was limited to putting coal-bombs onto locomotives as they left the country or hiding time-bombs, set to explode hours after leaving Yugoslavia, in wagons containing raw materials.

Through his friendship with Jebsen, Ivo met many other Abwehr officers in Belgrade and went out of his way to ingratiate himself with them, obtaining for them on the black market food and clothing unavailable in Germany and accepting promises of payment in marks. Ivo's greatest coup was to nurture a friendship with Martin Töppen, then head of the *Überwachungstelle*, the supervisory organisation entrusted with obtaining supplies from all the occupied territories. Töppen spent several days in Belgrade every month and always stayed at Ivo's home. The *Überwachung-stelle* was supposed to stamp out black markets, but in the Balkans it proved impossible and Ivo was responsible for buying and selling on the black market on the Germans' behalf, a duty he discharged by ensuring that the Germans obtained as little as possible of real value and that as much as possible disappeared from their reach. Ivo was in close touch with several Mihailovic aides in Belgrade and with their help he could ensure that whatever goods were in greatest demand by the Germans rapidly disappeared from the market.

Blessed with a powerful personality, Ivo had a natural ability to impress everyone he met. He covered his tracks so cleverly that the Germans never discovered what he was up to and considered him to be an utterly 'reliable' collaborator – so reliable, in fact, that on several occasions he was asked to attend conferences to advise the Germans on the best ways of keeping order in Yugoslavia. All this while he was passing information to the Mihailovic headquarters, often giving the Chetniks advance warning of German operations planned against them.

Towards the end of 1941 Jebsen suggested to Ivo that he could strengthen his position still further with the Germans if he was willing to recruit Yugoslavs for training as agents in Britain. Jebsen made it quite clear he did not much care if the recruits worked for Germany or for the Allies once they got to Britain, so long as he would be able to claim the credit for getting them to England. Ivo's plan from the start, capitalising on Jebsen's somewhat ambiguous offer, was to nominate Yugoslavs he knew were pro-Allies and instruct them to offer their services to British intelligence as double agents as soon as they arrived. They were presented to the Abwehr as fervent anti-Communists willing to work for Germany to ensure future good relations between Germany and Yugoslavia within the New European Order, which they viewed as the only alternative to Communism.

Ivo found two suitable candidates, but the Germans wanted them to make their own way to Britain to avoid arousing the suspicions of British intelligence. This was to cause major problems. First to arrive in London, in April 1943 after a hair-raising journey, was Eugen Sostaric, a Croat naval pilot who had been ADC to the young King Peter and had known Ivo for some years. Having been recruited by Ivo and accepted by the Abwehr as an agent, Sostaric planned his escape via Salonika and the Greek islands. In Salonika he began to worry that British intelligence might think he was a real German spy and unwisely decided to take out insurance by asking a friend, who he thought was in the Serbian resist-ance, to get word to the Yugoslav government-in-exile in London that he was a genuine patriot and was merely masquerading as a German spy in order to reach England. The friend was no friend at all and went straight to the Germans. Sostaric was arrested by the Gestapo and summarily sentenced to death.

Jebsen, courageously pulling every string he possessed, somehow managed to secure Sostaric's release and persuade his Abwehr bosses in Berlin that there had been a mistake and that the Yugoslav was still of some potential use to them – as a triple agent. Sostaric's position in Belgrade had become intolerable, Jebsen explained. He feared further denunciation, or arrest by the Gestapo or Serbian police, and was willing to go along with Jebsen's plan. Jebsen proposed allowing Sostaric to continue his journey and present himself to the British as a double agent, handing over the cover addresses and secret ink he had been given by the Germans. Once accepted by the British, he would begin secretly communicating with Lisbon using different cover addresses and different ink. Berlin agreed, presumably concluding that it had very little to lose.

Sostaric reached Madrid in March and immediately reported his triple-cross mission to the British, but London remained sceptical. By the time Sostaric reached Gibraltar by train, MI6 had reported that it could confirm 'little or nothing' of his story and advised that he be 'regarded with some suspicion until his bona fides are established'. Sostaric waited two weeks for a seat on a plane to England and was immediately interned, on arrival, for screening in an interrogation centre that had been set up in the Royal Victoria Patriotic School in Wandsworth, south London. Fortunately for the Yugoslav, almost everything he proceeded to tell his interrogators could be confirmed by Ultra intercepts. Sostaric refused to name the Yugoslav who had recruited him or the German who had rescued him from prison in Salonika, but by checking Ultra intercepts, MI5 was soon able to identify 'Dreadnought' and Jebsen.

Satisfied after three days that Sostaric was not a German plant, MI5 arranged for his release. The following day he found himself being entertained to an amiable lunch at Tar Robertson's club in St James's with Robertson, Ian Wilson and Popov. Sostaric was not told who Popov was and was extremely reserved throughout lunch, indicating that he was not particularly interested in intelligence work and was hoping that he might have the opportunity of joining the RAF as a pilot. Robertson pretended to be sympathetic, but pointed out that at the age of thirty-seven it was unlikely Sostaric would be accepted; whereas he could provide enormous assistance to Allied deception plans if the Germans believed he was a triple agent.

Popov had been asked to entertain Sostaric over the weekend and the moment they were alone together at Clock House, Popov identified himself as Ivo's brother. Sostaric's relief was palpable. He apologised for his earlier reticence, explaining that Ivo had warned him to be circumspect with British intelligence and not discuss Ivo's organisation until he had talked with his brother. Sostaric was still reluctant to go into espionage, preferring to fight in the open with his compatriots, but Popov was eventually able to persuade him that he would be more valuable to the Allied cause as an agent. He was recruited into Popov's network under the code-name 'Meteor'.

A few weeks after Sostaric's arrival in London, a second 'escaper' recruited by Ivo turned up. He was Stefan Zeiss, a twenty-seven-year-old multilingual Czech whose family lived in Belgrade. Zeiss had been stranded in Switzerland for close on a year and eventually made his way to Britain via Paris and Lisbon. He told British intelligence that in Paris he had met Ivo kitted out in the full dress uniform of an officer in the Wehrmacht. This startling news was later confirmed by Ultra intercepts – Ivo had so ingratiated himself with the Germans that in order to facilitate his travels around Europe on their behalf, in a private aeroplane, he had been issued with papers in the name of Hans Pol and appointed a *Sonderführer*, a rank equivalent to that of Lieutenant Colonel. Zeiss was described in MI5 files as having a 'discontented expression' and for this reason MI5 decided, unkindly, that his codename would be 'The Worm'. Along with 'Meteor', 'The Worm' was assigned to Popov's growing network and both men were soon busily writing to their German controls under the direction of the XX Committee.

Popov, meanwhile, had been reprimanded by Lisbon. 'People are again not satisfied with your work,' von Karsthoff wrote. 'The enormous amounts which you have received so far are absolutely not justified by what we in fact receive here in the way of information . . . You must in future report *many more details* about the formation and disposition of the army, about new weapons, important operations, about possible landings on the Continent . . .' This was followed by a long list of further questions about the organisation and strength of the Commando brigades.

Popov, typically, was unabashed:

> Surely you realise that what I send you has to be judged by its reliability and not merely by its quantity? You would not thank me for sending you pages of rumours which are unconfirmed. There are always stories and rumours . . . You must make it clear to those people higher up that my letters only contain fact and are much more valuable than if I invented details to make them look better . . .[2]

MI5, however, clearly decided that Popov should be seen to be trying harder, since on 28 April he supplied a detailed report about new Royal Navy ships, the building of tank-landing craft and assault craft, exercises taking place continuously in Scotland and on the west coast of England, the disposition of US troops on Salisbury Plain and the manufacture of chemical-warfare materials in the United States. All this was written under a letter to Armano Resende of Rua Pedro V/24, Lisbon, informing him that his 'dear cousin, Mrs Mario Elena Scott died on the 25th of April . . .'

The XX Committee was at this time using its double agents to persuade the Germans that the Allies were planning an invasion of

Norway, while in reality planners prepared for operations in the Mediterranean – the landings, in July, in Sicily. Popov reported large troop concentrations in Scotland, with landing craft being constructed in considerable numbers for amphibious operations and hospitals being cleared to make way for casualties. He also provided detailed analyses of the results of air-raids on London, designed to discourage the Germans by indicating that the attacks were becoming less and less effective. He reported that incendiaries dropped in west London near the Victoria and Albert Museum had caused no apparent damage; fire-watchers and wardens were dealing with incendiary bombs so quickly that little damage resulted. The general opinion, he said, was that loss of life and property was negligible. 'Air raid shelters have been so improved and the population are carrying out their directions so thoroughly that it is thought doubtful if even the biggest raids will have even a tenth of the effect of earlier raids on the morale of the people or in damage to property.'[3]

In fact, Popov was sick and tired of doing little but write letters at MI5's dictation, and the arrival of 'Meteor' had given him an idea about how he might get back into the action. On 11 May, during a long meeting with Masterman, he put forward an ingenious plan. He had discovered that the Yugoslav government-in-exile was anxious to arrange the evacuation of a number of officers who were marooned in Switzerland, having escaped from Germany or occupied territory. Popov proposed returning to Lisbon to organise their evacuation as a cover for renewing his contacts with the Abwehr and possibly recruiting Jebsen. 'Tricycle was in his best mood and had obviously thought long and hard about the plan,' Masterman noted. 'He wanted to get a move on, since he thought it was important he should get back to the UK in time to feed really effective disinformation before invasion of the continent.'[4]

Ian Wilson supported the plan, pointing out that Popov had been a double agent for two and a half years and must be regarded by Germany as 'one of their best men'. He felt the trip could prove extremely valuable in assessing the Germans' interests and intentions, as well as putting Popov in a good position to participate in the vital D-Day deception plans. In a coldly calculated analysis of the risks, Wilson pointed out that Popov knew nothing about the operational side of the deception plans; thus, if he was arrested and exposed as a double agent, the consequences would 'redound on his family' rather than MI5. 'The risk of Popov being arrested and giving away other agents', he concluded, 'is more than offset by the advantages that might be gained if the plan is carried through.'[5]

While waiting for the plan to be approved, Popov had plenty to keep him occupied. His MI5 file contains a letter, dated 3 May 1943, hand-written on American Red Cross paper:

> Dusko darling. I'll try to ring you today, but if I can't manage it this is to let you know I won't be able to see you tomorrow after all as Charlie is unexpectedly coming up to London!!! He won't be here long, though, so I'll try to ring you as soon as I can. I'm so sorry as I was all ready for you. Please try to be a quarter way decent till I can pick up where I broke off. You are a sweetie and I love you (a little!). Gwennie.[6]

As well as Gwennie (with whom Popov had been conducting an affair before he left for the United States), there was Mairi, who wrote from Flat 80, Grosvenor House, Park Lane: 'My darling . . . well, my darling, I don't think I have any more news at the moment but I shall write again soon; take care of yourself and as always all my love to you and more.'[7]

As well as Gwennie and Mairi, there was Ljiljana Bailoni, the twenty-one-year-old daughter of his friends, the Bailonis, to whom, MI5 noted, Tricycle had become 'rather attached'.[8] Popov had been making 'an infernal nuisance' of himself with MI5 trying to get visas for the entire Bailoni family to come to Britain. When that failed, he began pressing for a single visa to be issued to Ljiljana. The problem, as Ian Wilson readily accepted, was that in the Balkans it was routine for people with influence to do favours for friends. 'Tricycle is inclined to be rather a nuisance,' he admitted, 'in asking us to use our influence to further his personal whims.' Nevertheless he was still making heroic efforts on Ljiljana's behalf, even when Popov was back in Lisbon in August: 'As you know,' he wrote in a memorandum to the Foreign Office pleading her case:

> Tricycle is now in Lisbon. Before he left, he once more raised the question of whether at least the younger sister [of the Bailonis] could not come to this country, and, while no promises were given, he was told that the matter was not in the hands of those who ran his case but that as far as we were concerned we could see no objection to a separate application for a visa being made by Ljiljana, though whether or not it would succeed was not a matter for us.
>
> Evidence from various independent sources has recently reached us that Tricycle is paying considerable court to Ljiljana. Tricycle is doing an extremely good job of work under conditions of considerable risk at the present moment. He would undoubtedly be an easier agent to run if he became a little more settled in his domes-

tic habits, which he probably would be if this girl were here ... In these circumstances do you think the objections against this particular member of the family could be withdrawn and a visa granted?[9]

Two weeks after his meeting with Masterman, Popov heard that his proposal to organise an escape route for the Yugoslavs had been accepted in principle. He set up a meeting with Slobodan Jovanovic, the Yugoslav prime minister, who was aware of Popov's connections with MI5. Jovanovic was delighted with the plan and arranged for Popov to be appointed as an assistant military attaché, with diplomatic status and a diplomatic passport. He also made sure that Popov was excused any official duties, to the disgust of General Radovic, the military attaché, who was not let in on the secret and viewed Popov as nothing more than a worthless playboy with influential friends.

There was a red alert when MI5 learned, to its irritation, that not only had Jovanovic informed his Foreign Ministry that the British were backing Popov's trip, but that the ministry had promptly passed this information on to the Yugoslav Legations in Madrid and Lisbon. The more people who knew about Popov's activities, the greater the risk of his cover being blown. In the event there was no leak, but it caused a few anxious days at MI5 headquarters. Then there were considerable difficulties with visas. Spain would not issue a visa because Yugoslavia had broken off diplomatic relations with Spain after it had recognised what the Yugoslav government-in-exile called the 'puppet kingdom' of Croatia. Portugal would issue a transit visa only on condition that Popov was proceeding through Portugal to another country. In the end the Yugoslav acting war minister, Zivcovic, an old friend of Popov, who knew something about what he was doing, persuaded the Yugoslav Foreign Ministry to send him as a courier.

On 1 June Popov wrote to von Karsthoff to say that he would be visiting Lisbon soon and would be bringing 'material' with him. Wilson began putting together a package to impress the Germans, dealing first with the so-called 'missing letters'. Popov was supposed to have written thirty-six letters, each of which was numbered, to Lisbon. In fact seven were deliberately not written. The idea was to persuade the Germans that a cover address had been blown and that the censors had held up the mail, as might well have happened if Popov had been a genuine German agent. Wilson provided Popov with the information that would have been included in the 'missing letters', including the names of high-ranking officers, for which the Germans had asked several times. Von Karsthoff was always impressed when Popov produced documents, either stolen or photocopied, and Wilson sent an urgent request to the XX Committee for documents that Popov could take with him.

Much of the verbal intelligence Popov was required to deliver was intended to increase German paranoia about an impending invasion. MI5 relied a great deal on Popov's considerable talents as an actor, and thus he was told that he could talk freely on general matters like morale, food, air-raids in London and a general 'hotting up' of the atmosphere, but he was also given specific information to pass on. How, for example, it was getting very difficult to pick up casual information as officers were becoming much more discreet – he had witnessed, in both the Savoy and the Junior Carlton Club, the police being called when someone had been asking questions deemed to be too intrusive. The number of American troops on leave in London seemed to be increasing; he had overheard one group talking about Sherman tanks, but none was wearing divisional signs, although he had seen troops with 29th Rangers signs on their shoulders. There was a great deal of movement of British troops going on, along with training in cliff climbing and embarking and disembarking from gliders and aeroplanes – he had 'heard' that the standard time to disembark twenty-five men with full arms and equipment was forty-seven seconds. General Curtis, in command of British troops in the Salisbury Plain area, had made himself very unpopular by demanding a daunting amount of physical training. Popov's tailor had told him that he was very busy making battledress uniforms for senior officers. A friend, an officer in a Canadian division training for mountain warfare, had let slip that his unit had been turned into an infantry division. There were rumours that there was likely to be a serious shortage of hospital beds for civilians, as the military was insisting on more beds being reserved for soldiers. A deputation of senior officers in the Home Guard had recently asked permission to relax training so that their members could spend one or two Sundays a month in their gardens, but had been emphatically refused as 'the defence of the country would shortly be left to the Home Guard and training must be more intensive, not less'. On a weekend trip to Southampton with a girlfriend, he had seen air-raid shelters being constructed in preparation for the heavy attacks expected when the city became a supply base for the invasion.

At one point Wilson considered sowing further confusion by getting Popov to describe an entirely phoney divisional sign he had seen on the sleeves of American soldiers on leave in London. This plan was scuppered when the *National Geographical Magazine* inconveniently published a complete and up-to-date list of all American divisional signs. 'It occurs to me', Wilson noted in a memorandum, 'that it might not be wise for

Tricycle to claim to have seen a sign which does not appear in this magazine.'[10]

MI6 also bid to make use of Popov's services, asking if he could pump von Karsthoff about his personal enemies in Lisbon, the Abwehr's relationship with the Gestapo and arrangements made for evacuation from Portugal if the war took a still more unfavourable turn for Germany. 'It is possible', the MI6 request concluded mysteriously, 'that in the course of any discussions of future projects, Tricycle will be introduced to a naval officer of about 40, with a slight limp, a thin face and a rather hooked nose. If so, it would be an excellent thing if he could cultivate this man's acquaintance, and learn whatever he can of his past career or of the nature of his present activities and plans for the future.'[11] No name was attached to this individual.

While MI5 was working feverishly to prepare Popov for his trip, he announced, once again, that he had run out of money and was unable to pay the six months' rent due in advance on Clock House. Wilson suggested advancing him £250. 'If he comes back from Lisbon,' he reported (clearly he thought there was some doubt), 'we can ask for the £250 back, but Tricycle has undoubtedly been living on a much more reasonable financial scale since he has been in this country and I do not think we should grudge him this money even if we do not get it back later.'[12]

Popov finally left for Lisbon on 16 July 1943, carrying his reports in a Yugoslav diplomatic bag. A few days later MI5 was passed alarming intercepts indicating that the Germans were again suspicious that he was a double agent. There was concern in London that he was about to be arrested, but Popov, completely unaware of the danger he was in, employed his usual mix of charm, guile and gab with such effect that von Karsthoff was soon assuring Berlin there was nothing to worry about – Ivan was 100 per cent reliable.

It was Kammler, it transpired, who was mainly suspicious of Popov, largely on the basis of his belief that no real agent could have survived so long without being picked up by British intelligence. But Popov often had luck on his side and by that time relations between von Karsthoff and Kammler had soured to such an extent that the mere fact that Kammler voiced his suspicions of 'Ivan' turned von Karsthoff into a strong supporter. Von Karsthoff was also too lazy to bother with an investigation. Popov was left to dictate his report to secretaries who had 'a romantic admiration for him and questioned nothing',[13] and he was not interrogated in any way about his contacts or the sources of his information.

Popov had no trouble convincing von Karsthoff about the mission he had been given, organising an escape route for Yugoslavs stranded in Switzerland. He had had to accept the mission without consulting von Karsthoff, he said, as he had to act quickly and thought that any excuse to get to Lisbon should be taken up. He went on to explain how he had succeeded in playing off the Yugoslavs against the British, so that each of them thought the other knew all the details of how he was arranging the route. The British, he said, had been reluctant to give any assistance to a purely Yugoslav escape route because they feared that such a route would only be used to get out disgruntled pan-Serbs, intent on a Serbian-dominated Yugoslavia after the war, who would cause trouble as soon as they arrived in England. They had therefore insisted that the man chosen for the job should be someone known to them, such as Popov, who could be trusted to ensure that only Yugoslavs useful to the war effort would be allowed to escape. Popov had let the Yugoslavs think the British were really sending him out, while the British, on the other hand, thought it was a purely Yugoslav affair, the mechanics of which Popov would arrange on his own.

This involved story had been devised in London to account for the fact that Popov had no idea how to arrange any escape route, except with German assistance, and covered him against any leakage to the Germans from Yugoslav quarters that Popov had been sent out by, or at least assisted by, the British.

Von Karsthoff was intrigued and rose to the bait, just as MI5 had intended. The German immediately saw the possibility of using the escape route to infiltrate more agents into Britain at a time when they were sorely needed. On 23 July, British intelligence intercepted a signal from Lisbon to Berlin: 'Ivan may possibly be in position to enlist for us Yugoslav P/Ws who have fled to Huette [Switzerland]. At moment about 200 fugitives in Huette, nearly all officers. I report this for your consideration before the meeting in Meda [Madrid] as I consider this plan a good one. I still consider Ivan as reliable, if kept under strict supervision.'

Berlin approved von Karsthoff's proposal that the Abwehr help to organise the escape route in order to include its own people among the genuine escapees. Popov would naturally have to vouch for them, both to the Yugoslavs and to the British. Popov agreed, realising that von Karsthoff's nominees would almost certainly be recruited by his brother in Belgrade and that they would therefore pose no danger to the British.

Yet another cover story was drawn up, this time by the Germans. Popov would tell the Yugoslavs in London that he had met an old friend in Lisbon – Jebsen – who, afraid of the consequences of Germany losing the war, wanted to get on good terms with an Allied government and was therefore willing to ingratiate himself with the Allies by using the influence of his official position to help some Yugoslav prisoners of war escape. He was willing to obtain passports for ten or twelve Yugoslavs of Popov's choice, in return for an undertaking that when he felt the time had come to desert he would be given help, and when the war was over he would be allowed to live and work in Yugoslavia.

The escape route would be through occupied France on false documents provided by the Abwehr, then across the border into Spain, where Popov would meet them and hand them over to the British authorities in Madrid. Von Karsthoff said it was vital that Popov met the escapees in Spain so that he could learn as much as possible about the German nominees in the party, who would be posing as his friends, before they were handed over to the British. Von Karsthoff recognised that once the escapees were in Spain, Popov would need British help to get them out, but he said this would be easy as the British were constantly smuggling people out on false passports through Gibraltar.

Even Popov, whose buoyant optimism was a trademark of his character, was amazed at how easily the plan had fallen into place. Effectively he had persuaded the Germans to finance, organise and collude in a scheme that would only be of benefit to British intelligence.

Popov had not been long in Lisbon before Jebsen arrived from Berlin. The two friends found a place where they could talk – a quiet restaurant in Cascais, which would become a fashionable resort after the war, but at that time was still a small fishing village, about twenty-five miles from Lisbon. Despite their closeness, they still maintained, for their own protection as much as anything else, the charade that Popov was a genuine German agent. Popov was pretty sure that Jebsen knew he was working as a double agent, but never openly admitted it for fear of endangering his friend. Jebsen, for his part, never asked Popov directly if he was working for the British. Somehow, it was a *modus vivendi* that worked for both of them.

Jebsen had orders to use his influence to persuade Popov to work harder. Popov explained later in his debriefing report for MI5:

Before leaving Berlin Jebsen was told that my work during the last year, and especially during the last six months, was rotten. Müntzinger [the Abwehr officer in overall charge of Popov's case] explained that he felt the fault must be that I am overpaid; that they more or less always paid me and that, having seen that they are not complaining too much about it, I simply took my work lightly and did not want to run any special risks. Jebsen insisted that my work

in the future must be better. He said he did not care how I got my
information and where I got it (with a funny smile in his eyes), but
that I ought to write a lot and produce material, even if I had to take
it out of a film. Jebsen said that there are two types of people in the
office in Berlin: Nazis, who are damned idiots; and reactionaries. The
Nazis are too stupid to question my genuineness. The others might
think that I was not genuine but it would be absolutely against their
interests to let this be known or to discuss it.[14]

Jebsen confessed to his friend that he was in trouble with the Gestapo.
He did not go into great detail, but mentioned something about a black-
market foreign currency deal that had turned sour. Popov speculated
privately that Jebsen might have been too open in expressing his views
about the Nazis and the progress of the war and that word had reached
the Gestapo. They agreed that if Jebsen believed his life was in danger, he
would send a telegram to Popov, 'Because of illness cannot carry on with
business', whereupon Popov would do his best to get his friend evacuated
to Britain.

When Jebsen began talking freely about the Abwehr organisation, its
personalities and operations, Popov was in no doubt that his friend was
giving him information that he expected would be passed to British intelligence. Jebsen said that Admiral Canaris had recently been accused of
passing information to the Allies through the Vatican and, although he had
weathered the storm, his position was now a lot less secure. There had
been a large number of arrests. Canaris had told Jebsen privately that he
did not care if all the agents in Britain were fakes as long as he could go
to Field Marshal Keitel, the head of the German high command, and
report that he had twelve agents in Britain, each of them writing a letter
once a week.

The only man in Germany who still believed victory was possible,
Jebsen continued, was 'that idiot Hitler'. What was needed was a political
revolution: in his view, 90 per cent of the population would support it,
but there was no opportunity to organise, no places to meet and any
attempt at opposition was quickly crushed. He said that factory workers
in Cologne had recently gone on strike in protest against the bombing
and their working conditions. Several of them were executed as an
example to others and the remainder were deported. A favourite joke
going around was that Hitler, Goering, Goebbels and Himmler had all
taken refuge in a bomb shelter that received a direct hit. Who was saved?
Germany.

'In spite of not having told him that I am working for the British,'

Popov reported to MI5, 'I am absolutely sure that he knows it, although he has not said so to me. The way he talks to me and his whole behaviour shows this very clearly.'[15]

On 9 August, Popov called at the British Embassy, ostensibly to start making arrangements for the Yugoslav escape route, but actually to meet the MI6 head of station and pass over two charts of the Abwehr organisation, which he had drawn up after talking with Jebsen, and a copy of a questionnaire in German he had been given by von Karsthoff, dealing largely with invasion plans: 'All observations referring to an invasion of the continent are of interest . . . where are troops being concentrated, where are ships' concentrations, where are the Commandos stationed, what is being said in English military circles about the coming actions, how is the equipment of troops . . .?'[16]

The MI6 official reported to London that Tricycle had been in constant touch with von Karsthoff and Elizabeth Sahrbach, 'who have given him dinner several times and generally spoiled him', and Popov had also seen a good deal of Kammler and Jebsen. 'Tricycle thought it would be quite easy for us to persuade Jebsen to go to England and it is possible that Jebsen, convinced that Tricycle was in touch with the Allies, has put himself over big as anti-Nazi, hoping that Tricycle would put in a word for him when the time came.'[17]

As usual with Popov, his visit was marred by continuing arguments about money, particularly his insistence that in future he be paid in advance. After sometimes acrimonious and difficult negotiations with Berlin, during which Popov was constantly threatening to stop work altogether, it was finally agreed that he would receive $2,500 a month from the date of his return to England, plus a $2,000 bonus for carrying a radio transmitter back with him, and escudos for his living expenses in Lisbon.

Popov's position was strengthened by news from Berlin assessing the reports that he brought with him from England as 'very valuable' and urging him to return to Britain as soon as possible to gather more intelligence, particularly on invasion plans, shipping concentrations and Allied air operations. In preparation for his return to England, von Karsthoff sent to Berlin for a fake seal and rubber stamp to secure Popov's Yugoslav 'diplomatic bag'. In addition to a wireless transmitter, he was given a Leica camera (which he thought was von Karsthoff's own), six rolls of especially sensitive film for photographing documents, and a packet of crystals and instructions on how to make matches for secret writing. He was left to pack the bags himself, and so was able to slip in the notes, written in Serbo-Croat, of his conversations with Jebsen.

A few days before he was due to leave, von Karsthoff, in expansive

mood, threw a farewell dinner party for Popov. It was intended as a celebration of his achievements as one of Germany's top agents, but the mood
was spoiled by the news that came through earlier that day that Italy had
surrendered unconditionally to the Allies. Kammler offered odds of ten to
one that the war would be over by Christmas; von Karsthoff held to the
view that there would be a peace deal drawn up with the British.

On 14 September, Popov arrived back at Whitchurch airfield, where
the Security Control Officer had been asked by MI5 to ensure his bags
were not examined too closely and that he was not asked too many
'embarrassing questions'. He was taken by car to Bristol and caught a train
for London. Wilson and Robertson were waiting on the platform to greet
him as his train pulled in at Paddington station. After the usual hand-
shakes, they were driven to Popov's house in Knightsbridge, where they
discovered that none of them had a key. Some undignified acrobatics
followed during which Popov managed to climb in through a first-floor
window and open the front door from the inside.

In the sitting room at Clock House he broke the fake seals of the
Yugoslav Legation that secured his kitbags and displayed his booty. 'First
of all,' Wilson reported, 'a very large number of pairs of silk stockings and
similar articles tumbled out.'[18] He then handed over the wireless transmitter with instructions in English about frequencies and times of transmission, a Pelican edition of *The Country House* by John Galsworthy for
coding, von Karsthoff's camera and film, a small packet containing the
crystals to make secret ink, and a number of questionnaires. Finally he
produced his wages – an envelope with $2,000 in $100 notes and a packet
containing £2,500 in £5 notes (most of which were later discovered to
be very good forgeries).

Not for the first time, Wilson marvelled at Popov's ability to survive
and prosper at the Germans' expense. Just as members of the XX
Committee hardly dared believe that the committee controlled all the
German agents in Britain, so individual case officers like Ian Wilson
wondered how long their protégés would be able to pull the wool over
the Abwehr's eyes. Wilson worried every time Popov went to Lisbon and
constantly expected his cover to be blown ('If Tricycle returns from
Lisbon . . .'), yet each time he returned, self-confident and jaunty as ever,
this time having persuaded his controllers to part with what Wilson
considered to be 'exorbitant' sums of money. 'If it were not for the confirmation from independent sources,' he wrote, referring to Enigma
decrypts:

I would find it almost impossible to believe Tricycle's reports or that the Germans should not have discovered that Tricycle, his brother, and all the agents connected with them are working against them. These sources, however, make it clear that Tricycle's reports to us are accurate, that for the most part the Germans still believe him, and the connected agents, and that those members of the Abwehr who have reason to doubt him are so corrupt or so afraid of losing their positions by disclosing awkward facts that they are doing all they can to support him.[19]

Popov was vague about the detailed financial arrangements he had made with the Germans. 'I suspect the reason for his obscurity in this connection', Wilson concluded, 'is that various black bourse and/or gambling transactions took place between his receiving escudos and producing US dollars and £'s. I do not think it worth while to pursue further the details of the payments made to Tricycle.'[20]

In truth it was not the money, but the news from Jebsen, that really interested the MI5 men. Popov explained that Jebsen had advised him to move out of London because of the dangers posed by a new rocket being developed by Germany. British intelligence had been troubled for months by reports that Hitler was developing a new, and potentially devastating, secret weapon. Popov's dramatic intelligence prompted Tar Robertson to circulate an immediate memorandum to all members of the XX Committee:

The following conversation with regard to the 'rocket gun' is reported by Tricycle:

'Johnny advised me very strongly not to live in London because of the rockets which are going to be fired. I asked him what rockets. He said "Some new invention. From 120 to 250 are fired together, and each of them has the same effect as a 2,000-kilo bomb."

'I said to Johnny: "Don't be a fool, you are influenced by the German propaganda". He said "It is true". I said Goebbels had been talking about this for nearly a year, and Johnny said parts of them have been made in Friedrichshafen and another place which I did not know the name of and can't remember. Through the RAF bombing of Friedrichshafen a factory has been hit and production delayed for a certain number of months. I do think that about December will be the time that they will start firing the rockets. I asked where I should go and live, and he suggested Scotland, but said that the Midlands would do as they could be fired only from the French Channel coast . . .'

Tricycle has on this, as on former occasions, brought back a great deal of valuable information, much of which we know from other sources to be accurate, and nearly all of which came to him from Jebsen, who on this visit was, for the first time, acting as a conscious informant. It is therefore possible that he might be able to obtain valuable information [about the new weapons] and that he would be prepared to transmit this information to us.[21]

Popov insisted that Jebsen was ready to change sides if the right approach was made. Jebsen seemed, he explained, to be in some kind of trouble because of his anti-Nazi and defeatist views and he had hinted at the possibility of a deal with British intelligence if his situation became untenable.

Tar Robertson decided that the time had come to act and that Jebsen, who had already been given the codename of 'Artist', should be recruited by MI5 as soon as possible. Coincidentally, Jebsen was coming to the same conclusion.

11

Enter 'Artist'

JEBSEN, UNQUESTIONABLY, WAS IN TROUBLE, ALTHOUGH NOT, AS POPOV believed, because of his anti-Nazi and defeatist views; by the summer of 1943 such views were not unusual within the Abwehr. He was living in fear of the Gestapo as a result of becoming entangled in a foreign-currency scandal. Jebsen had been helping senior Gestapo officials move money abroad illegally, mainly to Switzerland, as a precaution in the event of a German defeat. The deal was just the kind of thing that Jebsen, with his wide range of business contacts, was good at, and all went smoothly until he discovered that certain Gestapo officers were palming forged notes onto him, leaving him out of pocket holding useless currency. Jebsen, unwisely, denounced them and made powerful enemies.

He was warned by friends several times that if he returned to Germany he risked arrest, or worse, and so his Abwehr masters – who had no incli-nation to cooperate with the Nazis – contrived to keep him abroad and out of the clutches of those members of the Gestapo seeking revenge. There was even talk of sending Jebsen to Britain to run the spy network there. It was thought he could perhaps make use of his family's business connections to obtain refugee status, since he claimed (untruthfully) that he had already been in touch with a member of the Rothschild family about getting a visa. Berlin turned the plan down, although it asked Jebsen to stay in contact with his business friends in case a visit could be arranged later.

While Jebsen believed he was being protected by the Abwehr he felt reasonably confident about his security, but when he arrived back in Madrid after his meeting with Popov in Lisbon, he was dismayed to be summoned to Abwehr headquarters in Berlin at once for 'discussions'. At the same time he received a telegram from a friend in the city warning him not to return. Jebsen immediately panicked. His first thought was that Kammler, who he knew was in Berlin, had discovered that he had been passing information to Popov and had decided to expose him.

Jebsen turned for advice to Hans Ruser, a fellow Abwehr officer in Madrid who held similarly vehement anti-Nazi views. Unknown to Jebsen, Ruser had contacted British intelligence a year earlier and offered his services as a spy. His offer was not taken up for fear of compromising Popov, but he was put on the books as a potential agent and given the codename 'Junior'. Ruser suggested that Jebsen should talk to the British.

On 18 September, Jebsen called at the British Embassy in Madrid in a highly agitated state to ask about the possibility of being evacuated. He told an attaché that he suspected Kammler had installed listening equipment in his apartment and that his 'secret understanding' with his friend Dusko Popov might have been exposed. 'He wanted to find out if the Abwehr were after him as well as the Gestapo,' the embassy reported to London. 'If they were, then Tricycle was blown, in which case Jebsen would fake his suicide and try, in a suicide note, to protect Dreadnought.'[1]

In fact Jebsen had already written a long, rambling and emotional 'suicide note', addressed to the head of Abwehr III in Madrid, to cover his expected disappearance. In it he explained that he had been driven to kill himself by a conflict of loyalty between his country and his friend Popov, who had confessed to him in Lisbon that he had been turned by the British some time ago. 'I know that it would have been my duty to report these facts immediately,' he wrote:

> I did not do this . . . I know that a Court Martial would condemn me to death for what I have done. By taking this step myself, I am hoping to save the Abwehr the shame and my wife the disgrace to bear a soiled name . . . Do not be afraid that there will be a scandal. I shall cover up all traces carefully. I shall send my things to my Father Confessor for the poor. Then I shall take poison and swim far out into the sea. It may be days before my corpse will be washed up and it will then be no longer recognisable . . .[2]

Jebsen emphasised in his letter that 'Paula' – the German codename for Ivo – was still genuine and could be relied upon to continue his work in Serbia. MI5 was sceptical that it would have provided any protection for Popov's brother: 'This may have been Artist's intention, but it is difficult to believe that it would have succeeded or that the whole of his plan for a faked suicide was other than a piece of extreme foolishness brought about by an excess of nervous strain.'[3] To the relief of MI5, the letter was never sent.

Ironically, MI5 knew from Ultra intercepts that Jebsen's fears were groundless – he was not being recalled to Berlin to be arrested or to face an inquiry into his conduct, but simply to make a routine report. He could not, however, be told that he had nothing to worry about without his realising that British intelligence was reading the Abwehr's radio traffic. The best MI5 could manage was to ask Popov to send a telegram to Jebsen in Madrid stating his conviction that none of their conversations could have been overheard. The British were anxious to persuade Jebsen that he did not need to be evacuated – he was of little use to MI5 in Britain, but could be an invaluable asset if he stayed with the Abwehr. As an MI5 memorandum observed: 'We should attempt to make capital from the démarche, should Johnny throw in his lot unconditionally with us.'

Over the next few days Jebsen recovered some of his confidence. He turned down an offer of sanctuary in the British Embassy and managed to avoid being recalled to Berlin by offering to report to the Abwehr leadership when Admiral Canaris and a retinue of senior aides were due to visit Madrid in early October. Once he had calmed down he began to regret making direct contact with the British. Although he was convinced that Kammler was still plotting against him, he judged the worst charge that could be laid against him was one of treasonable carelessness and indiscretion – a charge that other Abwehr officers had survived. However, if he continued his contacts with the British, the dangers he ran were grave. He was also smitten by a pang of conscience at the prospect of no longer being able to pretend he was anything other than a traitor to his country.

MI5, meanwhile, was anxious to draw Jebsen further into its embrace and maintained contact with him via the MI6 head of station in Madrid. There was discussion in London about advising Jebsen to take advantage of the Abwehr leader's visit to Madrid by telling Canaris personally about his difficulties with the Gestapo: 'It was thought that such a course might clear the air and possibly also result in Jebsen hearing things of interest from Canaris which might be reported back to us. It was decided, however, that as we have no knowledge of Canaris being in Madrid except from sources which must at all costs be protected it was impracticable to act upon this suggestion.'[4]

In fact Jebsen had already made plans to use Canaris' visit to test his position within the Abwehr. At his interview with the admiral he adopted the self-righteous attitude of one falsely accused, lodged a formal protest about Kammler's machinations in Berlin to discredit him – friends kept him informed about what Kammler was saying – and threatened to resign from the Abwehr unless he was given permission to return to Portugal to continue handling Popov's case under von Karsthoff. He reckoned that if he was still under suspicion, Canaris would insist that he returned to

Berlin, in which case Jebsen intended to ask the British to evacuate him without delay. In the event, he was given permission to return to Portugal.

Assured that his position within the Abwehr was secure, he tried, unsuccessfully, to cut off his contacts with British intelligence. He was advised, in no uncertain terms, that it was too late. 'At first, Artist wished to break off contact and continue as before,' MI5 noted. 'We have pointed out to him, however, that he has already taken an irrecoverable step and that if, as he says, he wishes to do everything possible to damage the Nazi regime, then he need have no scruples in playing with us.'[5]

On a different tack, Jebsen tried to protect himself by making discreet enquiries about the possibility of resuming his original Danish nationality. Although he was born in Hamburg, both his parents and his grandparents were Danish and he had held Danish nationality until the age of twelve, when his father became a naturalised German citizen and Johnny automatically followed suit. Resuming his former nationality would not only ease his conscience, but – in the event of his exposure, court martial and execution by the Germans – might offer some protection to his wife, Lore, an actress. Lore was living with her parents in Leipzig and saw little of her husband, partly because he was constantly travelling and partly because he kept a mistress in Paris. While their marriage was hardly perfect (at one point Jebsen wanted to marry a secretary at the German Legation in Lisbon), Jebsen felt a sense of responsibility towards Lore and felt she would be in less danger if she could argue that her husband had been working on behalf of his real Fatherland.

Friends in Copenhagen had assured Jebsen that it was feasible, in principle, for him to become a Danish citizen, but in reality it was virtually impossible. He would need to file his application in Copenhagen and, because of his continuing problems with the Gestapo, he was reluctant to travel through Germany en route to Denmark. Even if his application could be processed from a distance, it was certain to be reported to the Abwehr by German officials overseeing the administration of the occupied country.

Jebsen decided to ask his new 'friends' in MI5 if it might be possible to acquire citizenship via the Danish government-in-exile in London. 'The matter would, of course, require the utmost secrecy,' an MI5 report pointed out:

Artist emphasises that if he had Danish nationality he would be prepared to take greater risks on our behalf. He realises fully that if he were caught by the Abwehr, his Danish nationality would not save his life, but he is genuinely concerned as to his wife's position in the event of his execution and anxious to remove, in his own eyes, the stigma of treason.[6]

In the end, his application was overtaken by events.

Now that 'Artist' was apparently ready to succumb to the blandishments of British intelligence, there was concern in the higher echelons of MI5 that bringing him into the fold would entail unwarranted risks at a time when Operation Fortitude, the D-Day deception plan, was getting into gear. Jebsen knew too much. If he was arrested, it was likely he would reveal, under torture, that his friend Popov had been a double agent working for the British since the beginning of the war. This would mean that Popov's growing network would have to be dismantled. But there were also fears that Jebsen knew the identity of 'Garbo', an agent who was to play a pivotal role in Fortitude.

'Garbo' was the codename for an enterprising Spaniard by the name of Juan Pujol, who had created an entirely fictitious network of spies which was held in the highest regard by the Germans. A former poultry farmer and the manager of a small hotel, Pujol had offered his services to British intelligence early on in the war, but was rejected because of suspicions that he was a German agent. Undaunted, he made contact with the Abwehr and was recruited to spy for Germany from Britain with the codename 'Arabel'. In fact he stayed in Lisbon, concocting colourful reports using tourist guides and reference books that he found in public libraries and scanning British newspapers, which were widely available in neutral Portugal. He started recruiting sub-agents – all of them imaginary – to cement the Abwehr's belief that he really was in London.

By the spring of 1942 he was starting to have difficulty answering the Abwehr's ever-increasing demands for information and decided he could best advance his private war against the Nazis by making contact, once again, with the British authorities in Lisbon. 'Arabel' was well known to British intelligence through Ultra intercepts, and extensive efforts had been made to track him down. When MI5 realised that he had never set foot in England and had created a bogus network from scratch, it was an opportunity too good to miss. In the summer of 1942 Pujol was smuggled into England to continue his work for the Abwehr under the aegis of the XX Committee. By January of 1944 he had sent some 400 secret letters to Germany and transmitted nearly 4,000 messages by radio. The grateful Germans believed he had a network of fourteen sub-agents and eleven well-placed contacts, including one in the Ministry of Information, eventually awarded him the Iron Cross and paid him around £31,000 (more than £800,000 at today's values) to maintain his network.

He was too valuable to MI5 to be put at risk, and some members of the XX Committee argued that recruiting Jebsen would do just that, since he could not be trusted. Ian Wilson leaped to Jebsen's defence:

I entirely disagree that he is correctly described as unscrupulous and dishonest. As far as we are concerned there is abundant evidence that Artist, although he may be unscrupulous and dishonest towards the present German government, has not only been taking every care to protect the double agents of whom he has knowledge, but has been deliberately sending out agents with the knowledge that they would double cross and has supported Tricycle's brother in his anti-German activities on other lines . . . I am satisfied that on the whole Jebsen has been endeavouring to tell the truth to Tricycle and has been doing so in the knowledge that Tricycle will pass the information to the British.[7]

Wilson also held out an irresistible carrot: his belief that Jebsen had not, by far, told Popov everything he knew, and that he knew a great deal that would be of interest to MI5.

The sceptics were overruled and on 10 November 1943, Major Frank Foley of MI6 and Ian Wilson of MI5 flew to Lisbon to debrief Jebsen. Popov was on the same flight, but ostentatiously travelling alone. They made no acknowledgement of each other while passing through immigration controls at Lisbon airport and went their separate ways outside – the intelligence officers to the British Embassy, and Popov to his usual room at the Palacio in Estoril, carrying his Yugoslav diplomatic bag stuffed with undeveloped photographs, documents and voluminous notes from which he would dictate his report. The XX Committee, still anxious to bolster his status with the Germans, had provided him with intelligence that was an improvement, both in quality and quantity, over that with which he had previously been supplied.

Acutely aware that his luck could run out at any time, Popov had taken to carrying a gun (a Luger in a shoulder holster) while in Lisbon. He very nearly used it, with what would have been disastrous consequences, at his meeting with von Karsthoff. He had walked to the agreed rendezvous, been picked up by a car and driven to von Karsthoff's new villa, hiding in the back as usual as it was driven into the garage. He was met by a girl he did not recognise, a new secretary. She showed him into the drawing room and said she would let Herr Karsthoff know that he had arrived. Popov was standing by a pair of glazed doors looking out onto the garden when he heard von Karsthoff say, with what seemed at the time to be some menace, 'Turn around slowly, Ivan, and don't make any sudden move.' The German had entered the room without making a sound. Popov knew, at that moment, that the game was up. He had been betrayed; he was certain that von Karsthoff had a gun trained on him. He reached into his jacket for the Luger and began to turn, but as he did so he had a clear view of von Karsthoff's reflection in the glass of the door. The German was alone, completely unarmed, standing sheepishly in the centre of the room with a small monkey sitting on his shoulder.

Popov took his hand off his gun, turned to face von Karsthoff and burst out laughing with relief. Von Karsthoff pretended to be offended. 'What's the matter?' he asked. 'Do I look so ridiculous?' Popov, adrenaline still pumping, shook his head. The German explained that the monkey had been given to him a couple of days previously by an agent from south-west Africa and wasn't yet completely tame and might bite if startled. Popov said nothing about what had been going through his head, or that he had been preparing to kill the man he had got to know and like, almost as a friend.

Von Karsthoff was pleased with the material Popov had brought over, even though the photographs turned out to be over-exposed and worthless (they had been taken hurriedly by an MI5 photographer on the morning Popov left London). The German told Popov that Admiral Canaris had recently been in Lisbon and had expressed the view that 'Ivan' was not worth what he was being paid, but said that this new report might change his mind.

Jebsen was also in Lisbon when Popov arrived and the two friends were able to meet for the first time without play-acting and pretence. As events turned out, this new-found freedom in their relationship would be all too brief, but for the time being they could relax, with no barriers between them. It meant, for example, that Popov could ask Jebsen's opinion on the material he was due to hand over to von Karsthoff. Jebsen advised him to suppress one particular document, which he did not think that von Karsthoff would accept as genuine.

Popov's mission in Lisbon, ostensibly on behalf of his government, was to oversee the travel arrangements for the first 'escaper' from Yugoslavia. This was to be a test run before small groups of Yugoslav officers were moved along the same route – groups that the Germans intended to infiltrate with their own agents. The arrangement perfectly typified the byzantine complexity of deception operations. The first 'escaper' was to be another candidate recruited by Ivo in Belgrade, allegedly willing to spy for Germany from Britain, but actually ready to work for the Allies. The Abwehr was financing and facilitating the escape route as a means of getting agents into Britain and in the belief that it was being organised by the Yugoslav government-in-exile, whereas in fact it was entirely under the control of MI5. The Yugoslav government knew that Popov was working for British intelligence, but knew nothing of his activities as a double agent. At the centre of this web of deceit was Popov himself, cheerfully manipulating half a dozen different cover stories while his life hung by a thread.

By happy circumstance, the first 'escaper' was an old friend of the Popov family, the Marquis Frano de Bona. The scion of one of the oldest aristocratic families in Dubrovnik (de Bonas had lived in the city since the fifteenth century), the marquis was a lieutenant commander in the Yugoslav navy, just a year older than Ivo, who had little difficulty persuading him that he could perform valuable work in Britain as an Abwehr wireless operator secretly working for the Allies.

De Bona was first sent to Belgrade, where he was given a new identity, as a Herr Guttman, and an extensive briefing by Müntzinger, who was unusually forthcoming. Indeed, when de Bona was debriefed in London, some MI5 officers came to the conclusion that Müntzinger was using the Yugoslav as a messenger. The German made no secret of his view that the war was lost, and de Bona got the impression that he was speaking for some anti-Nazi faction within the Abwehr when he talked about a willingness 'on their side' to get rid of Hitler; to obtain terms; to bring into being any form of democratic government acceptable to the British and Americans; to withdraw from all occupied territories; to accept Allied conditions about frontiers (providing Germany remained untouched); and to come to any terms that would not impair Germany's ability to resist the threat of Communism. From his conversation with Müntzinger, de Bona felt that once the Germans believed there was a chance of a deal, the German government would find the means to approach the British government for terms, provided they could oust Hitler.

Müntzinger told de Bona he would be working with Ivo's brother, who was a very good agent, although very expensive. His primary mission was political. The marquis was to use his aristocratic background to join the right clubs and make friends with British 'lords', impressing upon them the dangers of Communism in the hope that they might lobby the British government to grant Germany terms. De Bona was to try and convince influential and aristocratic circles of the danger of forcing Germany to capitulate, thereby handing the whole continent to Bolshevik Russians. He was to inform the Abwehr, by wireless and secret writing, of his progress and pass on the names of people he found receptive to his ideas.

De Bona was ordered to report to Abwehr headquarters in Paris for training. Ivo accompanied him to Paris and was hoping to continue with him to Madrid to meet Dusko, but at the last minute he was recalled to Belgrade, to his great disappointment. The Abwehr had taken over the elegant Hotel Lutetia on the Boulevard Raspail; de Bona amused himself at the Lutetia by executing exaggerated parodies of the Nazi salute, accompanied by energetic clicking of the heels, without once raising an eyebrow among the humourless Germans.

After a brief training course as a wireless operator, he travelled south by train – first class, of course – to San Sebastián, on the Franco-Spanish border, where he was met by Jebsen, who smuggled de Bona across the border, hidden in the boot of a car with German CD plates; he then continued to Madrid for an emotional rendezvous with Popov, who had only just arrived in the Spanish capital, having been delayed by tedious visa problems in Lisbon. Popov, now wearing his hat as a representative of the Yugoslav government, handed de Bona over to the MI6 head of station, who was to arrange his passage to Britain via Gibraltar.

De Bona was supposed to have been accommodated in an MI6 safe house in the Madrid suburbs, but he turned up his aristocratic nose at the prospect and moved instead into a brothel in the city centre, where he stayed for four happy days. It was, he told Popov later, like living in a harem.

Given yet another identity, as 'Peter Benwin', a Canadian farmer, he travelled to Gibraltar on a refugee train and was escorted over the border by the local MI6 representative. While waiting for a flight to Britain he underwent a routine medical check and discovered that his sojourn in the brothel had left him, embarrassingly, with more than just happy memories. The naval doctor was not, however, unaccustomed to dealing with such problems. Bad weather forced de Bona to wait four days for a flight to Britain, where he arrived in mid-December.

In London he moved into Popov's rented cottage in Rutland Gate and was given the mystifying codename of 'Freak'. Some months later, according to MI5 files, a military investigation was mounted into allegations that 'members of the ATS [the women's Auxiliary Territorial Service] were being induced to Clock House for immoral purposes'. MI5 hastily called off the investigation and warned Popov and de Bona to 'stop drawing attention to themselves in this manner'.

After de Bona had left Madrid for Gibraltar, Jebsen and Popov returned to Lisbon by car, travelling a day apart. Jebsen seemed to feel that his problems with the Gestapo had, by then, been largely resolved. On 4

December, in conditions of great secrecy, he had the first of a number of meetings with Foley and Wilson, during which he handed over a wealth of information about the organisation of the Abwehr, operational intelligence and the internal situation in Germany, much of it in reports that he had typed himself in preparation for his debriefing. Some of what he had to say was rather embarrassing for British intelligence – he provided, for example, sufficient information about 'Garbo' for him to be arrested at once, had he not already been under British control. Foley and Wilson wanted to prevent Jebsen from learning which agents were under British control, but they recognised that it would be virtually impossible. If he supplied information about an agent and that agent continued operating, it would have been reasonable for him to conclude that the agent was controlled. They considered winding up the Tricycle network, evacuating Jebsen to Britain and using him as a 'reference library', rather than run the risk of leaving him at large in Spain and Portugal, but in the end they concluded that the advantages of continuing outweighed the risks.

They made a deal with Jebsen that after the war, provided they were satisfied he had helped them to the best of his ability and had concealed nothing, British intelligence would use its 'best endeavours' to help him regain his Danish nationality; would guarantee him freedom of travel to pursue his business interests; and would protect him from any charges that might result from his involvement in illegal currency dealing. Jebsen was also assured that any genuine German agents captured as a result of his cooperation would be spared the death penalty, and that his wife, Lore, would be 'looked after'.

In truth Jebsen had pretty much proved his *bona fides* with the British by tipping them off, the previous month, that Hans Ruser, 'Junior', was about to be recalled to Germany. Concerned that under questioning he might, intentionally or unintentionally, blow both Tricycle and 'Artist', British intelligence spirited him away in the dead of night. He emerged, several weeks later, in London under the protection of MI5. Acting on Jebsen's warning that Ruser was very close to his mother and that she probably knew as much as he did, the lady also disappeared from Germany and turned up in London for a tearful reunion with her son.

During his debriefings, Jebsen painted a picture of the Abwehr as an organisation riddled by petty jealousies and in a state of bureaucratic chaos. Müntzinger, the officer ultimately in charge of Popov's case, was not untypical: he had no filing system of any kind in his office and relied entirely on the memory of his assistant, who had recently been transferred to Budapest. The Abwehr, Jebsen said, was generally demoralised and cynical and the 'whole of the OKW [*Oberkommando der Wehrmacht,*

German Army High Command] had known for at least a year that Germany has lost the war'.

Jebsen confessed to Foley and Wilson that he had known from the start that the Yugoslavs being recruited by Ivo in Belgrade would double-cross Germany, and handed over a copy of a 'lengthy and ingenious'[8] memorandum which he had prepared for Berlin outlining the German end of the escape route. Under the plan, Jebsen was to present himself to the Yugoslavs and the British as a disgruntled member of HWK, *Handelsundwirtschaftskrieg*, the department for trade and economic warfare, who had no intention of returning to Germany, but was staying on the Iberian peninsula and endeavouring to curry favour with Allied governments.

To Foley and Wilson the plan was a real bonus, since it provided Jebsen with legitimate reasons to make contact with the Allies and perfect cover for delivering his reports. But, as always, they analysed the risk, attempting to anticipate every convoluted eventuality and explore the possible consequences. It was a byzantine game of second-guessing, played for the highest possible stakes:

> If the Germans ever become aware that the British have come to learn from some source or other (such as an Abwehr turncoat) that Artist was connected with the Abwehr and not H.W.K., then they might well argue that British suspicion must fall on the escape route and its organiser Tricycle; and if, after the British are assumed to have acquired this ground of suspicion, Tricycle's activities as an agent continued, the Germans might from this correctly conclude that he was controlled. There is no evidence that the Abwehr are likely to embark on this somewhat involved course of reasoning, but it remains a possible risk.[9]

Jebsen was also able to provide Ian Wilson with an insight into how other agents in Popov's network were viewed by the Germans. Wilson asked Jebsen if he thought it would be good idea for 'Balloon' (Dick Metcalfe, Popov's first sub-agent) to visit Lisbon. Jebsen was doubtful: it would require 'Balloon' to play his part exceptionally well and, as he was not regarded in the same favourable light as Popov, he might have a more difficult reception. 'Balloon' was not under suspicion, Jebsen added, but the Germans thought he was lazy, had no judgement and believed that while he was happy to sell information for money, he was unlikely, as an Englishman, to provide really vital intelligence detrimental to his country.

Jebsen said he had not seen the 'Meteor' traffic (confirming what the

British already knew from Ultra – that 'Meteor's' messages were passed direct to Berlin undeveloped), but he had heard that 'Meteor' (the Yugoslav, Eugen Sostaric) was regarded by the Germans as, potentially, an extremely valuable agent. No one, to Jebsen's knowledge, had expressed any doubts about him. Jebsen suggested that 'The Worm', who had been agitating about not receiving money or acknowledgements of his letters, should stop writing for a while, if for no other reason than that it could raise suspicions if all the agents kept writing without any hitch. Wilson sent a note to London recommending that 'The Worm' should send an ultimatum to Lisbon threatening to stop writing altogether if he was not paid immediately.

In a report to MI5, Foley and Wilson attempted to analyse Jebsen's 'highly complex' motives for cooperating with the British. They concluded that Ivo Popov, 'who by all accounts has a dominating person-ality', was a major influence and then listed other factors: a genuine dislike of Nazism; a belief in the British political system; a conviction, dating at least from the failure of the first German offensive against Russia, that Germany had lost the war; a fear of Communism in Germany, which could only, in Jebsen's view, be avoided by increased English influence in western Europe; a contempt for the inefficiency and corruption in the Abwehr; the realisation that his own future as an influential businessman depended on the restoration of normal trading activities in Europe, which he thought would be possible only after an Anglo-American victory; and a desire to reinsure himself.

'No doubt Artist is acting mainly out of self interest,' the report concluded, 'but of a clear-sighted and long-term character which, to a man of his undoubted intelligence, seems likely to prevent him from trying to deceive us.' Wilson added a personal note: 'I am convinced that Artist sincerely desires to continue to work wholeheartedly with us and is too far sighted to feed us with information which ultimately we would be able to prove was false.'[10]

While his friend was secretly closeted with British intelligence, Popov continued with his usual routine, meeting von Karsthoff frequently. He would later report that von Karsthoff seemed to being doing rather well for himself, having bought a new Cadillac and a *quinta* (farmhouse) near Colares, about five miles from Sintra. Popov's status with the Germans certainly seemed to be high: Jebsen had shown Ian Wilson a personal letter he had received from Müntzinger congratulating him on Popov's good work in fulsome terms. And when von Karsthoff returned from an Abwehr conference in Baden-Baden looking like a cat with two tails, he confided in Popov ('although I should not really be telling you this') that it was generally accepted that Popov was the Abwehr's best agent in Britain. Earlier von Karsthoff admitted he had had reports from Britain that Popov was associating with fervently pro-British Yugoslavs and congratulated him on maintaining such excellent cover.

None of this was cause for complacency, as Popov was quickly to discover when there was another scare that his cover was about to be blown. Out of the blue, a Portuguese by the name of Martins contacted British intelligence in Lisbon and confessed that he had been providing cover addresses for two German agents in Britain. Not only did he know their codenames – 'Balloon' and 'Gelatine' – but he also knew their real identities, as his firm had been used by the Germans to send payment to them. In London there was anxiety at this unexpected development. If 'Balloon' and 'Gelatine' suddenly stopped writing, the Germans would assume they had been arrested and that the 'arrest' of Popov would surely follow. If 'Balloon' and 'Gelatine' continued writing, Martins would in a short time suspect that they were controlled by the British and his suspicions might get back to the Germans, inevitably blowing Popov's cover, since he had introduced both to the Germans. While MI5 was pondering how to handle the situation, fate stepped in to deal with the problem. With impeccable timing, the Abwehr resolved MI5's difficulties by suddenly deciding that the ink being used by 'Balloon' and 'Gelatine' was insecure. Both were instructed to stop writing until new inks could be supplied – by the trusty Popov.

Along with the new secret ink, Popov was given a cover address, money and instructions to take back to England for 'Gelatine'. He was ordered not to disclose to her that he had acted as a courier, but merely to drop the material through her letter box. Von Karsthoff told Popov that while her work was quite satisfactory, she obviously did not know what was important. At times she reported a lot of rubbish, but occasionally what she picked up was of interest, and there was always the chance that, without realising it, she would pick up something of special importance. 'Balloon' was not similarly favoured: the Germans decided that in view of his recent disgruntled letters there was no point in supplying him with new ink without an accompanying large sum of money, and it was not possible to obtain authorisation for payment from Berlin before Popov left Lisbon.

Popov, unusually, had no cause to complain about his own finances. Capitalising on his newly augmented reputation, he was somehow able to persuade the Germans, for the first time, to pay him three months' salary ($7,500) in advance, on top of the three months he was owed in arrears. He insisted on payment in dollars to avoid being landed with more forgeries and deposited the cash, temporarily, in the safe at the Palacio

Hotel. A bizarre sequence of events followed. A German agent in the hotel, known to British intelligence as 'Viper', removed Popov's package from the safe and delivered it to the Abwehr in the belief that it contained important Allied diplomatic papers. Popov was highly amused when von Karsthoff told him what had happened and returned the money. MI5 was less amused and considered 'Viper' to be a potential threat to Popov's security. While the British were pondering how to remove him from his position at the hotel, fate intervened once again: 'Viper' was caught, red-handed, embezzling hotel funds and summarily fired.

With $15,000 deposited in a hotel safe, Popov might have had no cause to complain about money, but that certainly did not stop him. Von Karsthoff was all too familiar with Popov's cavilling litany and was provoked into an uncharacteristic slip one afternoon when the Yugoslav was lamenting the inadequacy of the funds he had been given for his growing network; which, he said, was keeping Lisbon informed of everything that was going on, 'short of a detailed account of Churchill's digestive processes'. Karsthoff suddenly snapped: 'We pay for what we get. You could earn millions if you gave us something really spectacular.' When Popov raised an eyebrow, the German justified his claim by asserting that 'huge sums' were being paid to another agent who was supplying 'incredible information'. 'Like what?' Popov asked. 'Like the minutes of the Teheran conference,' von Karsthoff replied triumphantly, referring to the meeting a few days earlier at which Churchill, Roosevelt and Stalin had agreed on a grand design for final victory against Germany and had signed a lofty declaration about ensuring a post-war world free of tyranny.

Popov began prodding the German for more details, but von Karsthoff would not be drawn, beyond saying that the man lived not far from Dubrovnik, but was not a Yugoslav. Popov passed this on to MI5, suggesting that if the agent was not Yugoslav, he would probably be Albanian, since that was the nearest border to Dubrovnik. He turned out to be Elyesa Bazna, the Albanian valet to the British ambassador in Turkey, Sir Hughe Knatchbull-Huggessen. Given the codename 'Cicero' by the Germans, Bazna had made a duplicate key to the ambassador's dispatch box and begun photographing vital documents, which he passed to the Germans. Over the course of some ten months Bazna was said to have been paid around £300,000 by the Germans, largely in counterfeit notes. He was never caught and after the war he attempted, unsuccessfully, to sue the German government for money he claimed he was still owed.

One of Popov's attributes as an agent was that he was always alert. One afternoon he was picked up for a *Treff* by two secretaries in an unmarked car and, as he slipped quickly into the back seat, he heard the driver say:

'It's easier with him than with Dickie – Dickie takes half an hour to manoeuvre his fat behind onto the back seat,' which made the other woman laugh. Popov knew someone called Dickie who was very fat and lived at the Palacio Hotel. Something of a mysterious figure, he was said to be an Austrian political refugee who worked in some menial role for the US Embassy, but apparently had sufficient means to stay at the Palacio. Popov knew little about him other than that he never had much success with women, refused to join in parties going to the casino or other places and spent much of his leisure time in the cinema. Popov determined to discover if he was the same Dickie mentioned by the German secretary.

Using a cinema to disappear for an hour or two was a routine ploy for a spy and so, the next time Dickie headed for the cinema in the casino complex, Popov was on his tail. He waited until the fat man had gone in before buying a ticket and settling into a seat in the back row. Ten minutes after the movie had started, Dickie got up from his seat and slipped out of a side door. Popov followed at a discreet distance. Very close to a rendezvous point often used by Popov, Dickie got into a parked car that Popov recognised as belonging to the Abwehr. The next day he reported what he had seen to MI5, which passed the information on to the US Embassy. The fat man was arrested, almost immediately confessed that he had been selling sensitive documents to the Germans and claimed he had been blackmailed. To try and save his skin, he denounced a young Portuguese servant working at the embassy, who was also in the pay of the Germans and who, when arrested, was found to be in possession of a duplicate key, newly made, to one of the embassy safes.

By mid-December 1943, Popov was pressing the Germans to allow him to return to London. He told them that as all the arrangements for the next batch of escapees had been made, he had no excuse to offer the Yugoslav government for staying on. The truth was that he wanted to be back in London because he had heard that MI5 had finally succumbed to his entreaties and arranged for the evacuation to London of his friend Ljiljana Bailoni from Lisbon. MI5 was not in the least motivated by a desire to accommodate another of their agent's love affairs, but was concerned that she might know too much about Popov. Thus it was thought wiser to get her out of the way.

Popov's departure was delayed because the Abwehr in Lisbon was endeavouring to obtain 'special questions' from Berlin, for which he was going to be paid a bonus. While he was waiting, Jebsen, acting on orders from MI5, recruited him as an unofficial informant for the *Sicherheitsdienst* (SD), the Nazi party's intelligence service, which worked alongside the

Gestapo. MI5 considered that currying favour with the SD might help Jebsen resolve his difficulties with the Gestapo and facilitate his early return to Germany on behalf of British intelligence. This was an attractive prospect since Jebsen had indicated that if he could get back to Germany, he could probably get some up-to-date information about the new rocket weapons Germany was developing.

One of Jebsen's contacts in Lisbon was his friend Klaus Henss, a former police officer who had been pushed into SD work rather against his will. The SD was forbidden from using Abwehr agents abroad and, when Henss complained to Jebsen about the difficulty of obtaining political information from Britain, Jebsen said he might be able to help. With the blessing of MI5, he arranged for Henss and Popov to meet. Popov accepted a long questionnaire about the political situation in Britain, industrial strikes, rationing, the views in City circles of the war and the significance of the recent change in Lord Beaverbrook's role in the War Cabinet to Lord Privy Seal. He also undertook to obtain copies of *Socialist Appeal*, *British Weekly* and the *Daily Worker*.

Popov spent Christmas with von Karsthoff and some of his friends in his *quinta*. They drank champagne and sang carols, but the mood was sombre. Berlin was under nightly attack by Allied bombers, much of the city had been reduced to smoking rubble and all the talk was of the coming invasion, following the announcement on Christmas Eve that General Dwight D. Eisenhower had been appointed supreme commander of the Allied invasion force. Von Karsthoff drew circles on a map indicating areas where the Allies could provide air cover and there was a long discussion about where, precisely, the enemy would choose to land.

After dinner they sat around a fire, but the logs – as if in sympathy with the atmosphere – refused to burn. Von Karsthoff threw a full package of candles into the fire and it blazed up suddenly. One of the guests, a naval attaché at the German Embassy, staring gloomily into the flames, said it was what Hitler should do: sacrifice some gains to defeat their most dangerous enemy, a coalition of extreme Bolsheviks and hardened capitalists. Popov asked who the candles represented. The attaché replied that everything to the south and west of Germany should be exchanged for a peace deal on the western front. He suggested that the Americans would jump at the chance of a deal, as no American wanted to die saving Russia. He continued in a similar vein about Germany being the saviour of Europe and its civilisation, shielding the world from the advance of Communism, all of which Popov would later faithfully report to British intelligence in London.

Early in the New Year Popov was given his final briefing by von

Karsthoff and was handed a lengthy questionnaire with the usual attention to detail:

> Information about air-planes must include exact number of each kind and if possible each type . . . It is absolutely necessary to give the correspondent dates of each information, for inst. the dates of dislocation or formation of a new unit, date of delivery of aircraft material to any of the above mentioned parts, date of the manufacture contract given to any firm. At least the date, as well as the source, of each obtained information should be given . . .[11]

As Popov was due to return to Lisbon in six to eight weeks, von Karsthoff advised him to use his new radio operator sparingly and to keep his messages brief; he could bring back the bulk of his information in person. The German also suggested to Popov that he should set up the transmitter outside London. 'It would be a silly thing', he said, 'for you to be killed by German weapons,' adding that there was no particular hurry since the new weapons would not be ready for at least another two months. Once again, this news significantly increased MI5's paranoia about the secret weapons being developed by Germany, although it would be June 1944 before the first V1 rockets – Londoners called them 'doodlebugs' – were unleashed against the south of England.

Popov returned to London on 5 January 1944 and was met at Paddington station by John Marriott, who took possession of all the papers he was carrying and asked if there was any urgent matter to be dealt with in the next few days. Yes, Popov breezily replied, he needed £250 in cash. Marriott sighed, but obliged.

On 11 January, Popov wrote in secret ink to Lisbon to report that he had arrived back safely and that the radio set would be in operation by 1 February. Meanwhile, he was also busy pulling strings on behalf of the lovely Ljiljana, who had moved into Clock House. On 12 January, J. C. Masterman wrote from the Reform Club to E. J. Passant at Sidney Sussex College, Cambridge, asking for help to obtain a place at Cambridge for a Lilian Bailony, twenty-one years old: 'One of our friends, known to you on paper though not personally, has become more or less the unofficial guardian . . . it would be really helpful and I think useful to the general cause if we could get the young lady into Cambridge . . . please do what you can for me in this matter.'

Jebsen, meanwhile, reported to MI5 that Colonel Georg Hansen, the head of Abwehr I, had described Popov as the Abwehr's best man in England. He wrote:

Their chief hope is to receive reports about the date of the landing in France. It would therefore not be clever of you to send no reports at all about the landing. Tricycle's camouflage will not be endangered if some dates are wirelessed with the remark that they are some General Staff officer's opinion, the accuracy of which it is not possible to check . . . It could also be reported that some General of importance had written a memorandum to prove that a landing before such and such a date would be undesirable and that this memorandum was being much discussed in General Staff circles . . . In any case, it is quite possible to deceive with regard to the date of the landing as, according to latest reports, Tricycle's reliability is no longer in doubt . . .[12]

12

Fortitude and Disaster

BY THE BEGINNING OF 1944, OPERATION FORTITUDE, THE MOST important and audacious of a multitude of ingenious plans designed to confuse and deceive the enemy about when the Allies would launch their assault on mainland Europe, was well under way. Managed centrally from the Cabinet office under the personal supervision of General 'Pug' Ismay, Churchill's chief of staff, its function was in essence to persuade the German Army High Command (OKW) that the Normandy landings were a feint and that the real invasion would come a few days later at the narrowest point in the English Channel – the Pas de Calais. The stakes were formidable: if Fortitude failed, there was every possibility that Hitler would pour his best troops into Normandy and sweep the invaders back into the sea with terrible losses, inscribing D-Day into the history books not as the greatest victory of the war, but as the greatest defeat.

Fundamental to the success of Fortitude was the need to convince the Germans that, at the very moment Allied troops were landing on the beaches of Normandy, a massive army of fifty divisions and one million men under the command of Lieutenant General George S. Patton was still encamped in southern England, waiting in the wings to undertake the real invasion. Thanks to reports from its spies in Britain (all under Allied control), the Germans believed this force was called the First US Army Group (FUSAG).

FUSAG did not exist. Its equipment, its landing craft, its tanks, its camps, its ammunition dumps, its field hospitals, its artillery and its trucks were all entirely fake, fabricated from scaffolding, poles, canvas, rubber and camouflage paint. One of Britain's leading architects, Basil Spence, designed and constructed an enormous 'supply dock' at Dover, covering three square miles of the foreshore, complete with jetties, storage tanks, pipelines and a power station – none of it real. Another imaginary formation – the British 4th Army – was allegedly stationed in Scotland, preparing to invade Scandinavia. This plan was Fortitude North, designed to keep the twenty-seven German divisions stationed in Norway pinned down and unavailable to help defend Normandy.

No one played a more important role in persuading the OKW to accept myth as reality than the double agents of the XX Committee, of whom there were fifteen still 'live', seven with wireless transmitters. From the beginning of 1944, the entire resources of the XX Committee were devoted to Fortitude. Case officers had daily meetings at SHAEF (Supreme Headquarters Allied Expeditionary Force) to concoct the information that would be fed to the enemy, like pieces of a jigsaw, to create a wholly false picture. The risks were horrendous. If one piece failed to fit, the whole charade could be exposed, leading to the danger that the Germans would start reading the agents' message 'in reverse' and thereby accurately divine Allied intentions. The analogy drawn by MI5 was musical: the 'orchestra' of double agents all needed to be playing the same symphony in tune. Those agents in whom the Germans reposed special trust were given the leading role in Operation Fortitude and were known as the 'first violins'. Tricycle, of course, was a 'first violin'.

In fact, the Tricycle group was initially banned from taking part in Fortitude for fear of repercussions if Jebsen was arrested, but Ian Wilson thought it was madness not to make use of one of their most valuable agents and lobbied hard for his inclusion. 'There can be no doubt that at the moment Tricycle's stock in the eyes of the Abwehr is extremely high,' he argued in a memorandum dated 23 December 1943; 'he was treated like a hero in Lisbon.'[1]

Wilson laid out a compelling case for using the Yugoslav. Doubts about Tricycle and Artist within the Abwehr had been 'completely dispelled' and the theory that Artist was in imminent danger was exaggerated. Even if he was arrested by the Gestapo and forced to confess that Tricycle's organisation was controlled by the British, it was unlikely the Abwehr would believe it. 'All Abwehr officers from highest to lowest have a vested interest in supporting the bona fides of Tricycle and I very much doubt if any of them would have the moral courage to admit that for years they had been fooled and had spent enormous sums of money running a British agent.'[2]

Wilson's argument won the XX Committee round and the ban on the Tricycle group participating in Operation Fortitude was lifted, although his assessment of the risk to Artist was grossly under-estimated, as events would soon prove.

In early February, Erich Vermehren, an Abwehr officer in Istanbul, defected to the Allies with his wife, the former Countess Elizabeth von

Plettenburg. Vermehren was a close friend of Jebsen, and Jebsen frequently visited Vermehren's mother, who was stationed in Lisbon as a foreign correspondent for a German newspaper. The connection was known to Berlin and instructions were sent to Lisbon to keep Jebsen under observation in case the Vermehrens tried to pass through Lisbon on their way to England.

Jebsen got wind of what was going on and contacted his MI6 controller on 14 February to warn him that he was again in trouble, tainted by his friendship with the Vermehrens. He had already made muddled plans to protect himself. If it came to a stand-off, he said, he would get word to the Gestapo that he had written a lengthy report containing everything he knew about the Abwehr and the SD, which he had lodged with a friend with instructions for it to be given to the British if anything happened to him. He would then try to break off relations with the Abwehr in such a way that Popov and his brother were protected and would continue to live quietly in Portugal. MI6 had little confidence that the plan would protect anybody.

A drama in Berlin far beyond Jebsen's control was soon to further endanger his position. In February, Admiral Canaris was summarily dismissed as head of the Abwehr. After some initial successes at the beginning of the war rounding up resistance networks in France, the Abwehr's reputation began to suffer after it failed to predict the Allied landings in North Africa in November 1942, and similarly failed to warn OKW of the invasion of Sicily in July 1943. Canaris was also involved in a long-running power struggle with Heinrich Himmler, who, as Reichsführer SS, controlled the Nazi party's own intelligence service, the SD. As the balance of power in Germany tilted increasingly against conservative elements like the Abwehr, in favour of hard-liners within the Nazi party (Himmler in particular), Canaris paid the price. Not long after the admiral's dismissal, Hitler announced that the Abwehr was to be merged with the SD to create a unified German secret service. It meant, effectively, that Jebsen was left high and dry, without the protection of his anti-Nazi friends in the Abwehr.

All this while Popov, in London, was making preparations for what would be his final, and most important, visit to Lisbon. As far as the Germans were concerned, his cover was to organise another batch of Yugoslav escapees. As far as MI5 was concerned, he was to deliver another movement of the symphony – a cunningly contrived package of deception material, including a large number of bogus observation reports on the order of battle, designed to conceal Allied plans to land in Normandy in June.

Popov visited all the areas mentioned in his observation reports so that he would be able to describe them, if necessary, under interrogation. Plausible stories were worked out as to where and how he had obtained all his information, which on this occasion was far more detailed than usual. Popov was also provided with many answers to the SD question-naire – and with an English raincoat as a gift for Klaus Henss, who had let it be known that he had always wanted one. With the writing on the wall for the Abwehr, MI5 was even more anxious that Popov should establish good relations with the SD.

At his final briefing, Ian Wilson was authorised to tell Popov that an account of his activities was given to Winston Churchill from time to time and that the prime minister showed 'considerable interest'. Popov was pleased, but anxious to get down to work, and began taking notes in Serbo-Croat of the report he was to dictate to the Germans:

> Preparations continue to be carried out but there are still no signs that invasion is imminent. I very much doubt if the date has even been finally fixed; I met an elderly officer whose duty it was to settle claims for damages done during military exercises in Kent and he was quite certain there was not going to be any invasion for a long time yet because in connection with his work he was supplied with details of forthcoming exercises in his area and they stretched right through the spring and summer. It was an 'open secret' that Montgomery had expressed great dissatisfaction with the state of training of the troops in England and that there were 'many indica-tions' that increased bombing activity is taking priority over invasion plans – Bomber Command seems to take priority in terms of manpower and supplies.

Popov was to point out that his information referred only to the inva-sion of France or the Low Countries; he had no knowledge of the threat to Norway from Scotland, as the utmost secrecy was maintained, but there were rumours that a large part of the east coast of Scotland was soon to be closed to the public. 'I know that members of the Norwegian govern-ment, who work in the same building as members of my own government at Kingston House, have great hopes of being home in Norway this summer . . . all the indications – security measures, close Anglo-Russian military co-operation, and political pressure on Finland – seem to point to Norway being the first target for assault.'[3]

Popov was also to try and get up-to-date intelligence about the devel-opment of the new secret weapons. He was to say that he was having difficulty finding a suitable house outside London for his wireless operator and was to ask if it was still really necessary. Fourteen days after his departure, 'Freak' was due to send a message saying he had found a place near Beaconsfield in Buckinghamshire and asking if he should rent it. MI5 hoped that the Germans' response would give them an idea of when the new weapons might be deployed.

Wilson impressed upon Popov that he was to take great care when meeting Artist and that he was to do everything possible to prevent him from becoming nervous or excited and doing something foolish; he was to reassure him, if he showed signs of agitation, that he was safe. These words would soon come back to haunt Wilson.

It was a measure of MI5's confidence in Tricycle that they allowed him to go to Lisbon at all at this critical stage in the development of Operation Fortitude. Alone among the deception orchestra, and certainly among the 'first violins', Popov was the only agent able to make direct, unsupervised, face-to-face contact with the enemy. All the other agents operated from the safety of Britain, communicating by wireless or secret writing, with MI5 controlling every word they transmitted or wrote. Popov, on the other hand, was trusted to deliver his intelligence personally, to lie with conviction, to act as if he really was a German spy, to survive interrogation and to socialise with his German controllers without ever making the fatal slip that would collapse the fragile house of cards being constructed by the XX Committee for the benefit of the German high command.

Two days before his departure, Popov had an audience with the queen mother of Yugoslavia, at her request. She told him she knew he was engaged in organising escape routes for Yugoslavs and asked if he could arrange for the escape of Branko Pogacnik, her private secretary, who was staying at the Hotel du Lac in Neuve Ville, Switzerland. Popov was the one man she could rely on, she said. She had no confidence in Yugoslav politicians, all of whom, in her view, were either looking out for their own private interests or those of their political factions, to the exclusion of the real interests of the country. Popov was impressed with her outlook and promised to try, but privately thought it was unlikely he would be able to help.

Popov left for Lisbon on 26 February 1944, carrying in a Yugoslav diplomatic bag an impressive portfolio of 'looted' documents, many subtly doctored to support Operation Fortitude and the notion of a great army gathering under canvas in the south-east of England. Included in the package was extraneous intelligence designed to indicate his continuing diligence as a spy: photographs of three Admiralty signals documents describing IFF [Identification Friend or Foe] apparatus; pilots' notes on a number of different aircraft; a doctored report by the Ministry of Home Security on the effect of German air-raids in 1943; a doctored reprint of a speech by the minister of production about the aircraft industry; an HMSO publication about rationing and food prices; and the *Exeter Express and Echo* dated 5 February, indicating that life was normal in the city.

He discovered when he arrived that von Karsthoff seemed to have been sidelined and he was to be debriefed by an SD officer, Oberstleutnant Alois Schreiber, who had a reputation for being a ruthless and brilliant interrogator. What followed made Popov's previous meetings with von Karsthoff seem like cosy fireside chats. The venue was a barren rented villa in Estoril, nothing like the comfortable quarters favoured by von Karsthoff. The questioning began at 7.30 in the evening and continued through the night, with only short breaks for beer and sandwiches. Schreiber, who seemed to need no sleep, spent the following day drawing pictures of Allied divisional signs, as described by Popov, to illustrate his report, and then the interrogation continued for another full night.

Ironically, Schreiber asked Jebsen to sit in on the debriefing; Jebsen played the role of hostile sceptic, asking barbed questions to ensure that Schreiber did not suspect any collaboration between them. While Schreiber had no reason to be suspicious of Popov, he cut no corners, taking Popov over his story again and again, questioning him closely on every detail of his report, particularly on all the places in Britain that he had visited and the sources for his hearsay information. Schreiber seemed especially interested in Popov's visits to Exeter, Kent and Hull. Much of the interrogation inevitably centred on the invasion. In accordance with the agreed plan, Popov said that while there were a lot of preparations, there was nothing pointing to imminent action. Specifically asked if he had seen larger-than-usual convoys of military vehicles passing through London, he said he had not; asked about the location of Eisenhower's headquarters, he said he thought they were in Grosvenor Square; asked if he had seen landing craft, he replied that he had seen small green boats made of canvas and wood on the back of lorries.

Popov stood up to the questioning well and only stumbled when he admitted he did not know what was in the photographs he had brought with him. He blustered, trying to explain it away by saying that he had copied the photographs from technical books that his wireless operator had obtained and had no time to try and understand the subject matter, although he had written down everything he could remember after meeting his air-force source. Schreiber chose not to pursue the matter.

Had Popov made a serious error – contradicting himself, for example

– during this marathon interrogation, he could have put at risk Operation Fortitude, not to mention his own life. As it was, he came through with flying colours. Baroness Marie Luise von Gronau, a secretary at the German Legation and a friend of Jebsen, who typed out Schreiber's notes, told Jebsen later that Schreiber had written a very laudatory report on the interrogation, that he had no suspicions and had committed himself to the view that Popov was an excellent agent, fit to be given most confidential tasks.

There followed an incident that would have played well in a slapstick comedy. In the febrile and uncertain atmosphere following Canaris' dismissal, many Abwehr officers were jockeying for position, looking for any opportunity to find favour with the new regime. Von Karsthoff was no exception. Since one of his primary assets was his network of spies in Britain, he was intent on having the honour of presenting Popov's report to Berlin, even if he had been prevented from taking part in the debriefing. He was, then, dismayed when a rival appeared on the scene.

Müntzinger, who had been nominally in charge of Popov's case since his recruitment, had been dismissed and replaced by one Wiegand, a peacetime lawyer similarly anxious to make a name for himself. When Wiegand arrived in Lisbon, apparently with the intention of collecting Popov's report, von Karsthoff was determined to thwart him. As soon as Marie von Gronau had finished typing the report, von Karsthoff picked up a copy and caught the first train for Berlin. Wiegand was furious when he heard what had happened and promptly began a frantic search for a flight that would get him to Berlin before von Karsthoff's train arrived. It seems that Wiegand won the race by a few hours, with disastrous results for von Karsthoff, who was removed from Lisbon and replaced by Wiegand. Von Karsthoff was eventually transferred to Austria, arrested by the Russians and executed. The antithesis of a hard-line Nazi, von Karsthoff had unconsciously played a significant role in Popov's success as a double agent. Like Popov, he appreciated the good things in life, and one of them was his comfortable posting in the amiable city of Lisbon, far from the war, where he enjoyed good food and wine and the company of his secretary/mistress, Elizabeth. Indolent and corrupt – he routinely took a 'commission' from payments made to Popov – his greatest concern was to maintain the status of his star agent as a German spy and thus protect his own position. The very last thing von Karsthoff wanted to happen was for his friend Popov to be revealed as a double agent. A more conscientious, less sociable individual might well have had doubts about Popov years earlier.

There was jubilation in London when, on 9 March, British intelligence intercepted a signal to OKW indicating that Popov's story about the Allies' order of battle had been swallowed whole:

> A V-mann [secret agent] . . . has brought particularly valuable information about the British formations in Great Britain. The reliability of the report could be checked [presumably with other double agents in Britain]. It contains information about three armies, three army corps and twenty-three divisions, among which the location of only one formation must be regarded as questionable. The report confirmed our own overall operational picture.[4]

An important part of the jigsaw that the XX Committee was constructing for the Germans had been put into place.

Popov, meanwhile, had discovered shortly after he arrived in Lisbon that the escape route (his cover for the visit) was falling apart. An attempt to send ten Yugoslavs along the route ran into trouble when two were arrested by the Gestapo crossing the Yugoslav frontier. They were subsequently released on the intervention of the Abwehr, but it was decided to abandon the idea of sending ten escapees at a time. When Popov got to Lisbon he found that the Germans had only arranged for one man to escape. He protested vigorously, insisting that the Germans produce more escapees or he would fail to satisfy his government and his cover would break down. Eventually other names were added to the list, including the queen mother's secretary, who was told he could join the escape route if he could make his own way to Paris.

For Popov, the highlight of the trip was unquestionably his long-awaited reunion with Ivo. He had insisted on his previous visit that the Germans arrange a meeting with his brother in order for them to discuss the organisation of the escape route. They were initially due to get together in Madrid, but when Popov was unable to get a Spanish visa, the Germans fixed documentation for Ivo to fly to Lisbon, where he arrived on 23 March, travelling with a false German passport in the name of Hans Poper.

Popov did not want to attract undue attention by waiting at the airport for Ivo's flight to arrive, so he arranged a rendezvous on the Lisbon–Estoril road. He parked on the hard shoulder in a car provided for him by the Yugoslav Legation, barely able to contain his excitement. Eventually Jebsen arrived in his Rolls-Royce with Ivo in the front passenger seat. It was the first time the brothers had seen each other for more than three years. They hugged, both of them close to tears, then retired to Popov's suite at the Palacio Hotel where, Popov recalled, they ate from room service and 'talked non stop for two days'.[5]

There was much to discuss apart from family news: three years of extraordinary adventures, with each brother, coincidentally and independently, playing a dangerous game of cat and mouse with the Germans. Ivo told his brother that a senior Abwehr officer in Paris had recently asked him if he thought Dusko was genuinely working for the Germans. Ivo replied that he had not seen his brother for three and a half years and in that time anyone could change, but he could not imagine Dusko, once having promised to work for the Germans, reneging on that promise. Ivo told the German he would make sure this was the case when he met his brother; he was planning to stop off in Paris on his way back to Belgrade to report that Dusko was 100 per cent reliable. Dusko laughed and offered to dream up hair-raising anecdotes about the many times he had narrowly escaped 'discovery' by British intelligence, which Ivo could pass on as proof of Dusko's loyalty to the Abwehr and willingness to take risks.

There was business to conduct, too. Popov had been asked by MI5 to get a full report from Ivo about the organisation and personalities of the Abwehr and the SD in Yugoslavia. No one was better qualified to provide this information than Dr Ivan Popov, who by sheer force of personality had managed to ingratiate himself with all the top German officials in his country. Popov told his brother that MI5 was on standby to arrange his immediate evacuation from Yugoslavia if he was in imminent danger. Ivo could call in their services by having a message – '*Macka je dobila devet macica*' ('the cat has nine kittens') – broadcast on the Yugoslav service of the BBC. After the message had been broadcast, Ivo was to go straight to Mihailovic's headquarters and report to the British Liaison Officer as 'Sveta Popovic'. Ian Wilson had arranged with the senior BLO that if a man calling himself Popovic arrived seeking protection, he should be given immediate refuge. Wilson cabled Ivo's description (height at least six foot one inch, slim, long fingers, green eyes, very large operation scar on stomach, speaks Serbo-Croat, French, German, Italian and a little English) to confirm his identity.

While Ivo was in Lisbon, the MI6 head of station arranged a discreet little dinner in his honour and sent a glowing report to London:

Ivo created the very best impression. He speaks with the authority and deep sincerity learned from his own experience of fighting for the Serbs under the cloak of collaboration with the Germans and witnessing the destruction of his country. This experience has left him his great personal charm but has given him a seriousness and depth of feeling which contrasts with Tricycle's expansive bonhomie.

Ivo was deeply moved whenever he spoke of Serbia, but never lost control of voice or power of expression. He explained the Abwehr organisation in Belgrade and how the two top men were not on speaking terms, enabling him to play one off against the other. 'I got the impression that he had carried this art of playing off one department of the Abwehr against the other to a high degree of perfection and that almost all his activity is conducted in this way.'[6]

Before Ivo left for Belgrade, via Paris, Popov made an attempt to persuade him to disappear until after the invasion, but Ivo insisted that he could not desert his friends in the resistance and that he must return. Popov warned him that if his friends were 'blown', he (Ivo) would be the first to be put up against a wall and shot. It made no difference, as Popov knew in his heart that it would not. Ivo was a man with a strict code of behaviour and well-defined views on duty and morality. He refused to discuss the matter further and left Lisbon the next day.

In truth, both brothers were gloomy about the future of Yugoslavia. Staunch royalists and supporters of General Mihailovic's underground army, the Chetniks, they were dismayed by the Allies' decision, after the Teheran conference in November 1943, to withdraw backing for the Chetniks in favour of the Communist-dominated Partisans under Marshal Tito. Tito was preferred because of his policy of maintaining active operations against the Germans, regardless of the cost to the civilian population. Mihailovic, by contrast, was appalled by the scale of reprisals wrought by the Germans and opposed the policy, arguing that other means of resistance were equally effective. To Popov, a future Yugoslavia under Communism was quite as bad a prospect as Yugoslavia under the heel of the jackboot. Certainly his dreams of returning home as British consul in Dubrovnik would have little chance of becoming reality, since Tito would have no use for such offices.

Acutely conscious of the fact that Communism was unlikely to foster the kind of economic environment in which an entrepreneur could flourish, Popov decided the time had come to cash in on the promises he had been given by the Germans of substantial business interests in Yugoslavia after the war. He asked for a meeting with his new controller, Wiegand, pointed out that in the event of Communist domination of Yugoslavia his family possessions would be worthless, and insisted that the Germans should either make binding arrangements for his future financial security or provide the necessary permits for him to transfer his assets to Lisbon.

As an example of chutzpah it was hard to beat – making his most outrageous demands of the Germans at a time, with the Allied invasion looming, when he might have been expected to avoid causing trouble.

Wiegand was still in the honeymoon period of dealing with Popov, and liked to boast in Paris and Berlin about running the Abwehr's best agent in Britain, so he was perhaps more inclined to humour his protégé than might have been expected. But Popov wanted more. He required an advance payment, he said, of $150,000 for further information about Allied invasion plans and a guarantee of safe passage – navicerts – for two oil tankers, currently in Sweden, which an oil company wanted to purchase. He claimed that obtaining safe passage for the ships from Sweden to Portugal would result in his being appointed to the board of the firm concerned and would ensure his post-war employment as a consideration for past services for the Germans.

Weigand promised to do his best to negotiate with Berlin on Popov's behalf, but his memorandum pleading Popov's case landed on the desk of Oberstleutnant Wilhelm Kuebart, an officer who in the past had frequently voiced suspicions about Popov's true allegiance. Kuebart was unsympathetic, particularly after discovering that Jebsen had concocted the oil-tanker scheme and that he and Popov were intending to sell the navicerts for a large sum, without the knowledge of the Germans.

Kuebart sent a representative to Lisbon to inform Popov that there was no question of payment in advance for any report, and that the navicerts could not be obtained. The best Berlin could offer was a three-year contract with a Swiss import/export company, which would guarantee him a minimum of 1,500 Swiss francs a month. Popov, affecting anger that his services were so poorly valued, turned the deal down flat and declared that unless his demands were met in full, he would no longer work as an agent for Germany.

MI5, who knew nothing of all this, would have been furious if Popov had terminated his relationship with the enemy in pursuit of personal financial gain. Popov later sought to justify his intransigence to MI5. He had always made it clear to the Germans, he said, that he worked for them solely for financial reasons. It would have been out of character if he did not at this stage in the war fight as hard as possible to safeguard his assets, even to the extent of threatening to stop work. He added that if his bluff had been called, he could always say that Jebsen had persuaded him at the last minute to carry on working.

Kuebart, who was no fool, called Wiegand back to Berlin and once again raised his doubts about Popov, pointing out that it was highly unlikely a truly independent agent could afford to threaten the Abwehr in this manner. Wiegand swore that he had complete confidence in Popov, that he was the best Abwehr agent in England and was doing invaluable work providing intelligence about the Allied invasion plans. He pointed out that Popov was not a German and was not morally bound to constantly risk his life for Germany; that his motives were clear and some way had to be found to avoid falling out with him, probably by redeeming in some form the promises given to him years earlier of post-war benefits. Wiegand did not mention that Jebsen had offered him a share in the profits, if he could help obtain navicerts for the two tankers in Sweden. Kuebart remained unconvinced and the issue was still unresolved when the time came for Popov to return to London.

While the Germans expected Popov to return to Lisbon in about eight weeks, Popov explained that it might be difficult as he was not sure he could get his government to send him out again on the same mission. Wiegand told him not to return if the invasion seemed imminent; he would be more valuable staying in London and reporting up-to-the-minute news of what was happening there. The airmail service between Britain and Portugal came to a sudden halt a few days before Popov left, cutting off one of the Abwehr's information supply lines – letters in secret ink. Popov was warned to be very careful using the radio when he returned to Britain, and not to stay on air for more than eight to ten minutes at one transmission; if he wanted to break off, he was to do so, whatever his control might say. Wiegand said they would listen out every day between 2.00 and 2.30 p.m. British time.

The day before he was due to leave, Jebsen warned his friend that Schreiber was intending to interrogate him again and that Popov should go through his report once more to refresh his memory. It seemed that Schreiber was acting on orders from Berlin, possibly in a last-minute attempt to trip Popov up, but his heart was not in it and he only went through the motions, explaining to Popov that he was hoping to get more details from him that he might have forgotten during his initial debriefing.

Popov was given two new questionnaires, but Schreiber emphasised that he was to concentrate on the invasion. He was told there would probably be some diversionary raid at the start and it was of the greatest importance to the Germans to know which operation was a diversion and which was the real thing. Popov was asked to try and find out what troops were taking part – information that could indicate whether a landing was merely a raid. As he lived in London, he might get a sense about the date from passing convoys, or from talking to officers and families; one of his girlfriends might have heard from a brother or a husband when it was likely to occur. Schreiber produced a map of Britain with areas outlined in red, mainly port towns along the south and east coasts, and Popov was told to visit as many as possible.

Popov arrived back in London on 13 April to discover that a 1,000-pound bomb had fallen outside his London house, but had failed to explode. Wilson was waiting to meet him to put together a detailed report on his visit. 'As usual,' he noted:

> the story verges on the improbable, but can be fully checked on a number of points from Most Secret Sources. Tricycle freely voluntteered the information, even on his financial negotiations with the Abwehr, during the course of which he carried the threat of ceasing to work for the Germans further than we would have dared authorise. Our fears that he might not explain some of his financial negotiations, of which we had knowledge from a source [Ultra] which made detailed questions impossible, proved to be unjustified. I have no hesitation in accepting the truth of Tricycle's account of his dealings, and his confidence that all those with whom he personally has had to deal believe in him seems fully justified.[7]

Perennial doubters, MI5 officers routinely checked and cross-checked every scrap of information, even when supplied by a trusted and high-calibre agent like Tricycle.

As well as the two questionnaires from the Abwehr, Popov brought back five reports from Artist, another political questionnaire from the SD, a number of messages from General Mihailovic to King Peter (which had been passed to Popov verbally by Ivo), $1,000 for 'Gelatine', $1,000 for 'Freak' and $14,000 for himself – more, in fact, than he had been paid by the Abwehr. MI5 concluded that the balance was made up in part by 'successful gambling'.

The SD questionnaire contained thirty-nine points, many concerning the prime minister:

> What are Churchill's prospects at the moment of remaining at the helm? How is his health? Is Churchill's loss of prestige through his last much criticised radio speech really so great that his position has been shaken? Does he by any chance already think of retiring and, if so, when? Who, with the present changed political situation in England, might be considered as his successor?[8]

In fact Popov had not thought his first report for the SD, compiled by dictation from MI5, particularly good and he had been prepared to explain that he had been unable to give it sufficient attention because he had been too busy working for the Abwehr. To his surprise it was judged to be excellent and seemed to be having the desired effect of protecting Jebsen. After it had been analysed, Henss told Jebsen that the Gestapo orders to arrest him at the German frontier had been withdrawn. Instead, the SD would send someone to Lisbon at the end of April or beginning of May to meet Jebsen and clear up outstanding allegations against him in SD files, relating to questionable financial deals. Jebsen was confident he could handle it. Most of the allegations against him were false, he told Popov, and the Gestapo had been mistakenly informed that he was involved in more currency rackets than was the case.

Jebsen's confidence was misplaced: a net was closing inexorably around him. His good friend Baroness von Gronau did her best to warn him. First she was ordered by Schreiber not to have any contact with him, under any circumstances. She ignored the order and met Jebsen secretly to tell him he was under some kind of suspicion. He ridiculed the idea, just as he did when von Gronau asked him directly if he was a British agent. From then on he denied that he was a British agent so frequently that it confirmed her suspicion that he was. Sometimes when he pumped her for information she would jokingly ask whether it was for the British or the Americans.

The two of them had had a close relationship for some time. They both lived in Estoril, and Jebsen often gave the baroness a lift to and from the office in his car. She was intrigued by him and he became besotted by her, eventually asking her to marry him. Since she knew he already had a wife, and a mistress in Paris, it was not difficult for her to refuse, but they remained friends. Despite his pale unhealthy complexion, his nicotine-stained teeth and fingers and the fact that he always wore a dark homburg, a dirty raincoat and unpolished shoes, she found him excellent company and greatly admired his intelligence. Jebsen talked often about 'friendship stretching across international boundaries regardless of war or peace' and had a wide knowledge of the world. Whenever he was out of town, the baroness looked after his large house and kept his four servants on their toes.

In early April, von Gronau was shown a top-secret telegram by the chief secretary in her office announcing the arrival in Lisbon of an RSHA (*Reichssicherheitshauptamt*, the organisation that controlled the SD) mission from Berlin to investigate Jebsen and his activities. She immediately warned Jebsen and he again ridiculed the threat, claiming that he knew so much about the SD they would not dare investigate him. On 18 April von Gronau was ordered to leave Portugal and report to Berlin within forty-eight hours. She unwisely spent her last day in Lisbon quite openly with Jebsen, who drove her to the airport. The baroness would end up in a concentration camp, although she survived the war.

Unknown to Jebsen, a business colleague by the name of Brandes, a man he considered to be a friend, was secretly reporting his activities to Schreiber. On 17 April, Schreiber sent a long telegram to Berlin making a number of wild allegations against Jebsen: that he owned both German and British diplomatic passports; that he was planning to buy up Swiss francs through nominees of Rothschild banks, and smuggle thirty million Swiss francs from Germany into occupied territory; that he was involved in other shady deals; and that he possessed a letter of recommendation from a Rothschild to the British Embassy in Madrid requesting that he should be given every assistance in the event of difficulties with the Abwehr. All this information presumably came from Brandes, since while Jebsen had talked about contacting the Rothschild family in Britain, he had never actually done so.

That same day both Jebsen and Schreiber were ordered to attend a meeting in Biarritz on 21 April to discuss Popov's financial demands with Major Bohlen, the administrative head of all the KOs (*Kriegsorganisationen*, or war stations). Jebsen confided to Brandes that he thought the meeting was a trap and he was certain he would be arrested. He added that if he detected any further signs of mistrust towards him on the part of Berlin, he would 'draw his own conclusion'. Brandes immediately reported this conversation to Schreiber, who passed it on to Berlin by signal.

Jebsen's excuse for not going to Biarritz was that it would 'blow his cover', but Schreiber would have none of it. He warned Jebsen that such an action would be considered desertion, since Jebsen must consider himself a soldier with a special mission in a neutral country and thus subject to military law. Jebsen remained adamant. Schreiber said he would have to report Jebsen's refusal to Berlin. In response, Berlin sent another telegram to Jebsen ordering him to report and a separate one to Schreiber that he should go alone, if Jebsen still refused.

MI5 was intercepting the increasingly frantic traffic between Berlin and Lisbon, but its assessment – tragically mistaken, as it turned out – was that Jebsen was not in any particular danger and that he was in such a state of nerves that he imagined traps where none existed. Jebsen could not be told that MI5 was listening in to the traffic, but he was warned at a routine meeting with MI6 in Lisbon that he should not trust Brandes.

It seemed, for a few days, that MI5's assessment of the situation was correct. Jebsen was suddenly told he would be receiving $75,000 as a first payment of the money demanded by Popov – proof, he was sure, that all was well. Schreiber had let him know that Popov's reports had made a tremendous impression in Berlin, reflecting well on Jebsen, and that his last report had been classified as being 'good as sure', an almost unparalleled evaluation. To cap it all, Schreiber informed Jebsen that he was to be awarded a medal, the *Kriegsverdienstkreuz* first-class, an honour shared by no one in Lisbon. It later transpired there was no evidence of any such award and that it was part of a plan to lure him into a trap.

On 21 April, the day he was supposed to be in Biarritz, Jebsen wrote a chirpy letter to his friend:

> Dear Dusko,
> . . . I congratulate you on being my Beloved Führer's best agent, who is genuine without any doubt . . . because, after having hesitated for some time, the Abwehr decided that the money should be transferred to you as arranged here with Schreiber and Wiegand. I got 75,000 dollars, of which I shall send you 50,000 today. To Ivo I shall send the 20,000 Swiss francs tomorrow, and I take from them my share; we might settle our accounts later on . . .

He went on to explain how he intended to handle the money and concluded: 'Be a good boy, and try to behave. Yours always, Johnny.'

Schreiber went alone to the conference in Biarritz, where he met Kuebart and his adjutant, Sonderführer Weiss. Kuebart revealed he had been given verbal orders to ensure, personally, that Jebsen reached German-occupied territory and to thwart any attempt on his part to defect. Jebsen's desertion was to be prevented by any means, as Berlin had proof, Kuebart claimed, that Jebsen had been working for both sides for some time and was now preparing to go over to the Allies. Schreiber could see the writing on the wall: that he was going to be given the task of dealing with Jebsen. He protested that the affair was a matter for Abwehr III, counter-espionage, and that the execution of the order was a police matter. Both Kuebart and Weiss agreed, but said it had been decided that the case was primarily of military interest and therefore an exception was to be made. Neither Abwehr III nor the German police in Portugal were to be informed what was going on. Schreiber, still trying to extricate himself, insisted on personal confirmation from Berlin that he was to deliver Jebsen to Reich territory. It arrived the following day.

While Schreiber was in Biarritz, Jebsen had another clandestine meeting with his MI6 contact in Lisbon, who reported to London that he was in very good spirits, much calmer, and absolutely confident that the Abwehr was now satisfied as to his own *bona fides* and those of Popov. Jebsen was certain that Popov's position as an 'ace' agent was assured and that the General Staff would act on the information he passed. He was no longer concerned that an investigation into his activities would be reopened.

On 28 April, Jebsen wrote another cheerful letter to Popov, telling him that he was in the clear and that doubts about his genuineness had been swept away. The proof, he said, was that he had been awarded a medal, a KVK first-class. 'First class was probably given', he joked, 'because you double-crossed them first class.' Jebsen confessed to feeling a little ashamed for getting a decoration when Popov and Wilson had done all the hard work and said he had decided to send it to Wilson as a curiosity. He ended with a light-hearted allusion to the complications of life as a double agent:

> Last time I forgot to send my best greetings to Frano ['Freak']. This was because at the time I didn't remember that he should know that I know what after all we all know. I sometimes forget to whom I have to cover what, and what I have to cover to whom. I hope you will give my love to all you can give it to without spoiling your, my, or anybody else's cover. To you I can give my love anyhow, which I do . . . Yours, as always, Johnnie.

This affectionate note was the last Popov would ever hear from his friend.

Back in Lisbon, Schreiber learned that a close friend of Jebsen, Moldenhauer, had arrived and was staying with him at his villa in Estoril. Moldenhauer was employed in the Abwehr's Cologne office, but was known to have good connections in Allied circles. Schreiber believed that he and Jebsen were planning to desert together and decided that Moldenhauer should be abducted as well. If he was innocent, he deduced, he would have no trouble clearing his name with the authorities in Berlin.

Schreiber called Jebsen and Moldenhauer to a meeting in his office in the late afternoon of 30 April. The plan was to knock them unconscious, drug them by injection and lock them in two large trunks, which could be shipped by car that same evening into Spain and across the French border into Biarritz. He chose two accomplices: Bleil, a signal officer in whose name the car that would be used was registered; and Karl Meier, a civilian motor officer who could repair it, if necessary. At noon Schreiber and Meier purchased two metal trunks big enough for humans and fitted with openings for ventilation. Schreiber bought a sleeping draught from a Lisbon pharmacy.

At 6 p.m. Jebsen and Moldenhauer arrived together at Schreiber's office, apparently unsuspecting of any plot. After a short general conver-

sation, Schreiber asked Jebsen to step into another room, where he
announced that he had orders to take him to Berlin, by force if necessary.
Jebsen made a leap for the door, but Schreiber, who was fitter and
stronger, grabbed him. Meanwhile, Meier had overpowered Moldenhauer
in the adjoining room. Schreiber told them that he was going to knock
them out with drugs, and both men – according to Schreiber's interrogation by the Allies after the war – submitted. The party set out for Badajoz
with the two drugged victims in the boot of a large Studebaker sedan
with CD plates. At around 2 a.m. they crossed the Portuguese-Spanish
border without incident (both Bleil and Meier knew the guards from
previous trips). The Spanish-French border was crossed at Irun, and in
Biarritz both men were turned over to the SD. Schreiber and his assistants
returned to Lisbon; Jebsen and Moldenhauer were transported to Berlin
in the personal aeroplane of Colonel Georg Hansen, head of military
intelligence in the newly unified intelligence service.

The news that Artist had disappeared set alarm bells ringing in London
and provoked dismay, not so much prompted by concern for his well-
being, but by the potential damage to Operation Fortitude. If Artist
revealed, at the hands of the Gestapo, that Popov was a double agent
controlled by the British, the Germans would know that all the intelligence he had been passing to the Abwehr was suspect. Since this information neatly slotted in with reports from other agents in Britain, the
entire network of controlled agents could be compromised. If the
Germans concluded that the messages they were receiving from Britain
were the opposite of the truth, then they would deduce that the Pas de
Calais was not the real objective and that the invasion, when it came, was
not a feint.

There was little doubt in MI5 that Artist had been abducted to
Germany, but no one could be sure precisely why he had been arrested.
The general tenor of intercepts indicated that the Germans were worried
Jebsen was about to go over to the British, rather than that they knew he
was already a traitor. If this was the case, Ian Wilson and others thought
there was a good chance that Jebsen would not be subjected to the kind
of pressure that would break him. But if he had been arrested as a traitor
and was subjected to sustained torture, there was no such guarantee.

J. C. Masterman, chairman of the XX Committee, was gloomy:

> The fact that Artist, who is fully cognisant of the Tricycle network
> and who has some knowledge or at least some inkling of the other
> cases, has fallen under suspicion and been removed to Berlin by the
> Abwehr, prima facie, threatens the whole cover plan. We cannot tell

why Artist has fallen under suspicion – we only know that he is regarded as 'unreliable'. Such indications as there are suggest that his 'unreliability' may be connected with his financial operations, his intrigues with the S.D. . . . and not with his dealings with Tricycle at all. There is no proof that treason on the part of Artist is part of the charges. But obviously under interrogation in Berlin Artist may betray all, or perhaps more than all, he knows. We must act on the assumption that the Tricycle case may be blown . . .[9]

The XX Committee discussed the options at length, even contemplating whether it was necessary to shut down the whole deception operation. In the end it was decided that the Tricycle network would no longer take part in deception activities, although 'Freak' was to continue operating his wireless transmitter to try and provoke a reaction from Lisbon that might indicate how Tricycle was regarded. If he was confirmed in a position of trust, he could continue as before; in the meantime the Tricycle network was to be suspended, to minimise the risk to Operation Fortitude. Masterman observed:

> The danger of continuing with other agents is that if they were all blown their traffic could be read in reverse and interpreted accordingly. In spite of this danger I incline to the view that they should continue. If the situation deteriorated we could use agents to fill the German mind with confusion. If it was decided they were blown we could take the extreme step of shutting down everything and denying any intelligence to the enemy at a time when they need it most.

But Masterman thought the danger of the enemy deducing the plan was minimal: 'I do not believe that even a lengthy and exhaustive study would sift the truth from the falsehood.'[10]

Popov was not given the news about his friend until 7 May. He returned from a convivial lunch to find Tar Robertson and Ian Wilson waiting in his sitting room at Clock House with grim faces. He always kept the front-door key in the same place and the bar well stocked, so it was no surprise to find friends already ensconced and enjoying his hospitality when he returned home, but this time it was different. Johnny had failed to keep an appointment with his MI6 contact on 5 May, Robertson said solemnly, and enquiries revealed that he had not been seen at his house since 29 April. Without exposing Ultra, they were not able to tell Popov that they knew Jebsen was already in Germany, in the Gestapo prison in Berlin, but Popov was no fool and realised immediately that his friend had probably been arrested. He was distraught; the best he could hope for was that Johnny had been taken in because of his shady financial dealing. If that was the case, he stood a chance. The alternative was grim.

Robertson and Wilson also had to break the news to Popov that his network was being suspended until his status with the Germans could be established. It was necessary, they explained needlessly, to protect Fortitude until Jebsen's fate was known. Popov protested that Johnny would never betray him, but in his heart he knew that he might. He had absolutely no doubt that Jebsen would never give him away under any normal interrogation, but both Popov and Ivo had discussed what might happen if Johnny was arrested and both doubted his ability to withstand physical violence.

All that remained active of the Tricycle network was 'Freak's' radio transmitter. Popov suggested that the Germans should be pressed to live up to their promises to continue operating the Yugoslav escape route, as a means of assessing whether they still believed in him. Wilson agreed. A message to Lisbon, followed by two reminders, elicited an ominous response from Wiegand on 16 May. He said that the escape route could no longer be operated 'for technical reasons' and that other methods were under consideration. The following day, frustrated beyond belief by the uncertainty, Popov suggested parachuting into Yugoslavia to join Ivo's operation; Wilson gently talked him out of it.

The post-mortem within British intelligence into what had gone wrong in the Jebsen case revealed considerable acrimony. Felix Foley of MI6 bitterly accused his MI5 colleagues of leading Jebsen 'up the garden path' and doing insufficient to save him, when intercepted signals clearly indicted that he was in serious trouble. He could have avoided the trap, Foley suggested, had he been warned. MI5 was unrepentant. Robertson wrote to Foley to point out that careful consideration had been given to warning Jebsen, but everyone had agreed that the risk of revealing the existence of Ultra was 'unacceptable'. Thus was Artist, an informant praised in a recent MI5 report for the 'very high standard of accuracy'[11] of his intelligence, sacrificed at the altar of security. Certainly the need to protect Ultra was paramount and, in the view of MI5, worth a life, but little consideration seems to have been given to evacuating Jebsen to Britain before the net closed around him.

There was some hope, in fact, that Jebsen was holding out. Had he been forced to confess everything, MI5 would have expected that Abwehr and SD officials closely connected with him would themselves have been arrested, or at least removed from their posts. But at the end of May there was no indication that any of his colleagues had been compromised. Indeed, Schreiber had received a special telegram from Colonel Hansen conveying appreciation and thanks for 'undertaking Dora' (the codename for the operation to abduct Jebsen).

Artist's arrest did not ultimately jeopardise Operation Fortitude; indeed, Fortitude exceeded all expectations, largely due to the artful fiddling of the 'first violins'. In May 1944 the German high command believed the Allies had under their command an enormous army comprising some ninety divisions, plus seven airborne divisions. The true figure was thirty-five divisions, plus three airborne. And at dawn on 6 June 1944, when the Allies stormed ashore on the beaches of Normandy, Germany's formidable 15th Army remained resolutely in place, 175 miles to the north, defending the Pas de Calais, its sentries posted along the shoreline searching the empty grey waters of the English Channel and scanning the horizon, day after day, for the invasion that never came.

13

In Search of Revenge

WHILE MEN AND EQUIPMENT WERE POURING INTO THE NORMANDY bridgehead and the front-line troops were pushing deeper into France, Popov was invited to a 'little dinner' at the Hyde Park Hotel in London. He arrived to discover that the 'dinner' was a full-scale banquet in his honour attended by virtually everyone he knew in MI5. After the meal, Tar Robertson got to his feet to make an elegant speech, at the end of which he announced that Popov had been recommended for an OBE in recognition of his invaluable and courageous service with British intelligence.

'It would be false modesty to say I wasn't grateful,' Popov noted in his memoirs, 'although I did squirm in my seat at the exaggerations of some of the feats attributed to me . . . It would have been a splendid evening if I could have kept my thoughts on the festivities and not on Johnny.'[1]

Jebsen weighed heavily on Popov's conscience. There was little information about his whereabouts, although the latest intelligence was that he was probably still alive, that he had not talked and that friends were still trying to secure his release. But within MI5 there was not much optimism that Artist would survive. The manner of his abduction indicated that the SD was determined to bring charges against him, and a long list of Abwehr officers had already been executed in the witch-hunt following the dismissal of Admiral Canaris.

At the time of the banquet MI5 was endeavouring, without much success, to persuade the FBI to allow Popov to return to the United States on a brief mission on behalf of his government. The Yugoslav government-in-exile wanted Popov to represent it at a United Nations conference in New York on post-war reconstruction and relief, and to persuade influential Yugoslavs in the United States to support a potential rapprochement being hammered out between King Peter and Marshal Tito. Robertson had written a discreet personal letter to Hoover, assuring him that Tricycle would not be reporting to the Germans and that his mission had nothing to do with British intelligence. 'We feel we owe it to Tricycle himself to facilitate him in any work he may be doing for his own Government,' Robertson wrote:

> There has inevitably been some criticism of Tricycle by his compatriots, who could not be told of the most valuable and courageous work he was doing for us, and who therefore felt that Tricycle was not playing his part in the war effort. It will no doubt assist Tricycle to discount the criticisms of himself among his compatriots if his services are now made use of by his government.[2]

Hoover remained implacably opposed to Popov's visit, having been reminded by his staff that Popov had been turned back to the British because he was 'a spendthrift and expended his energy wholly in living lavishly'. Somehow the reminder failed to mention the Pearl Harbor questionnaire, or the microdots, or setting up a direct radio link with the enemy. In fact Hoover's memory left a lot to be desired – within a couple of years, in embarrassing circumstances, he would pretend to have no idea who Popov was. Eventually Hoover's opposition and visa problems caused so much delay that there was no point in Popov's trip.

In early August 1944 a doodlebug dropped close to Clock House and blew out all the windows. Hitler's dreaded 'secret weapon', the V1 rocket, had been launched against London a few weeks earlier to devastating effect. A V1 scored a direct hit on the Guards Chapel, close to Buckingham Palace, on Sunday 18 June, killing nearly 200 Guardsmen and a number of civilians. In a single twenty-four-hour period that month, no fewer than 244 V1 flying bombs were launched against Britain from sites in the Pas de Calais. The doodlebug was a terrifying psychological weapon. When flying overhead, its strange put-put engine could be clearly heard and Londoners soon learned that in the terrifying silence when the engine stopped they had only about fifteen seconds to find shelter. In September the doodlebug was replaced by the more sophisticated V2 supersonic rocket, which completed its journey from launch to detonation in less than four minutes and gave no warning. It is estimated that some 8,500 flying bombs were launched against Britain between June 1944 and March 1945, killing around 9,000 civilians and injuring 25,000. Astonishingly, public morale held up, boosted by reassuring news of the Allies' advance in Europe.

Like everyone living in London, Popov's nerves were stretched by the flying bombs, but he was also greatly concerned about his family and the fate of Jebsen. After Clock House had been made uninhabitable, he asked MI5 if he could take a break.

Wilson suggested he should go to Scotland and learn fly-fishing. He recommended the Fisherman's Inn, in the Highlands, fifteen miles from Tain. After London, the Highlands were an oasis of tranquillity. Popov found an elderly retired colonel who was delighted to give him lessons in the arcane art of fly-fishing and settled down for a complete rest. Two days later he was woken in the middle of the night by the innkeeper, who told him there was a police motor-cyclist waiting outside: a telephone call had been received from the War Office ordering him to report back to London immediately. Popov was taken to a military airfield on the back of the police motor-cycle and flown south to an airfield in Surrey, where an MI5 driver was waiting. He had no idea what was going on until he arrived at Waterloo station, where Ian Wilson was waiting. Wilson was clearly excited, but refused to tell Popov what was afoot – only that he should be patient. Thirty minutes later a train pulled into the station and Popov's brother, Ivo, looking thin but tanned, stepped out onto the platform. Popov could hardly believe it. He was, Wilson later reported, 'overjoyed'.

Much had happened to Ivo since the two of them were last together in Lisbon in March. On his return to Belgrade he discovered that a *Sonder-Kommission* (special commission of inquiry) of the SD had been convened to investigate corruption among German officials. Corruption was rife at all levels in Belgrade, particularly among SS and SD officers, many of whom had accepted bribes from Ivo. Fortunately the *Sonder-Kommission* was careful not to inquire too deeply into SS and SD corruption, concentrating instead on misdemeanours committed by Wehrmacht officers and officials who were not party members. Some forty Wehrmacht officers were arrested and seventeen were shot, along with a large number of Yugoslavs alleged to have had corrupt dealings with them.

Ivo, who had personally corrupted any number of Germans while organising economic sabotage operations, was inevitably called before the *Kommission* and grilled about his financial dealings. He calmly refused to answer most of the questions put to him, on the grounds that he was involved in secret work for the Abwehr and was therefore not authorised to discuss his activities. If he thought he had got away with it, he was wrong.

On 16 April, the Popov family house in Belgrade was destroyed during an American air-raid. Miraculously, no one was hurt. Four days later, Ivo was arrested, taken to a Gestapo prison and severely beaten. Transferred to an officers' prison, where his treatment was somewhat better, he was interrogated every day by members of the *Kommission*, on one occasion for seventeen hours without interruption, but continued to deny he had any financial dealings with the Abwehr. After a week he was released on orders from Berlin, issued (he thought) by Colonel Georg Hansen, whom he had met several times and cultivated as a friend. They had last met in Paris, where Hansen entertained Ivo to a sumptuous dinner, then got horribly drunk and embarrassed Ivo by his repeated and excessive expressions of gratitude on behalf of the Reich for the wonderful work Ivo and his brother were doing. Ironically, it was around this time that Hansen was arranging for Jebsen to be abducted from Portugal and brought to Berlin.

Almost immediately he was released, Ivo was asked by Mihailovic to undertake a mission that could easily land him back in prison. Mihailovic, who after the war was captured by the Partisans and executed for 'collaborating with the enemy', wanted to get rid of two individuals who were causing particular difficulty for the Chetniks – the chief of the Serbian Special Police and a Gestapo officer called Brandt, who headed the section fighting Mihailovic forces. Mihailovic knew that Ivo had evidence that both men had accepted bribes from time to time and wanted him to denounce them to the *Sonder-Kommission*. Ivo did not hesitate, even though he knew he would be making powerful enemies. The Serbian police chief was sent to Germany within twenty-four hours of being denounced by Ivo, but Brandt simply went on leave for a week and resumed his former position when he returned, bent on revenge.

Ivo was hoping that his contacts within the Abwehr would protect him, but the Abwehr was in the process of being taken over by the SD and purged of Canaris loyalists. Abwehr officers were in touch with Ivo almost every day pleading with him not to reveal to the *Kommission* that he had given them money, food or other assistance. While they had a strong personal interest in helping Ivo to clear himself with the *Kommission*, they no longer had sufficient influence to help him if he got into serious trouble. The one person he had always been able to rely on was Jebsen, who seemed to have assumed personal responsibility for ensuring the safety of the entire Popov family. Ivo had no way of knowing, at that time, that Jebsen was locked in a prison cell in Berlin.

On 13 June, Ivo was conducting his regular morning surgery in Belgrade when four Gestapo officials burst in, ordered the waiting patients to leave, and hustled Ivo into a waiting car. At the Gestapo headquarters in the centre of town he was informed by an SS colonel from Berlin, who had previously interrogated him, that he should consider himself under arrest. Ivo, with a sinking heart, asked why. His greatest concern was that the Germans would discover his underground activities on behalf of the British and he almost laughed out loud when the SS colonel accused him of giving false evidence about paying a bribe to Brandt. Ivo denied knowing anything about it and protested that he ought not to be arrested because the head of the *Kommission* had given him his word of honour as an officer that no Serb would be arrested as a result of the information he gave to the *Kommission*. The colonel smiled thinly and informed Ivo that he was not being arrested as a Serb, but as a *Sonderführer*.

Incarcerated in Glavnyaca prison awaiting a trial that could result in his execution, Ivo was allowed to receive food parcels from outside. One included a packet of cigarettes with a miniature drawing of a floor plan inserted between the layers of cigarettes. The plan showed a door opening onto a flight of steps and leading to a forest, a Serbian symbol for freedom. At first Ivo had no idea what building it depicted (there was no description) and it was some time before he realised it could be the first floor of the Gestapo headquarters, where he was regularly interrogated. The routine was for a group of about fifteen prisoners, deprived of shoes and belts, to be driven under guard in the back of a truck to the headquarters, and made to stand in a line holding a piece of paper against the wall with their noses, so they could not see what was going on. The door to 'freedom' was at the end of the line. Ivo was due for another interrogation within a few days; this time he pretended he had hurt his foot and was last out of the truck so that he would be last in the line. A light over the door to the interrogation room indicated when the next prisoner should be brought in, and Ivo silently counted how many seconds it took for the guard to hustle the prisoner into the room. When the next man went in, Ivo made his move. He stepped sideways out of the line, opened the door, bounded down the steps and was out on the street, barefoot and holding his trousers up with one hand. Ivo knew central Belgrade intimately and within minutes he was knocking on the door of a friend's apartment.

That night, equipped with a borrowed belt and a pair of shoes two sizes too small, he left the city and walked six miles to his sister-in-law's villa in Beli Potok, just outside Avala, where Dragica and his son had taken refuge after their house in Belgrade was bombed. He told Dragica that he was going to join the Chetniks in the mountains and admitted to her, for the first time, that he had been working for the Allies almost since the start of the war. If she had any difficulties with the Partisans or the Russians when she returned to Belgrade, she was to contact the British and ask for 'Mr Wilson'. Ivo then left for Resnik, where the Chetniks had a base, and stayed there for fifteen days while waiting for orders from the Mihailovic headquarters. Dragica saw him every day, walking three hours through the forest to meet at a halfway point between Beli Potok and Resnik.

Ivo eventually spent six weeks travelling with Mihailovic and took part in a raid on a Partisan base, during which documents were captured that proved what the Chetniks had long suspected – that the Partisans were using Allied-supplied arms and ammunition to attack the Chetniks rather than the Germans. Anxious for these documents to be seen in London, on 7 July he sent a wireless message from the Mihailovic headquarters to Ian Wilson, requesting evacuation to Britain. It was picked up by the Allied base in Bari, on the heel of Italy, but subsequently misrouted. When Ivo heard nothing from Wilson, he hitched a lift to Bari on an aeroplane that was evacuating American airmen who had baled out over Yugoslavia. He left behind his typewriter and a number of sheets of paper signed 'Paula', his German codename; an intelligence officer with Mihailovic promised to send out letters from time to time to persuade the Germans that Ivo was still in the mountains.

It was early August before Wilson received a message from MI6 in Bari: 'Dr Ivan Popov escaped from the Gestapo, is here with us and wishes for exit from this country. There is the possibility of sending him with the American aviators who are here with us. He requests that arrangements be made to secure his reception at Foggia. He travels under name of Dr Pedrag Ivanovic.' Ivo was travelling under an alias in the hope of concealing from the Germans that he was on his way to Britain and thus avoid bringing further trouble to his family. He arrived in London on 15 August 1944, the day the Allies launched Operation Anvil, the landings in southern France.

The Popov brothers checked into adjoining rooms at the Savoy (Clock House was still uninhabitable) and caught up on each other's news. When they had covered all the family matters, Popov told his brother about Jebsen, unburdening the guilt he felt about what had happened to his friend. The most recent intelligence about Jebsen was that at one point he had been held in Oranienburg concentration camp on a charge of high treason, although it was not known if he was still there, or even still alive. Popov pumped his brother for the names of anyone who might know what had happened to him. Ivo suggested Mihail Glusevic, a rich Yugoslav who had lived in Paris for thirty-five years, was a member, with Jebsen, of the secret group working against the German state economic system and was deeply involved with Jebsen on a number of financial deals. He also mentioned Frederick Hahn, a close friend of Jebsen and a top official in the Reichsbank, or Ministry of Economics. Hahn was engaged to a beautiful French girl, Jacqueline Blanc, and stayed at her apartment on the Rue de la Pompe when he was in Paris. Popov jotted down the names and addresses.

Ten days later, on 25 August, Paris fell to the Allies. General Dietrich von Choltitz, the German commander, defied Hitler's orders to destroy the city and surrendered to the French general Jacques Leclerc, ending four years of Nazi occupation. Popov immediately began pestering MI5 for permission to go to Paris to seek out Jebsen's friends and find out what had happened to him. Bill Luke, his former case officer, was handling his request. Luke told Popov he did not think it would be possible to find out anything that MI5 did not already know, but Popov disagreed and insisted that as he was mainly responsible for Jebsen's misfortune, he owed it to his friend to find out if he was still alive, or, if he was dead, to do something for his widow. It took nearly six weeks for permission to come through.

Popov arrived in the newly liberated city on 9 October 1944 and first sought out Jacqueline Blanc. Her apartment was on the second floor of an elegant nineteenth-century house in the smart 16th *arrondissement*. Popov trudged up the stairs and banged on her door, but although he thought he could hear someone moving about inside, there was no reply. He went downstairs, stood on the opposite side of the street and looked up at the windows of the apartment. When he saw the curtains twitch, he went back up the stairs and banged on the door more forcefully, calling out in French for her to open up. Eventually the door opened, on a security chain, and Mademoiselle Blanc stared out at him through the crack. Popov quickly assured her that he meant her no harm and only wanted information about his friend Jebsen, a man to whom he owed his life and whose debt he wished to repay. Mlle Blanc reluctantly slipped the chain off the door and silently gestured him to enter. She was wearing, Popov recalled, a silk dressing gown and was, as Ivo had said, exceptionally beautiful. She regarded Popov coolly as he took a seat, but the moment he started to ask her questions, she denied knowing anything. Herr Hahn was in Germany, she said; she knew absolutely nothing of business affairs and nothing about anyone called Jebsen.

Popov thought she was lying and threatened to expose her as a collaborator – there had been ugly scenes on the streets of Paris of women, their heads shaved, being marched through jeering crowds for associating with the Germans. Mlle Blanc paled and looked desperately for help towards a door, slightly ajar, leading into an adjoining room. It opened and a man walked in with a revolver in his hand, pointed at Popov. He introduced himself, politely, as Frederick Hahn, apologised for the subterfuge and asked what it was that Popov wanted. Popov felt he had nothing to lose by being honest, and gave Hahn a potted version of his relationship with Jebsen and their undercover work for the Allies. All he wanted, he said, were the names of people who might know what had happened to his friend. Hahn was nervous. He wanted time to think about it, he said. He had been told that he would be arrested if he returned to Germany and he did not want any further trouble. Popov offered to put in a good word for him with the Allied authorities if he would help. Hahn asked him to return that evening, when he would give his decision.

Popov returned at eight o'clock quite expecting Hahn to have disappeared. To his surprise, the German opened the door and ushered him in. He had decided, he said, to tell Popov all he knew. Jebsen had been in the Gestapo prison in Prinz Albrechtstrasse, but had recently been transferred to Oranienburg, a concentration camp for transients outside Berlin. The SS officer in charge of his interrogation was Sondar Eggar, but others often took part. The man to worry about was *Obersturmbahnführer* Walter Salzer, who worked with Ernst Kaltenbrunner, a senior officer in the SD. Salzer was Kaltenbrunner's *Mädchenfüralles* – the man who did his dirty work – and if an 'accident' befell Jebsen, Popov could be sure that Salzer was behind it. Coincidentally, Hahn said, Salzer had worked for one of Jebsen's companies prior to the war. Before he left, Popov gave Hahn a telephone number to call if he needed help from British intelligence.

Popov then called at the address on the Rue de Franqueville, also in the 16th *arrondissement*, that Ivo had given him for Mihail Glusevic. The Yugoslav proved as reluctant to talk as Hahn, particularly about his financial affairs, but Popov eventually convinced him that his only interest was in trying to save his friend. Glusevic had made a lot of money on the black market and was not inclined to broadcast the fact, but admitted that Jebsen was involved in many of his illicit deals. He swore he had not seen Jebsen since he was last in Paris at the end of March, but he knew that Jebsen was in trouble. On 10 August the Gestapo had surrounded his house and he was taken away for questioning for several hours. The questions were all about Jebsen's financial affairs; Glusevic believed that Jebsen could not have told them much because they did not seem at all well informed. He was pressed to say where Jebsen was, but thought that was only because the Gestapo wanted to cover up the fact that he had been arrested. His house was searched, apparently for money or valuables that the Gestapo thought Glusevic was hiding for Jebsen. They also asked him to produce a small trunk that Jebsen had left with him. As it was obvious they knew he had it, Glusevic complied. They broke open the lock, but found only some coffee, chocolate and a few personal belongings – clearly not what they were looking for. Glusevic neglected to tell them that Jebsen had earlier left a small case with him containing papers, money and gold, but had then sent instructions for it to be forwarded to a contact at the Hotel Lutetia, the Abwehr headquarters.

Glusevic agreed to arrange a meeting between Popov and Jebsen's mistress, Madeleine Schmidt, but it was entirely unproductive. She was unable to shed any light on what had happened – the last she had heard from Johnny was a letter delivered in April; since then, nothing.

Popov returned to London no wiser about Jebsen's fate than when he had left. Ian Wilson privately expressed the view that since the Gestapo seemed to know very little about Jebsen's financial dealings, the likelihood was that he had already been executed, or had perhaps committed suicide. But Popov clung grimly to the notion that his friend was still alive.

At the end of November he received a mysterious letter from Switzerland, signed only 'Ulla', to say that Johnny would be visiting her in Zurich shortly before Christmas and would be staying at the Hotel Baur au Lac. There was no contact address for 'Ulla'. Popov did not know what to make of it – he felt sure that if Jebsen was free to visit hotels in Switzerland, he would have been in contact – but, grasping at any straw, he was reluctant to dismiss it as a hoax. He returned to Paris, bought a small front-wheel-drive Citroën and drove to Zurich, checking in to the nearby Zum Storchen Hotel. He called at the Baur au Lac twice a day every day for two weeks, asking if Herr Jebsen had arrived or if there was any message for him. The answer was always no. Popov never discovered who had sent him the letter, or why.

Back in London, Popov met Tar Robertson and Wilson and suggested reopening contact with the Germans. There was no indication that Jebsen had been forced to blow the Tricycle network, he argued, and no reason to believe that the Germans suspected him of supplying deliberate misinformation, so there was no reason why he could not go back to work. His proposal was discussed at a high level within MI5, but it was decided there was not much to be gained by reactivating the network at that stage of the war. Wilson's view was that if the Tricycle network was ever resurrected, it would be more useful to penetrate the Russians, and that if Jebsen survived he could perhaps offer his services, including those of Popov, to the Russians.

Meanwhile there was growing concern over the safety of Popov's family still in Yugoslavia, particularly that of Ivo's wife, Dragica, and their three-year-old son, Misha. Tito and his Partisans were by then firmly in control of the country and conducting a purge of fellow Yugoslavs thought to be too pro-German or too pro-Mihailovic. Popov suggested that the time had come to reveal to the Yugoslav government the work that he and his network had been undertaking on behalf of British intelligence in order to offer some kind of protection to their families. The problem was Jebsen. While there was a chance, however remote, that he was still alive, it was vital not to let the Germans know that the Tricycle network was controlled. Wilson told Popov that MI5 was ready to explain the true nature of their activities to the Yugoslavs 'when the time was right', but could not do so yet because of the danger to Jebsen – the information was sure to leak to the Germans, sealing his fate. If the Germans discovered that the Tricycle network was controlled by British intelligence, Jebsen was doomed.

In an attempt at a palliative, the British ambassador in Belgrade was asked to discreetly raise the matter of the families' security with Dr Subasic, the Yugoslav prime minister. Subasic's advice was to contact General Velebit, Tito's military representative in Britain and the probable next ambassador, and warn him that a false impression may have been created about the work which the Popov group had been doing. Subasic said that Velebit was the only Yugoslav in Britain with sufficient power to order the protection of the families.

Not much good seems to have come from this initiative, since Wilson called the Tricycle network together for a meeting in January 1945, to impart bad news: there was nothing MI5 could do to help their families. 'I made it clear', he reported:

> that while we regarded it as being incumbent upon us to protect them from any harm coming from mistaken reports that they were collaborating with the Germans, we could not protect them, or their families, from troubles which arose from political difficulties in Yugoslavia and I pointed out that in so far as any of them were politically regarded by the Partisans with disfavour, the only assistance we could give them was to permit them to remain in this country.[3]

The Yugoslavs had no alternative but to accept this mealy-mouthed compromise and it was agreed that no attempts would be made to rehabilitate them with the Yugoslav government until the political situation was more settled.

By a curious coincidence, General Velebit's mistress in London was also a former lover of Popov and he had remained on good terms with her. She told him she had learned from Velebit that Dragica was in serious trouble with the Partisans in Belgrade because of Ivo's alleged collaboration, and that she and her son had only been saved from being shot by the intervention of a British liaison officer. Dragica had been robbed of her jewellery and forced to perform menial tasks for the Partisans.

This news did nothing to calm Ivo's fears about his wife and son. As it happened, the feisty and beautiful Dragica was more than capable of taking care of herself. After her husband left for Britain she returned to Belgrade and found a small apartment, where she was soon visited by Brandt, head of the local Gestapo, angrily demanding to know where Ivo was. Dragica was completely unintimidated. She told him that Ivo was so furious about the way he had been treated by the Germans, having worked so hard for them, that he had gone to Berlin to complain to Goering, whom he knew personally. Brandt swallowed hard and swiftly changed his tune, pretending he had actually come to warn her that the Russians were poised to cross into Yugoslavia and to offer her safe conduct to Vienna. She would certainly be shot by the Partisans if she stayed, he said. Dragica haughtily replied that she had no intention of leaving; that she would rather run the risk of being killed than leave Serbia; and that, while her husband had worked for the Germans, she never would. Brandt left without another word.

Dragica stayed in hiding while a fierce battle raged through the streets close to the central station, where the Germans stubbornly held on until 20 October, when the city finally fell to the Russians. Not long after order had been restored, she was telephoned by a Russian officer who asked for a room. Dragica had been born near Kiev and spoke fluent Russian; she replied in Russian and agreed to let a room in her apartment. Her tenant was a Soviet war correspondent who spoke no Serbo-Croat and he persuaded her to work as his translator for a few weeks until he left for the front in Budapest. Dragica then worked for Brigadier Fitzroy Maclean, the head of the British Military Mission, giving him Russian conversation lessons. Maclean, a friend of Churchill, a diplomat and acclaimed author, was very taken with her, and made sure she was invited to parties and receptions at the mission.

Dragica's frequent visits to the mission inevitably attracted the attention of the NKVD, the Russian secret police, and in January 1945 she was picked up and taken in for questioning in the former Gestapo building. She was interrogated for twelve hours without a break about the whereabouts of her husband, his activities during the German occupation, the reason for her frequent visits to the British mission and the nature of her relationship with Maclean. Dragica knew she was in quite as much danger from the Russians as she was from the Germans. She played the role of an empty-headed housewife to perfection, cried a lot, claimed she had no idea what her husband was doing, that he always locked himself away whenever he had visitors so that no one could disturb them, and offered up a mass of pointless information about the foibles and idiosyncrasies of her husband's friends, which only served to confuse her interrogators.

In truth, Dragica was shaken by what the NKVD revealed: they knew the names of all the Germans and most of the Serbs with whom Ivo had been working, they knew every detail of Ivo's movements and even of a chance meeting she had had with his friends. They knew everything about Jebsen and his visits to Lisbon, his work for the Abwehr and the fact that he could speak Russian fluently. They knew that Martin Töppen, the Abwehr paymaster, had invited her to a concert in early 1943, but she had not gone because Töppen insisted he had to be in uniform. When they asked her if she discussed politics on her visits to the British Mission, she laughed and said she was not interested in politics in the slightest (in fact she discussed politics endlessly with Maclean). 'What Mrs Popov was to learn during the course of the interrogation through which the NKVD put her', MI5 later reported, 'would have shattered the confidence and composure of any ordinary man or woman and one can only wonder at the success with which she came through the interrogation.'[4]

Having drawn a blank with threats, the NKVD tried again three weeks later with blandishments. She was taken to a different office and interviewed by an avuncular Russian, who hinted strongly that it would be in her best interests to answer his questions. The Partisans were difficult to control, he said. They knew her husband had worked for the Germans and she might well need the kind of protection that the Russians could offer her. He asked her if she was suffering from the cold and, when she admitted she was, he said he would arrange for two cubic yards of wood and a ton of coal – an unbelievable quantity of fuel at that time – to be delivered to her apartment. Still she told him nothing.

Dragica was extremely anxious to join Ivo in Britain, but could not leave without exit permits from both the NKVD and the OZNA, the Yugoslav secret police, which were unlikely to be forthcoming. She thought her only hope was to present her case to Tito personally. She got the telephone number of General Bakic, Tito's private secretary, from Maclean and tried to call him several times a day for two weeks, without success. Then, by chance, a friend introduced her to the wife of one of Tito's ministers who promised to raise her case with her husband. He refused to help.

On 27 February 1945, Field Marshal Sir Harold Alexander arrived in Belgrade on an official visit of inspection. The British Military Mission organised a reception in his honour and Maclean promised to wangle an invitation for Dragica. She arrived to find she was the only woman present, apart from members of the Belgrade theatre and female Partisan leaders in uniform. Among the guests was General Bakic, to whom she quickly contrived an introduction. The general, much taken by her beauty, asked her to do him the honour of opening the ball with him at 10 p.m. and during the waltz Dragica explained her situation. Bakic was sympathetic, expressed surprise that she was having so much difficulty and promised to see to it straight away.

Two days later she received official permission from the Yugoslav government to travel abroad, but she still had to obtain from the Partisans a certificate of 'political blamelessness', certifying that she had never worked against the Partisans and was in sympathy with the movement. This involved a nightmare round of interrogations, lasting up to twelve hours, by different OZNA groups. No fewer than six separate groups questioned her about the political sympathies of her family and friends and about Ivo's movements and activities. While OZNA had none of the detailed information possessed by the NKVD, it was obvious that they had had her under constant surveillance since the withdrawal of the Germans. OZNA seemed anxious to establish whether Ivo had worked for British intelligence, but Dragica reverted to the role of dumb housewife. When her interrogators demanded that she sign a statement confirming that Ivo was a British agent, she replied that she could not sign because her husband never told her anything about what he was doing. But if her husband *had* been working for the Allies, she asked wide-eyed, did that not mean they were all friends? This left her interrogators nonplussed.

OZNA was also very interested in Maclean and his political sympathies, but Dragica insisted, as a 'mere woman', that she had never discussed politics with him, although she was sure he was well disposed towards the Partisans. 'Who wouldn't be?' she added ingenuously. When she was asked about Maclean's views on a possible war between Britain and Russia, she professed to be astonished, had never heard of such an idea and couldn't understand why anyone would imagine such an event could come to pass – were the two countries not allies? 'Mrs Popov is an extremely astute and nimble-witted woman,' MI5 noted admiringly after her debriefing in London.

On 18 March, Dragica was at last issued with a passport valid for four months and a visa for entry into Britain. She was warned by OZNA to be extremely careful in Britain, because they had agents there who would be watching her and reporting on her behaviour and her contacts. She was also told not to mention the interrogations to anyone. (Almost the first thing she did when she arrived in Britain was to give a full report to MI5.) Dragica and Misha left by plane for Bari on 23 March, from where they were driven to Naples to await a flight to Britain. They arrived in London, for a loving reunion with Ivo, on 11 April, as the war in Europe was drawing to a close.

At the end of the month, as Russian T-52 tanks tore into the heart of Berlin, Hitler and his mistress, Eva Braun, committed suicide in a bunker under the Chancellery. A week later, in a small schoolhouse in Rheims, General Alfred Jodl, the German army chief of staff, signed the instrument of unconditional surrender. The following afternoon, 8 May 1945, Churchill broadcast to the nation, announcing that while Japan remained to be subdued, the war in Europe would end at midnight. Thousands of people took to the streets in London, blowing whistles, dancing, waving flags, throwing confetti, even kissing and hugging total strangers, in scenes of unrestrained joy repeated across the country.

By VE Day most of the concentration camps in Germany, including Oranienburg, had been liberated, although there was still no sign of Jebsen. Popov was obsessed by a burning need to find out what had happened to his friend, but information was hard to come by in the chaotic days at the end of the war. MI5 received a report about a man called Hjalmar Schact, who had been in the next cell to Jebsen in the prison in Prinz Albrechtstrasse; he recalled Jebsen being brought to his cell after a vicious beating with blood covering his shirt and calling out to his guards as the cell door clanged shut: 'I trust I shall be provided with a clean shirt.' Popov savoured the story and took some comfort from it.

Jebsen's friend, Baroness von Gronau, was also interviewed at length, but was unable to offer any solid information. She said she thought Jebsen had been charged with high treason and, when this could not be proved, he was accused instead of *Devisenverbrechen* (currency fraud) in connection with twenty million French francs. The baroness's brother called at Jebsen's family firm in the ruins of Hamburg to enquire about him and was informed, mystifyingly, that he had died in Shanghai in 1936. Jebsen had told the baroness that if she was at a certain restaurant in Flensburg three days after the end of hostilities, a British pilot would call there and take her back to England. The baroness wrote to the proprietor of the restaurant to ask for news of Jebsen, but received no reply.

On a visit to Switzerland to organise his father's release from an intern-ment camp, Popov was given the name of an Obergeheimrat Quitting, who might have some information. He wrote to Wilson asking if it might be possible to find Quitting among the thousands of German prisoners. 'If you have luck and find the man,' he wrote, 'keep him alive until I come, I would love to have a few words with him.'[5] No trace of Quitting was found.

The most promising lead came from Frau Petra Vermehren, who thought she was the last person to have seen Jebsen alive. Frau Vermehren was arrested as soon as she returned to Germany from Lisbon, after the defection to the British of her son and daughter-in-law, and was sent to Oranienburg concentration camp. She was the only woman in the camp and received word through the camp barber that Jebsen had arrived. She found his cell and threw stones against his window until she got his attention. This was in September 1944, although she believed he had arrived in July. Some of his ribs had been broken during his interrogation, so he lay on his bed for the first few weeks. He told her he had been abducted and smuggled out of Spain in a box because he had divulged information to the British. Jebsen and his friend Moldenhauer were taken away from Oranienburg in February 1945. Frau Vermehren made discreet enquiries, but was unable to obtain any information as to his fate. On 12 April Moldenhauer returned and was surprised that Jebsen was not there. He thought Jebsen might have been sent to another concentration camp at Sachsenhausen. On 15 April, with the Russian advance close by, most of the inmates were marched away. Those prisoners left behind were shot, probably including Moldenhauer. Frau Vermehren was certain that Jebsen was dead.

Popov, too, could come to no other sensible conclusion. Bitterly conscience-stricken that he had not been able to save his friend, as his friend had saved him so often, he resolved to track down whoever was responsible for Jebsen's death and avenge his murder. Every time he ran through the list of possible suspects one name always came to the fore: Walter Salzer, Kaltenbrunner's *Mädchenfüralles*. Popov returned to Paris to talk to Hahn in the hope he might know where Salzer could be found. Hahn had no idea, but he did provide Popov with a detailed description of the man he was hunting – early forties, medium height, receding brown hair, blue eyes, a crooked smile deformed by a sabre scar on his left cheek, his left hand badly scarred by burning so that he almost always wore gloves.

Dressed in the uniform of a lieutenant colonel – his nominal rank – in the British army to facilitate his travels, Popov set out for Germany at the wheel of a jeep to find Salzer. He was appalled by the devastation wrought by Allied bombers and the plight of the thousands of refugees clogging the roads, but he pressed on, from one ruined city to another, checking the records in every prison camp where former members of the SD were being held. He drew a blank everywhere.

Eventually he ended up in Hamburg, searching through the rubble of the city centre for Avelhofstrasse, where Salzer had worked for one of

Jebsen's companies before the war. He was hoping the company records might reveal some clue to Salzer's whereabouts, but there was nothing left in Avelhofstrasse except piles of blackened bricks. Sitting in his jeep, smoking a cigarette and pondering what to do next, he saw a small boy emerge from a hole in the ground, presumably leading to a cellar. The boy stared at him uncertainly. Popov beckoned him over and offered him a chocolate bar. The boy grabbed it without a word, ripped off the foil and crammed it into his mouth. Popov asked him, in German, where he lived and he pointed to the hole in the ground. The boy said he lived with his father, who used to be a janitor before the street was destroyed. Popov gave the boy another chocolate bar and asked him to fetch his father. He ran off, disappeared down the hole and re-emerged with a man who looked old enough to be his grandfather. It transpired that he was not the janitor of the Jebsen office, but of the building opposite. He did not know Salzer, but he knew someone who used to work there – a man called Mayerdorf, who was living with his daughter-in-law in the suburbs.

Herr Mayerdorf admitted he had worked for Jebsen, but claimed he could not remember any of his colleagues, and certainly not anyone called Salzer, until Popov produced a carton of cigarettes, which miraculously cleared his memory. Yes, perhaps he could recall someone by the name of Salzer. He did not know where he was now, but Dr Ziegler, a director of the company, would know. Ziegler and Salzer were friends. Unfortunately Dr Ziegler had moved to Cologne; he did not know the address, even when Popov produced more cigarettes.

It took eight hours to drive from Hamburg to Cologne, but less than an hour to discover that his journey was fruitless. Every German had to register with the local police; a bad-tempered clerk in the registration office agreed to look up Dr Ziegler's address and was unashamedly pleased to inform Popov that Dr Ziegler had moved back to Hamburg. After another eight-hour drive Popov at last obtained, from the police in Hamburg, an address for Dr Ziegler. It turned out to be a rented room in a grim boarding house. Ziegler was not at home when Popov called, but the landlady was happy to gossip. Popov reassured her that he was not on official business, but was merely looking for a friend, a man called Salzer who was also a friend of Dr Ziegler. She did not recognise the name, but when Popov described Salzer it was immediately clear she knew who Popov was talking about. Salzer, it seemed, had visited Ziegler shortly after he moved in about a month ago; he had been obliged to stay the night, she added disapprovingly, because of the curfew. Popov thanked her for her time and said he would call again to see his 'friend'; he was certain she would tell Ziegler that a British officer had been looking for him.

By happy circumstance, Ian Wilson's cousin, Clive Aldridge, was in charge of the British military intelligence office in Hamburg and Popov knew he could beg a favour. Popov asked Aldridge if he could arrange for Ziegler to be arrested and held in the military cells overnight prior to being 'interrogated' by Popov the following day. Aldridge was happy to oblige.

When Dr Ziegler was ushered into Popov's borrowed office the following morning he was fuming with rage at having been locked up and indignantly demanded an explanation. Popov stared at him coldly, told him to be quiet and pretended to consult a file, before looking up and asking him if he knew Walter Salzer. Ziegler admitted that he did, but claimed he had not seen him since the previous year. Popov consulted his 'file' once more and advised Ziegler not to lie; he knew, he said, that Salzer had visited Ziegler as recently as four weeks ago. But Ziegler was far from cowed. It took Popov several hours to break down the German's resistance and only after serious threats to his continuing freedom did Ziegler grudgingly disclose the address, in Minden, where Salzer was living under the assumed name of Ulrich. Popov was going to let him go, but then suddenly asked if he knew what had happened to Jebsen. He died in a concentration camp, Ziegler replied. How did he know? Popov asked. Because, he said, Salzer told him.

At that moment Popov knew he was going after the right man. He still had every intention of killing Salzer and planned a careful alibi. He checked into the officers' mess at the British headquarters in Bad Oeynhausen, and over dinner let it be known that he would be leaving for Paris very early the following morning. At first light he was on the road to Minden, a fine old city reduced to ruins, like so much of Germany. He found Salzer's address without much difficulty, knocked on the door and asked for Herr Ulrich. The housekeeper said he was out, shopping, and would probably be some time. She suggested that Popov should return, but he said he would wait and without asking took a seat in the hall. The housekeeper looked over his uniform, shrugged and left him.

Popov sat there all morning, smoking one cigarette after another and ignoring the curious stares of the other residents walking in and out of the house. At around two o'clock the front door opened and Salzer walked in, carrying a sack of potatoes. Popov recognised him immediately from the scar on his cheek and the glove on one hand. Salzer walked past Popov as if he had not seen him, but as he climbed the stairs Popov called his name. He stiffened for a moment, but continued up the stairs. Popov again called his name. This time he turned and was about to protest that his name was Ulrich, but Popov had already drawn his revolver. Salzer seemed resigned to whatever was going to happen, as if he no longer cared. Following Popov's instructions he dropped his sack of potatoes and walked out of the house to the jeep, with Popov close behind him.

Popov told him to drive and gave him instructions on which direction to take. They ended up on a lonely track leading through a wood outside the town, which Popov had reconnoitred earlier that morning. When the jeep stopped in a clearing, Popov was tempted to shoot Salzer there and then and get it over with, but he needed to know first what had happened to Jebsen. He motioned Salzer to get out of the jeep and told him to stand with his back to a tree. Salzer realised he was going to be killed and sank to his knees with a whimper. When Popov began to question him, he was so frightened he could barely speak. Popov asked him if he knew why he was there; Salzer shook his head. Popov asked why he had changed his name; Salzer said everyone who had been in the SD was being arrested. Popov asked why Jebsen had been kidnapped; Salzer said it was on Kaltenbrunner's orders. He kept repeating, over and over again, that he was only following orders, but eventually admitted, between great racking sobs, that one of those orders was to execute Jebsen.

For Popov it was the end of the trail – final confirmation that his friend was dead. But he was so sickened by the slobbering man in front of him that he could not bring himself to pull the trigger. He hit Salzer full in the face with his fist, hoping to provoke him into a fight, but the German remained on his knees imploring Popov to spare him. Popov hit him again, and again, then pummelled him with both fists in a fury, completely out of control. Salzer did not even try to protect himself. Thoroughly disgusted, Popov finally walked to his jeep and drove away, leaving Salzer still on his knees at the base of the tree, covered in blood and sobbing pitifully.

If Popov could not find the level of cold-bloodedness to avenge his friend's death, he did everything else he could. He went to great lengths to find Jebsen's actress wife, Lore. She was living in Leipzig, in the Russian zone, and was desperate to get out. Popov organised her rescue, arranged all the documentation she required and found her a place to live in Krefeld, in the Allied controlled zone of Germany. He cleared her debts, provided her with sufficient money to live on and then asked MI5 to pull strings to find her work as an actress by introducing her to theatre directors in the British zone, reminding Wilson in a letter that when Jebsen agreed to work for the British, one of the few things he asked in return was that if he was killed, his wife would be looked after. Popov wrote:

Neither Mrs Jebsen nor I have the desire to impose her upon a theatre, but there is no doubt that a recommendation from a very high British level in Germany would help enormously. If pressure is done from a very high level the director without any doubt will be delighted to see Mrs Lore Jebsen and it is then up to her to prove she has talent. I have done all that I can do in my power and shall continue to do, if nothing else to ease my conscience.[6]

Unable, or at least unwilling, to return to a Yugoslavia under a Communist regime, Popov became a naturalised British subject on 12 June 1946, a process that was hurried through official channels as an indication of the government's gratitude for his work during the war. Supporting his application, Bill Luke wrote: 'He has in my view done more to deserve British citizenship than most other people. I believe that it is possible to speed up the naturalisation of aliens if they have given notable service to the Crown and Tricycle's case would certainly come under this heading.'

Ivo, too, was rewarded with the KMC, the King's Medal for Courage. The citation read:

From the time when his country was invaded, [he] did everything in his power to help the Allied cause by assisting escaping prisoners of war, and in other ways. He himself, at great personal danger, remained in Yugoslavia, and without having contact with the British authorities took steps in 1942 to provide the British Intelligence Service with reliable agents whom they could use for the purpose of deceiving the enemy. The plan was successful and ultimately Popov was able to get in touch with the British authorities in neutral territory to whom he gave most valuable information. This agent acted all along on his own initiative and penetrated the German Intelligence organisation to a remarkable extent and with complete disregard for his own safety. As a result of his valuable work he himself, and his family, suffered great inconvenience and he had to flee from Yugoslavia in 1944 when his position became compromised, prior to which he had twice been arrested by the Gestapo.[7]

The citation for Dusko's OBE was couched in similar terms:

Dusan Popov originally offered his services to the British Embassy in Belgrade at a time when his own country was neutral and the prospects of a British victory did not look favourable . . . His active work extended over a period of three and a half years during which time he showed courage and resourcefulness. At one time, when he was under suspicion and it was thought that his contact with the enemy would have to be discontinued, he persuaded the British authorities to allow him to take the risk of meeting the enemy with empty hands and although he was subjected to a close interrogation, he came through with flying colours . . . The work of this agent was invaluable to the Allied cause and the channel of communication played an important part in deceiving the enemy prior to the Normandy invasion. At all times this agent has co-operated with the British authorities to the fullest extent at great danger both to himself personally and to his relatives in Yugoslavia.[8]

Popov was not officially presented with his OBE until 28 November 1947. Normally, he would have been called to an investiture at Buckingham Palace and awarded his decoration by the king, but MI5 was still coy about parading its agents in public and so a different, more discreet venue had to be found. Everyone who knew Popov agreed that there could be no more appropriate location for the ceremony than somewhere like the Ritz Hotel in Piccadilly. In the cocktail bar, of course.

Postscript

AFTER THE WAR POPOV SETTLED IN PARIS, AT 3 RUE DOSNE IN THE fashionable 16th *arrondissement*. He set up a small publishing business and astonished all his friends in MI5 by suddenly getting married, at the age of thirty-four. The ceremony took place at Megève in the French Alps on 6 March 1946. His bride, MI5 recorded drily, was an eighteen-year-old French girl by the name of Janine, 'who is apparently entering this matrimonial adventure with her eyes open'.[1]

In the summer of 1946, on a business trip to the United States, Popov again clashed with J. Edgar Hoover, the director of the FBI. MI5 had had to put in a special plea to the US Embassy in London for him to be issued with a visa: 'His consistent loyalty to the Allied cause has been proved beyond the shadow of doubt . . . and his success as an agent was due in no small measure to his own initiative and courage.'[2]

In April 1946, Hoover had put his name to a fanciful article in *Reader's Digest*, under the headline 'The Enemy's Masterpiece of Espionage', in which he explained how the FBI had 'discovered' the existence of microdots. Almost nothing Hoover wrote about the discovery was true, and certainly no mention was made of the pivotal role played by Dusko Popov. In the article, Hoover described how a 'Balkan playboy' suspected of being a German spy had been stopped and searched when he entered the United States, and how a laboratory agent had suddenly noticed a gleam of reflected light on an envelope among his possessions. 'Under the microscope it was magnified 200 times. And then we could see that it was an image on a film of a full-sized typewritten letter, a spy letter with a blood-chilling text . . .'[3] Once the 'Balkan playboy' realised the game was up, Hoover wrote, he began to 'gush information' – although curiously the director made no mention of the fact that the information being gushed included an early warning of the attack on Pearl Harbor.

The article was illustrated by a picture of a telephone memorandum note on which the microdots were glued. Unfortunately it was addressed to a friend of Popov and made the friend look like a Nazi collaborator. Popov was furious, both on account of the slur on his friend and the fact that Hoover had made no mention of Pearl Harbour – evidence, he felt, of the director's guilty conscience.

When Popov wrote an angry letter of complaint to Hoover, the director was smitten by an inexplicable memory loss, scrawling a note on Popov's letter: 'Just who is this?' Any of his assistants could have told him that he had signed literally hundreds of memoranda about Popov only a few years earlier, at a time when he seemed to be morbidly obsessed with the 'Balkan playboy's' love life. Popov called at the FBI headquarters in Washington in an attempt to see Hoover, but was fobbed off by aides. For the time being, however, he had to leave matters where they stood.

In 1948, Janine gave birth to a son, Dean. Popov's business interests rapidly expanded into Germany, where he was involved in developing the textile industry in Krefeld and had obtained a licence for importing Peugeot cars. Energetic and enthusiastic about the prospect of a new Europe arising from the ruins of the war, he was later nominated as secretary-general of the European Movement, a lobby group founded to promote European unity in 1948. Ivo, meanwhile, was living in Rome and working with the Christian Democratic Party to oppose a threatened takeover by the Communists.

On 17 January 1951, Ivo's wife, Dragica, died when an Alitalia flight from Paris crashed while attempting to land in Rome; only three people on board survived. Dragica was travelling in place of her husband and many members of the family believed that the aircraft was sabotaged by the UDBA, the Yugoslav secret intelligence service, to kill Ivo. Several attempts had already been made on his life, since he remained a prominent and outspoken opponent to the regime of Marshal Tito.

That same year Popov bought the Château de Castelleras, an extraordinary stone castle on a hilltop overlooking Nice in the south of France, and embarked on a major programme of renovation. The Château de Castelleras would become the venue for some memorable parties during the years Popov was in residence. In 1954 he acquired a 220-acre farm nearby and set about planting 10,000 olive trees. Castelleras was eventually sold for development and Popov moved into La Grande Bastide, the former summer palace of the bishop of Grasse, which adjoined his farm in Opio. He had lost none of his taste for living in style.

Popov's first marriage was not to endure and in 1961, at a dinner party on a business trip to Stockholm, he met a ravishing Swedish student, Jill

Jonsson. Popov was bowled over by her beauty and not in the least deterred from pursuing her by the fact that she was eighteen and he was approaching fifty, or by her father's stern disapproval. 'Dusko was such fun,' she said, 'so full of energy':

> He was like a magnet, everyone was drawn to him. Every day he sent me flowers. Then he asked me if I would go to Cologne with him, for the carnival, but my father said no. I cried for three days, pleaded with him to let me go and eventually he relented and said I could go if I telephoned home every day. I did call every day but I was so excited that my father thought I was drugged and contacted Interpol. When the time came to leave Dusko kissed me and I cried all the way home. I didn't care what people thought. I knew that I could not live without him and he could not live without me.[4]

Popov and Jill married on 14 June 1962, in Opio. Her father did not attend the ceremony. 'He did not like Dusko's reputation with all these women,' Jill explained, needlessly. Despite the disparity in their ages, they were idyllically happy. Jill bore Dusko three sons, Marco, Boris and Omar, between 1963 and 1969. He rarely talked about the war, never told her that he was a double agent and did not even mention that he had been awarded an OBE. All she knew was that he had been obliged to leave Dubrovnik early on in the war, but what he did after that she had no idea. This was not just modesty on Popov's behalf. He was a man who lived for the moment, always looking forward rather than back.

Jill took little interest in Dusko's business affairs other than being acutely aware that there were significant ups and downs in their fortunes. At one moment they would be riding around in a Rolls-Royce and hosting extravagant parties, at another moment the Rolls would suddenly disappear and Dusko would be advising her, with an indulgent smile, to wait a while before she bought a new pair of expensive shoes. 'Dusko never worried about money,' she recalled. 'He always believed he could make it.'

In the mid-1960s Dusko briefly emerged into the limelight as an 'international financier' with an ingenious plan to rescue the Atlas Aircraft Corporation of South Africa by repatriating millions of rands owned by foreign investors, which had been frozen by the South African government to prevent the flow of capital out of the country. This was breathlessly described as 'one of the most brilliant financial schemes of the century', and Popov had apparently won the backing of the Reserve Bank in Pretoria to raise $15 million for the Atlas Corporation by issuing 1,500 bearer certificates at \$10,000 each and offering them for sale in Switzerland at a 10 per cent premium to investors looking for a way of getting their funds out of South Africa. It meant that blocked rands could be converted into dollar bearer certificates repayable in ten years at an annual interest rate of 5 per cent.

The announcement of the scheme made headlines in all the newspapers in South Africa and led to angry questions being asked in parliament as to why the Reserve Bank was underwriting a loan being negotiated by a 'comparatively unknown financier' who was reaping a substantial commission for himself. Journalists besieged the Johannesburg hotel where Dusko and Jill were staying. The *Sunday Times* dubbed him a 'man of mystery' and described how, during an interview, the telephone in his suite was ringing constantly and telex messages were clattering in from London, Geneva and New York. 'He deals with governments, multi-million dollar corporations . . . He is also a delightful person and for the half hour of our interview charmingly told me practically nothing that I wanted to know. Then he showed me to the door and returned to his world of millions and mystery.'

In another newspaper Popov claimed he was in the process of negotiating multi-million-dollar loans for a number of other South African companies. His role, he airily explained, was to bring together borrowers and lenders. Asked what it took to be a financier, he replied: 'You have to be something of a dreamer, to have ideas, and enough concentration to ensure those dreams come true.'

In the end, although Popov professed himself to be entirely satisfied, the blocked rand scheme was under-subscribed. Some analysts suggested, nevertheless, that he had grossed a commission approaching \$1.5 million; others believed he had barely made enough to cover his expenses. On the subject of profit, Popov kept his own counsel.

Little more was heard of the 'international financier'. Popov and Jill returned to the quiet life in Opio, where they played a lot of tennis and devoted themselves to bringing up their children. Ivo, who had remarried, moved into the mill house next door to La Grande Bastide with his French wife, Brigitte, and their two young sons.

Popov might have remained in happy obscurity for the rest of his life if the existence of the Pearl Harbor questionnaire had not been revealed more than twenty-five years after the end of the war. In 1972, to the fury of MI5, Yale University Press published in book form a history of the XX Committee, which Sir John Masterman had written for the internal use of British intelligence. In the teeth of opposition from the British government, Masterman had tried, and failed, to find a publisher in Britain. *The*

Double-Cross System in the War of 1939 to 1945 included not only a copy of
the entire questionnaire, but also Masterman's conclusion that it represented 'a sombre but unregarded warning of the subsequent attack upon
Pearl Harbor'.

Masterman only identified the double agent who obtained the questionnaire as 'Tricycle' and did not mention J. Edgar Hoover by name, but
he made clear his own view that a grave error had been made, pointing
out that fully one-third of the questions dealt with Hawaii and Pearl
Harbor and were much more specific than the questions on other topics.
'It is surely a fair deduction', he wrote, 'that the questionnaire indicated
very clearly that in the event of the United States being at war, Pearl
Harbor would be the first point to be attacked and that plans for this
attack had reached an advanced stage by August 1941.'[5] The *Herald Tribune*
agreed, describing it as 'an unmistakable intimation of Axis plans to attack
Pearl Harbor four months before the event'.

In response, the FBI issued a statement pointing out that the questionnaire was neither the first, nor the most important, item of intelligence
indicating that Pearl Harbor was a target; the Bureau, as coordinator of
intelligence, had fed repeated warnings about Pearl Harbor to both the
War and the Navy Departments.

Until the publication of Masterman's book, Popov had never thought
about telling his own story; indeed, he imagined he would be forbidden
to do so by MI5. But Masterman had opened the door and Popov saw no
reason why he should not walk through. In 1974 he revealed himself to
be Tricycle in his book *Spy/Counterspy*, a racy account of his adventures
that read like a James Bond novel. Fundamentally accurate, if occasionally
embellished, its most sensational charge was to accuse Hoover of stupid-
ity and gross negligence by ignoring the Pearl Harbor questionnaire and
allowing Japan to inflict upon the United States the greatest naval disaster in its history.

Hoover had died two years earlier, but the Bureau did its best to stop
publication of Popov's book and, when that failed, mounted a damage-
limitation campaign branding him as a liar. Popov, meanwhile, was galli-
vanting round the country on a nationwide promotion tour, charming
every interviewer and being fêted as 'the real James Bond', an appellation
he modestly disclaimed, often pointing out that James Bond wouldn't
have lasted forty-eight hours in the real world of espionage. More than
one commentator pointed out that his glamorous wife more than fulfilled
the qualifications to be a 'Bond girl'.

Clarence Kelley, Hoover's successor as director of the FBI, attempted to
discredit Popov by issuing a denial that Popov and Hoover had ever met

(as Popov claimed in his book) and insisting that the Bureau had never received information indicating that the Japanese would attack Pearl Harbor. It is true that none of the FBI files contains a written record of any meeting between Hoover and Popov, but Hoover was notoriously secretive and often had 'off-calendar' meetings. Popov certainly reported the meeting to MI5 when he was debriefed on his return to Britain. William Stephenson, the head of British Security Coordination, confirmed to his biographer that Popov had met Hoover, although he was not prepared to go public with the information because he did not want to upset Anglo-US relations. 'Our conversation was not for publication at the time,' Stephenson's biographer recalled, 'but he was very clear. He said Popov had indeed met Hoover – he knew all about it. He thought it was a terrible failing in Hoover, who had this strait-laced attitude that shut him off completely from realities. Stephenson had no doubts about Popov's credibility and he thought the FBI had totally failed to pick up on what Popov was trying to tell him about Pearl Harbor.'[6]

Bureau attempts to limit the damage to Hoover's reputation were fruitless: the damage was done and the wound of Pearl Harbor was reopened as historians entered into a furious debate about the extent to which Hoover was culpable. Most agreed that the questionnaire deserved more credence than it had been given, particularly in the light of its provenance. 'Regardless of Hoover's assessment of Popov's character,' John Bratzel and Leslie Rout wrote in the *American Historical Review*, 'the director's failure to transmit the entire Popov questionnaire to the White House and to military and naval intelligence agencies showed both a poverty of judgement on his part and the crippling consequences of rivalry among those governmental agencies charged with gathering and evaluating information essential to the United States at a critical time in its history.'[7]

Some experts suggested that Hoover, who was paranoid by nature, was influenced not only by his loathing of Popov, but by his suspicion that the British were trying to draw America into the war. FBI files indicate that at one point Hoover apparently considered the possibility that the questionnaire might have been concocted by British intelligence for just that purpose. Rear Admiral Edwin Layton, Fleet Intelligence Officer at Honolulu in 1941, undertook a major study of the Japanese attack and concluded that Hoover 'dropped the ball completely' in his handling of the Popov information. 'His failure represented another American fumble on the road to Pearl Harbor.'[8]

After it had been made public, the questionnaire was analysed and re-analysed by researchers and proved to be conveniently ambiguous. Supporters of Popov insisted that it was a clear warning of the attack on

Pearl Harbor; sceptics asserted, on the contrary, that the questions were insufficiently detailed to be of use and those concerning Hawaii dealt almost entirely with installations, hangars, depots and workshops, subjects that would not really have been of much interest to the Japanese, particularly as they had an efficient espionage system operating in the Honolulu consulate, which was feeding naval intelligence back to Tokyo on a regular basis.

In the view of Thomas Troy, the official historian of the CIA, Popov was nothing more than a 'troublesome playboy'. Troy mounted a staunch defence of Hoover, accusing British historians of propagating the post-war controversy about the questionnaire as 'examples of the cleverness of British intelligence sabotaged by American incompetence'. Troy suggested that the questionnaire might not have been for the Japanese at all and could easily have ben interpreted as simply a desire by the Germans to update their files, since they were already in possession of detailed reports on all US military bases, including Pearl Harbor. And if British intelligence really believed that an attack on Pearl Harbor was imminent, why did they not inform the United States through official channels? 'Why would they rely on the persuasive abilities of a 29-year-old Yugoslav who arrived in the US with thousands of dollars in his pocket and a desire to party?'[9]

Some revisionist historians now believe that the questionnaire was an irrelevance, as President Roosevelt knew about the impending attack and allowed it to happen to legitimise the entry of the United States into the war at a time when 80 per cent of the American public were against becoming involved. 'He was forced', wrote Robert Stinnett, a Pacific War veteran who spent seventeen years researching Pearl Harbor, 'to find circuitous means to persuade an isolationist America to join in the fight for freedom.'[10] The Japanese strike sank or seriously damaged eighteen naval vessels (including eight battleships), destroyed 188 planes and left more than 2,000 people dead. There were eight investigations into the disaster. Washington was absolved of any responsibility, and blame was firmly attributed to 'dereliction of duty' by the military commanders on the ground. No mention was made of Popov or his questionnaire during any of the investigations.

Popov was unperturbed by his detractors and remained utterly convinced, until the end of his life, that Hoover was guilty of failing to act on the intelligence he had provided. It was a view largely shared by British intelligence officers. As Tar Robertson said:

> The mistake we made was not to take the Pearl Harbor information out and send it separately to Roosevelt. No one ever dreamed

Hoover would be such a bloody fool. We knew from 'special intelligence' how Hitler was courting the Japanese and trying to do them
favours, and this married in with a verbal report from Tricycle that
his friend, the senior official in the Abwehr who had originally
recruited him as an agent, had just recently helped a high ranking
naval member of a special Japanese mission to Berlin to go on a visit
to Italy, which he regarded as being vitally important. Taken
together, the questionnaire and this report formed a strong indication that, to put it no higher, the Japanese might try a surprise raid
of this kind of Pearl Harbor.[11]

After the furore generated by his book had died down, Popov once
more stepped out of the limelight and returned to his beloved Opio,
where he was obliged to explain to his sons why he had never thought to
mention to them that he had been a double agent in the war. Ivo, meanwhile, had become interested in alternative therapies and, with his
brother's help, had opened a rejuvenation clinic in the Bahamas. Both
brothers continued to smoke and drink, despite warnings from their
respective doctors.

Ivo died on 16 December 1980, at his home outside Nassau. Dusko
died on 10 August 1981, at Opio, at the age of sixty-nine. 'He lived', his
widow said, 'how he wanted to live.'

APPENDIX I:

The Pearl Harbor Questionnaire

THIS IS MI5'S ENGLISH TRANSLATION OF THE QUESTIONNAIRE GIVEN TO
Popov in Lisbon by his German controller in August 1941, and which he
handed over to the FBI in New York four months before the Japanese
attack on Pearl Harbor:

Naval information –
Reports on enemy shipments (material foodstuffs –
combination of convoys, if possible with names of
ships and speeds).
Assembly of troops for overseas transport in USA and
Canada. Strength – number of ships – ports of assembly – reports on ship building (naval and merchant
ships) – wharves (dockyards) – state and privately
worked wharves – new works – list of ships being
built or resp. having been ordered – times of building.
Reports regarding USA strong points of all descriptions especially in Florida – organisation of strong
points for fast boats (E-boats) and their depot
ships – coastal defence – organisation districts.

Hawaii
Ammunition dumps and mine depots.
  1. Details about naval ammunition and mine depot
     on the Isle of Kushua (Pearl Harbor). If
     possible sketch.
  2. Naval ammunition depot Lualuelei. Exact posi-
     tion? Is there a railway line (junction)?
  3. The total ammunition reserve of the army is

supposed to be in the rock of the Crater
Aliamanu. Position?
4. Is the Crater Punchbowl (Honolulu) being used
as ammunition dump? If not, are there other
military works?

Aerodromes
1. Aerodrome Lukefield – Details (sketch if
possible) regarding situation of the hangars
(number?), workshops, bomb depots, and petrol
depots. Are there underground petrol installations? – Exact position of the seaplane
station? Occupation?
2. Naval air arm strong point Kaneche [actually,
Kaneohe]. – Exact report regarding position,
number of hangars, depots and workshops
(sketch). Occupation?
3. Army aerodromes Wicham [actually Hickam]
Field and Wheeler Field. – Exact position?
Reports regarding number of hangars, depots
and workshops. Underground installations?
(Sketch.)
4. Rodger's Airport – In case of war, will this
place be taken over by the army or the navy?
What preparations have been made? Number of
hangars? Are there landing possibilities for
seaplanes?
5. Airport of the Panamerican Airways. – Exact
position (if possible sketch). Is this airport
possibly identical with Rodger's Airport or a
part thereof? (A wireless station of the
Panamerican Airways is on the Peninsula
Mohapuu.)

Naval Strong Points Pearl Harbor
1. Exact details and sketch about the situation
of the state wharf, of the pier installations,
workshops, petrol installations, situations of
dry dock No. 1 and of the new navy dry dock
which is being built.
2. Details about the submarine station (plan of

situation). What land installations are in existence?

3. Where is the station for mine search formations? How far has the dredger work progressed at the entrance and in the east and southeast lock? Depths of water?
4. Number of anchorages?
5. Is there a floating dock in Pearl Harbor or is the transfer of such a dock to this place intended?

Special tasks

Reports about torpedo protection nets newly introduced in the British and USA navy. How far are they already in existence in the merchant and naval fleet? Use during voyage? Average speed reduction when in use. Details of construction and others.

1. Urgently required are exact details of the armoured strengths of American armoured cars, especially of the types which have lately been delivered from the USA to the Middle East. Also all other reports on armoured cars and the composition of armoured (tank) formations are of greatest interest.
2. Required are the Tables of Organisation (TO) of the American infantry divisions and their individual units (infantry regiments, artillery 'Abteilung' and so forth). These TO are lists showing strength, which are published by the American War Department and are of a confidential nature.
3. How is the new light armoured car (tank)? Which type is going to be finally introduced? Weight? Armament? Armour?

1. Position of British participation and credits in USA in June 1940. What are England's payment obligations from orders since the coming into force of the Lend Lease Bill? What payments has England made to USA since the outbreak of war for goods supplied, for estab-

lishment of works, for the production of war
material, and for the building of new or for
the enlargement of existing wharves?

2. Amount of state expenditure in the budget
years 1939/40, 1940/41, 1941/42, 1942/43 altogether and in particular for the army and the
rearmament.

3. Financing of the armament programme of the
USA through taxes, loans and tax credit
coupons. Participation of the Refico and the
companies founded by it (Metal Reserve Corp.,
Rubber Reserve Corp., Defence Plant Corp.,
Defence Supplies Corp., Defence Housing Corp.)
in the financing of the rearmament.

4. Increase of state debt and possibilities to
cover this debt.

All reports on American air rearmament are of greatest importance. The answers to the following questions are of special urgency:

1. How large is:

(a) the total monthly production of aeroplanes?
(b) the monthly production of bombers?
(c) the monthly production of fighter planes?
(d) the monthly production of training planes?
(e) the monthly production of civil aeroplanes?

II. How many and which of these aeroplanes were
supplied to the British Empire, that is to
say:

(a) to Great Britain?
(b) to Canada?
(c) to Africa?
(d) to the Near East?
(e) to the Far East and Australia?

III. How many USA pilots finish their training
monthly?

IV. How many USA pilots are entering the RAF?

<u>Reports</u> <u>on</u> <u>Canadian</u> <u>Air</u> <u>Force</u> <u>are</u> <u>of</u> <u>great</u> <u>value.</u>
All information about number and type (pattern) of
front aeroplanes. Quantity, numbers and position of
the echelons are of great interest. Of special
importance is to get details about the current air
training plan in Canada, that is to say: place and
capacity of individual schools and if possible also
their numbers. According to reports received every
type of school (beginners', advanced, and observer
school) is numbered, beginning with 1.

APPENDIX 2:

The Lisbon Memorandum

THIS WAS THE MEMORANDUM (NO. 324) PREPARED BY MI5 IN NEW YORK to cover Popov's return to London via Lisbon. Its aim was to explain to the Germans why Popov had not been working effectively in the United States. MI5 believed the chance of it succeeding was less than 50:50.

1. Your objective in passing through Lisbon is to satisfy the Germans that you have been genuinely acting as an agent for them and that any faults they may have to find with your information or activities since you have been in the USA are solely due to their failure to keep you supplied with funds.

2. Before you leave you will be given verbally some information to give to the Germans and we will settle together from what sources you obtained it. You will make your own notes to take with you so that you can repeat the information in Lisbon.

3. You will also take with you photographs of the Naval Conference Notes mentioned [by letter] on February 2nd and of the aero-engine mentioned in March. Also cuttings from various technical papers which are being prepared.

4. As soon as possible after arriving in Lisbon, you will go to the British Embassy to ascertain the time of your departure for London. This will have been arranged so as to give you at least three clear days in

Lisbon, but no more, unless there is no
aeroplane available on the fourth day. The
date fixed must be adhered to, and you must,
if necessary, tell the Germans that you
cannot extend your stay without arousing
suspicion.

5. Apart from this you should have no contact
   whatever with the British authorities in
   Lisbon except that in case of extreme
   personal danger you should try and telephone
   [number deleted].

6. In seeking instruction for the future you
   should explain that both the British and the
   Jugo-Slav governments know that your cover
   job in the USA is finished and therefore
   must assume that you will be available for
   some sort of war service in England. It will
   therefore be relatively easy for you to
   undertake any mission for the Germans in
   England. While you are willing to try and
   get back to the USA, or other parts of the
   world, if the Germans so desire, you cannot
   be sure of being able to arrange it.

7. On entering England you will not have diplomatic immunity and can therefore take in
   only what you are prepared to smuggle. As
   far as money is concerned, it is illegal to
   take Sterling over £10 into England but you
   can take dollars, explaining if necessary to
   the English authorities that they are the
   remains of the personal funds you had in the
   USA.

8. You should refuse to visit the German
   Legation or otherwise lay yourself open to
   British suspicion, particularly because (a)
   you were questioned about your brother's
   letter; (b) you have been depressed by the
   round up in Rio and the various American spy
   trials; (c) you do not know if Ivan II and
   Yvonne are free from suspicion.

9. You cannot extend your stay in Lisbon or

avoid going on to London as to do so would
arouse British or Jugo-Slav suspicions. You
had the greatest difficulty in persuading
the Ministry of Information to let you
return by way of Lisbon. To do so, you
required Jugo-Slav influence which you
obtained by assuring them that if they
assisted you to go to Lisbon you could
settle claims which the Bailonis had asked
the Jugo-Slav Minister to make against you.

10. In any event, you cannot return to Jugo-
Slavia or go to Germany because this would
indicate to the British and the Jugo-Slavs
that you had influence from and worked for
the Germans; and while they could protect
you – except in Jugo-Slavia – during the
war, such protection might not be effective
after the war. You therefore prefer to run
the risk of avoiding discovery by remaining
in Allied countries whether or not you
continue to be an active agent.

11. You will insist on the Germans providing
what they already owe you and making proper
provision for your future payment if you are
to continue to be active on their behalf.

12. Financial difficulties have disrupted your
work in the USA. Since June you have had no
funds to continue buying information from
the journalist, Cassini. You were offered,
but unable to buy, more drawings through the
Indian. You have had to reduce tremendously
the scale of your standard of living, thus
being unable to make useful new contacts or
to obtain further information from past
contacts.

13. Your own money was exhausted in the purchase
of your car and furnishing your apartment.
What they have paid you kept you going only
up to May. Your salary from the Ministry of
Information was trifling – $500 a month.
Since then you have existed only by spending

the BAILONIS' money and borrowing from Mlle Simon.

14. A rough statement of your receipts and expenditures, as seen through German eyes, is attached and shows that (a) you have spent at least $20,000 on direct expenses; (b) at the outset you were spending some $2,500 a month on entertaining and social life, generally over and above the current expenses of your apartment. This you had to reduce in June and thereafter bring down to next to nothing.

15. Three people only in the United States have reason to know what you have been doing. These are (a) the Indian who constructed your radio and sold you the aero-engine drawings; (b) the Croat wireless operator; and (c) the Russian-American journalist who sold you the production figures.

16. All items of information which you have given and which, from their nature, could have been obtained in the course of conversation, you will connect up with some of your actual contacts. For example, the story of the submarine nets which you took to Rio came from a Naval officer you actually know and the rubber figures came from Stimson's partner, Robbins.

17. A large part of your information has been too detailed to have been acquired in normal conversation and requires you to have had direct or indirect access to documents or exact figures. The dates and sources are as follows:

18. From September 1941 onwards your chief informant on air matters has been EDWARD L. BACHER, an employee of the Aeronautical Chamber of Commerce. Some air information also came from your Flying School and detailed aircraft production figures through the journalist, Cassini, which you were, to

some extent, able to check through BACHER.

19. In September or October 1941, a very pro-British Congressman – Sol Bloom, Chairman of the House of Representatives Foreign Affairs Committee – let you have the War Department appropriation figures. He knew you were connected with the British Government and used the figures in support of his contention that the US were making all possible preparations to intervene.

20. From October until you went to Rio you got particulars of tanks and armoured cars from Major George STARR whom you actually met with Terry RICHARDSON. In January you got details of explosives from him. Shortly after that he was sent overseas in February.

21. The Tables of Organisation which you took to Rio you stole from the offices of the Jugo-Slav Military attaché early in October.

22. The Naval Conference notes, of which you are now taking a photo, were obtained from Lieut. Commander Frank WALDRON in January. Using Mlle Simon's presence to attract him, you used to invite him to your apartment and on one occasion persuaded him to go straight there to dine and for the night, on his way back to New York from a Washington Conference. You provided a girl for him and took the photo while he was occupied with her in your bedroom and he thought you were in Mlle Simon's room.

23. From March until June you were regularly buying production figures from CASSINI – guns, steel plate, planes, tanks, copper and all war metals, and the list of companies making tanks and tank armaments.

24. Igor CASSINI is a Russian now naturalised as an American. He writes a column mainly about the private lives of high members of the US administration for the 'Washington Times Herald'. He is thirty years old – weak face,

curly hair, clean-shaven. Very anti-British.
He boasted to you how he was in the habit
of obtaining confidential figures for his
paper by bribery – particularly from the War
Production Board. You discovered he was open
to accept bribes himself by offering him
money to publish pro-British material. You
then disclosed that you were really as anti-
British as he was and arranged to pay him
for the production information received. He
refused to give you his source but you
believed it was really in W.P.B. as his
detailed figures accorded with the general
figures you got conversationally from your
social contacts.

25. When you promised information about manoeu-
vres in June, you intended to visit a girl
called Eleanor (nickname: Raven) known to
Johnny Jebsen, who is married to a Lieut
DECKER, who was taking part. Through them
you could have contacted many Army officers;
but owing to lack of money you could not get
to Phoenix to see her.

26. Edward L. BACHER of the Aeronautical Chamber
of Commerce you met at the Flying School
shortly after your arrival – long before
they advised you to make a contact in the
Chamber of Commerce. He lives in Washington
but comes regularly to the New York office.
You have a story of how you won his confidence and got him to think that you were
engaged in collecting information for the
Jugo-Slav Government, who felt they were not
fully informed by the British. You also have
the story of how he went to Ottawa and got
information on the Conference there from the
Norwegian airman, Captain SLATTEN. Your
failure to get to Ottawa yourself can, if
necessary, be explained in accordance with
the facts – that your exit permit proved
defective. The delay in transmitting the

information was due to BACHER being uncertain of the accuracy of what SLATTEN had
given him and you therefore thought it
better not to use the information until you
yourself checked it as far as you could, in
conversation with your contacts and BACHER
has confirmed it after discussion with
others in the Aeronautical Chamber of
Commerce.

27. You are familiar with the detailed story
which has been discussed on your relations
with the Croat radio operator, Nicolas
POLIC, and the house you provided for him at
Oyster Bay, Long Island. The set has been
dismantled and stored away at the house and
you have arranged to write to him care of
General Delivery, Glen Cove, L.I., where he
will call for letters once a fortnight, from
the middle of November onwards, about the
'car', in order to give him his instructions
what to do with it according to whether you
are to want it on your return to the USA or
if he is to destroy it. You did not discuss
with him the possibility of anyone else
wanting it and you will show extreme reluctance (owing to the danger of discovery) if
the Germans suggest it might be made available for some other agent. If driven to it,
you will agree to instruct POLIC to deliver
the wireless set in such a manner as the
Germans may direct, but you will try to
avoid this and will try even more to talk
them out of any suggestion of their sending
an agent to call at the house.

28. We have also discussed in detail, and I will
not repeat, the story of the Indian, Mohamed
ALI KHAN, who built the radio set for $600
and sold you the aero-engine drawing for
$400, of which he took $100. Later, he
offered you more drawings but you did not
take them because (a) you were by then short

of funds; (b) you had not been shown how to
transmit documents; and (c) you did not know
if the drawings he got were of any value. He
would not tell you where the drawings came
from (beyond saying it was another Indian)
because he was afraid you would buy direct
and save his 'cut'

29. The fact that you were living above your
apartment income did not cause trouble with
the authorities because they would know of
the large sum you originally brought over
and did not, of course, know that $36,000 of
it had been handed over to Samuel Sand. It
did cause certain gossip in social circles
which you quieted by explaining the financial position and by proving to one of the
gossips that your visa had been obtained at
the request of the Ministry of Information.

30. The receipt of the escudos caused you some
embarrassment but you managed this by
explaining to Sir Anthony Rumbold that you
had left jewels for sale in Portugal and he
arranged for the Treasury Department to
'unfreeze' any moneys that might be sent to
you.

31. The letter from Ivo caused a great deal of
difficulty. It was picked up by the censors
and instead of being delivered by post was
handed to you by Butler of the Ministry of
Information who asked you to explain it. He
apparently accepted your explanation that
you presumed that your brother was trying to
put through some black market transaction of
which you yourself knew nothing and warned
you not to answer the letter as it was
illegal for you to communicate, even through
Switzerland, with anyone in Jugo-Slavia.

32. You must have a show-down with Johnny and
Karsthoff on the money question. The last
wireless message will deny receipt of the
$10,000 and you will have to resist all

persuasion by Johnny to the contrary. It is
impossible here to judge what the true facts
are and it is to be hoped that you will get
them from Johnny before you meet Karsthoff.
We can only leave it to your discretion to
handle this situation as best you can in the
light of what you discover in Lisbon. You
will have your brother's letter with you so
that you can, if necessary, prove to
Karsthoff that Johnny caused the letter to
be written as the envelope is in his handwriting.

33. You know nothing above the activities of
    IVAN II and YVONNE since you left England
    except that, at the Germans' request, you
    rebuked IVAN II for his bad work and got an
    indignant letter from him in reply; and you
    wrote to YVONNE with a new cover address but
    she did not answer your letter.

34. Ralph [Popov's alleged radio operator] has
    formed no part of the set up since you left
    England. Your earlier requests for money for
    him were because an 'all-in' figure had been
    agreed to cover you and him and you saw no
    reason why that figure should be reduced.
    Also you had promised Ralph that you would
    put something aside for him in the USA and
    at intervals after you arrived, when you had
    money, you have sums amounting to $4000 to
    Reynolds & Company, Brokers, of 120
    Broadway, to invest in railroad stock on his
    behalf.

35. You, yourself, did the coding and decoding
    of messages and the operator does not know
    the code but merely transmitted messages
    already coded. Therefore you must make quite
    sure that you fully understand the code.

36. You yourself took and developed the photo-
    graphs of documents which you are taking
    with you.

37. You have not sent them secret ink letters

since the difficulties with the wireless
operator began because (a) you were expecting every day to be put into a position to
pay him so that he could transmit as before,
and (b) you were rather frightened to use
secret ink as it became obvious from the
newspaper reports of the spy trials that
some inks at least were liable to detection.

38. You will not take any secret ink with you
from the USA. If they want you to write in
secret ink from England, they must (a) give
you some to take in a form which you can
smuggle, and (b) reassure you that the type
of ink is reasonably secure.

39. IVAN II knows a good deal about wireless and
could no doubt operate a set if they
provided him with one or parts and instructions to construct one, but we do not wish
you to suggest this yourself or press for it
even if they suggest it.

40. Your work for the Ministry of Information
consisted of propaganda among the Jugo-Slav
immigrants to the USA etc., and you were
also asked to give to the British, information about the various Slav minorities in
accordance with the detailed story which we
have discussed.

Notes

1. The Arrival of a Spy

1 Public Records Office, National Archives, Kew, KV2/852
2 Tape loaned to author by Popov family
3 KV2/866
4 KV2/845
5 KV2/845
6 KV2/866
7 According to MI5 records, Popov was 'introduced' to Friedl on 28.2.41.
8 Popov, Dusko, *Spy/Counterspy* (Grosset & Dunlap, New York, 1974)
9 In fact there is no record of Popov ever reporting back to 'C', although the British government has not yet released the papers of Sir Stewart Menzies.
10 KV2/845
11 Masterman, J. C., *The Double-Cross System in the War of 1939 to 1945* (Yale University Press, New Haven, CT, 1972)
12 KV2/845
13 KV2/845

2. An Unlikely Agent

1 Popov, op. cit.
2 Ibid.
3 Public Records Office, National Archives, Kew KV2/845
4 KV2/845
5 Popov, op. cit.

3. The Great Game Begins

1 Montagu, Ewen, *Beyond Top Secret Ultra* (P. Davies, London, 1977)
2 Masterman, op. cit.

3 Ibid.
4 Ibid.
5 Masterman, J. C., *On the Chariot Wheel: An Autobiography* (Oxford University Press, London, 1975)
6 Montagu, op. cit.
7 Masterman, *The Double-Cross System*, op. cit.
8 Taped interview loaned to author by Popov family

4. The Lisbon Connection
1 KV2/845
2 Ibid.
3 Ibid.
4 Ibid.
5 Ibid.
6 Tape loaned to author by Popov family
7 KV2/845
8 KV2/846
9 KV2/846

5. Plan Midas
1 Taped interview loaned to author by Popov family
2 KV2/847
3 Popov, op. cit.
4 Ibid.
5 Tape loaned to author
6 KV2/846
7 KV2/846
8 KV2/847, report by W. E. Luke, dated 5.5.41
9 KV2/847
10 KV2/847
11 KV2/848
12 KV2/848, letter from Cavendish-Bentinck to Luke, 8.6.41
13 KV2/847
14 KV2/847
15 KV2/847, memo from W. E. Luke, dated 3.5.41
16 KV2/847
17 Hansen is believed to be his real name, but MI5 has never officially released it.
18 KV2/846
19 KV2/863
20 KV2/863

21 KV2/848

22 The attack at Taranto marked the point at which the aircraft carrier and its strike planes became the dominant weapon of naval warfare. For that reason the Japanese displayed great interest in the operation.

23 KV2/849

24 KV2/849

25 Tape loaned to author by Popov family

26 See Appendix 1

27 KV2/849

28 KV2/849

29 KV2/849

6. The Pearl Harbor Questionnaire

1 All quotes are from FBI files, unless otherwise credited.

2 KV2/845

3 Popov, op. cit.

4 Popov may have mistakenly combined two meetings as one in this account. While the record shows that on 14 August Foxworth forwarded to Hoover a typewritten copy of the Pearl Harbor questionnaire, along with a sample of Popov's secret ink and details of the code he would be using to write to Lisbon, it seems Popov did not hand over the microdots until 19 August, when he met Lanman in a room at the Lincoln Hotel.

5 The Mann Act of 1910 was originally designed to prevent white slavery, but was extended in 1917 to enforce private morality.

6 Popov's account of his career as a double agent is largely confirmed by the record, although he seems to have embroidered an anecdote here and there, probably to help sales.

7 Popov, op. cit.

8 KV2/849

9 After publication of *Spy/Counterspy* in 1974, the FBI vigorously denied that Popov had ever met Hoover and there is no record of such a meeting. But Hoover never publicly acknowledged Popov's existence, despite bulging files full of reports about him.

10 Tape loaned to author by Popov family.

7. Radio Games

1 Montagu, op. cit.

2 Ibid.

3 Ibid.

4 Ibid.

5 Popov, op. cit.
6 Ibid.
7 KV2/849
8 All quotes are from FBI files, unless otherwise credited.
9 KV2/849
10 KV2/849
11 KV2/852
12 KV2/849
13 KV2/849
14 KV2/849
15 Montagu, op. cit.
16 Ibid.

8. Hoover on the Rampage

1 KV2/852
2 Summers, *A., Official and Confidential: The Secret Life of J. Edgar Hoover* (Putnam, New York, 1993)
3 KV2/850
4 KV2/849
5 See Appendix 2
6 KV2/850
7 KV2/850
8 Popov, op. cit.
9 Tape loaned to author by Popov family
10 KV2/850
11 KV2/850
12 KV2/850
13 KV2/850
14 KV2/850
15 FBI files
16 FBI files
17 KV2/850
18 KV2/850
19 FBI files
20 KV2/852
21 Tape loaned to author by Popov family

9. Back in the Game

1 KV2/851
2 KV2/851
3 KV2/851

4 KV2/851
5 KV2/851
6 KV2/851
7 KV2/852
8 KV2/850
9 KV2/868
10 KV2/863
11 KV2/853
12 KV2/850
13 KV2/852
14 KV2/850
15 KV2/852
16 KV2/851
17 KV2/851
18 KV2/851

10. The Yugoslav Escape Route
1 KV2/868
2 KV2/864
3 KV2/863
4 KV2/852
5 KV2/856
6 KV2/852
7 KV2/853
8 KV2/854
9 KV2/854
10 KV2/853
11 KV2/853
12 KV2/853
13 KV2/859
14 KV2/859
15 KV2/859
16 KV2/854
17 KV2/853
18 KV2/859
19 KV2/859
20 KV2/854
21 KV2/854

11. Enter 'Artist'
1 KV2/854

2 KV2/847
3 KV2/859
4 KV2/847
5 KV2/854
6 KV2/857
7 KV2/857
8 KV2/857
9 KV2/859
10 KV2/859
11 KV2/856
12 KV2/856

12. Fortitude and Disaster

1 KV2/856
2 KV2/856
3 KV2/864
4 OKW Intelligence Summary, 9.3.44
5 Popov, op. cit.
6 KV2/857
7 KV2/867
8 KV2/864
9 KV2/858
10 KV2/858
11 KV2/859

13. In Search of Revenge

1 Popov, op. cit.
2 KV2/859
3 KV2/859
4 KV2/859
5 KV2/860
6 KV2/861
7 KV2/870
8 KV2/861

Postscript

1 KV2/861
2 FBI files
3 *Reader's Digest*, April 1946
4 Interview with author
5 Masterman, *The Double-Cross System*, op. cit.

6 Macdonald, Bill, *The True Intrepid: Sir William Stephenson and the unknown agents* (Timberholme Books, Surrey, BC, 1998)

7 Bratzel, John F. and Rout, Leslie B., 'Pearl Harbor, Microdots and J. Edgar Hoover' (*American Historical Review* 87, December 1982)

8 Summers, op. cit.

9 Troy, Thomas F. 'The British Assault on J. Edgar Hoover: The Tricycle Case' (*International Journal of Intelligence and Counter Intelligence* 3, no. 2, 1989)

10 Stinnett, Robert B. *Day of Deceit: The Truth about FDR and Pearl Harbor* (Simon & Schuster, New York, 2001)

11 Knightley, Philip, *The Second Oldest Profession* (André Deutsch, London, 1986)

Select Bibliography

American Historical Association Committee for the Study of War Documents, 'Guides to German Records Microfilmed at Alexandria, Virginia, Washington, DC, 1959–1965'

Andrew, Christopher, *Secret Service* (William Heinemann, London, 1985)

Bratzel, John F. and Rout, Leslie B., 'Pearl Harbor, Microdots and J. Edgar Hoover' (*American Historical Review* 87, December 1982)

Breuer, William B., *Hoodwinking Hitler: The Normandy Deception* (Praeger, New York, 1993)

Brown, Anthony Cave, *Bodyguard of Lies* (Harper & Row, New York, 1975)

——*C: The Secret Life of Sir Stewart Graham Menzies* (Macmillan, New York, 1987)

Bruce-Briggs, B., 'Another Ride on Tricycle' (*Intelligence & National Security* 7, no. 2, April 1992)

Chapman, John W. M., 'Tricycle Recycled: Collaboration Among the Secret Intelligence Services of the Axis States, 1940–41' (*Intelligence & National Security* 7, no. 3, July 1992)

Costello, John, *Mask of Treachery* (William Collins, London, 1988)

Cruickshank, Charles, *Deception in World War II* (Oxford University Press, Oxford, 1979)

Cull, Nicholas John, *Selling War: The British Propaganda Campaign Against American Neutrality in World War Two* (Oxford University Press, Oxford, 1995)

Delmer, Sefton, *The Counterfeit Spy* (Harper & Row, New York, 1971)

Dunlop, Richard, *Donovan: America's Master Spy* (Rand McNally, Chicago, 1982)

Farago, Ladislas, *The Game of the Foxes: The Untold Story of German Espionage in the US and Great Britain During World War Two* (David McKay, New York, 1971)

Gentry, Curt, *J. Edgar Hoover: The Man and the Secrets* (W. W. Norton, New York, 1991)

Handel, Michael I. (ed.), *Strategic & Operational Deception in the Second World War* (Frank Cass, London, 1987)

Hesketh, Roger, *Fortitude* (The Overlook Press, New York, 2000)

Hinsley, F. H. and Simkins, C. A. G., *British Intelligence in the Second World War IV: Security & Counter Intelligence* (HMSO, London, 1990)

Hoover, J. Edgar, 'The Enemy's Masterpiece of Deception' (*Reader's Digest*, April 1946)

Hyde, Montgomery, *Room 3603* (Mayflower-Dell, New York, 1964)

——*Secret Intelligence Agent* (Constable, London, 1982)

Jones, R. V., *Reflections on Intelligence* (Heinemann, London, 1989)

Kahn, David, *Hitler's Spies: German Military Intelligence in World War II* (Hodder & Stoughton, London, 1978)

Knightley, Philip, *The Second Oldest Profession* (André Deutsch, London, 1986)

Lewin, Ronald, *Ultra Goes to War: The Secret Story* (Hutchinson, London, 1978)

Macdonald, Bill, *The True Intrepid: Sir William Stephenson and the unknown agents* (Timberholme Books, Surrey, BC, 1998)

McLachlan, Donald, *Room 39: A Study in Naval Intelligence* (Weidenfeld & Nicholson, London, 1968)

Master, Anthony, *The Man Who Was M* (Blackwell, Oxford, 1984)

Masterman, J. C., *The Double-Cross System in the War of 1939 to 1945* (Yale University Press, New Haven, CT, 1972)

——'The XX Papers' (*Yale Alumni Magazine* XXXV, February 1972, pp. 7–11)

——*On the Chariot Wheel: An Autobiography* (Oxford University Press, London, 1975)

Mintz, Frank P., *Revisionism and the Origins of Pearl Harbor* (University Press of America, Lanham, MD, 1985)

Montagu, Ewen, *The Man Who Never Was* (Lippincott, London, 1953)

——*Beyond Top Secret Ultra* (P. Davies, London, 1977)

Mure, David, *Practice to Deceive* (William Kimber, London, 1977)

——*Master of Deception: Tangled Webs in London and the Middle East* (William Kimber, London, 1980)

Pearson, John, *The Life of Ian Fleming* (McGraw Hill, New York, 1966)

Peis, Gunter, *The Mirror of Deception: How Britain Turned the Nazi Spy Machine against Itself* (Weidenfeld & Nicolson, London, 1977)

Perrault, Gilles, *The Secret of D Day: From the Secret Files of German and Allied Intelligence, the Untold Story of the Fantastic Espionage War* (Little Brown, Boston, 1965)

Popov, Dusko, *Spy/Counterspy* (Grosset & Dunlap, New York, 1974)

Powers, Richard Gid, *Secrecy & Power: The life of J. Edgar Hoover* (Free Press, New York, 1987)

——*Washington Post National Weekly Edition*, 7–23 November 1994

Prange, Gordon W., Goldstein, Donald M. and Dillon, Katherine, *Pearl Harbor: The Verdict of History* (McGraw Hill, New York, 1986)

Reibling, M., *Wedge: The Secret War Between the FBI and the CIA* (Knopf, New York, 1994)

Stephenson, William Samuel (ed.), *British Security Coordination: The Secret History of British Intelligence in the Americas, 1940–45* (Fromm International, 1999)

Stevenson, William, *A Man Called Intrepid: The Secret War of 1939–45* (Macmillan, London, 1976)

Stinnett, Robert B., *Day of Deceit: The Truth about FDR and Pearl Harbor* (Simon & Schuster, New York, 2001)

Summers, Anthony, *Official and Confidential: The Secret Life of J. Edgar Hoover* (Putnam, New York, 1993)

Swearingen, M. Wesley, *FBI Secrets: An Agent's Exposé* (South End Press, Boston, 1995)

Theoharis, Athan G., *From the Secret Files of J. Edgar Hoover* (Ivan R. Dee, Chicago, 1991)

——*J. Edgar Hoover, Sex and Crime: An Historical Anecdote* (Ivan E. Dee, Chicago, 1995)

Toland, John, *Infamy: Pearl Harbor and its Aftermath* (Berkley Books, New York, 1983)

Trefousse, Hans L., 'The Failure of German Intelligence in the United States, 1939–45' (*Mississippi Valley Historical Review* 42, no. 1, June 1955)

Troy, Thomas F., 'The British Assault on J. Edgar Hoover: The Tricycle Case' (*International Journal of Intelligence and Counter Intelligence* 3, no. 2, 1989)

Walker, David E., *Lunch with a Stranger* (Allan Wingate, London, 1957)

West, Nigel, *MI5: British Security Operations 1909–1945* (The Bodley Head, London, 1981)

——*MI6, British Secret Intelligence Service Operations 1909–1945* (Weidenfeld & Nicolson, London, 1983)

Wighton, Charles and Peis, Gunter, *Hitler's Spies & Saboteurs: The Sensational Story of Nazi Espionage in the US and Other Allied Nations* (Holt, Rinehart and Winston, 1958)

Winks, R., *Cloak and Gown* (Collins Harvill, London, 1987)

Winterbotham, F. W., *The Ultra Secret* (Dell Books, New York, 1974)

Index